Master Narratives of Islamist Extremism

Master Narratives of Islamist Extremism

Jeffry R. Halverson, H. L. Goodall, Jr.,
and Steven R. Corman

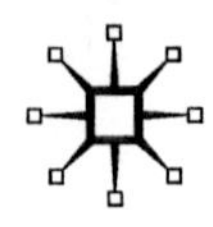

MASTER NARRATIVES OF ISLAMIST EXTREMISM

First published in 2011 by PALGRAVE MACMILLAN® in the United States – a division of St. Martin's Press LLC, 175 Fifth Avenue, New York, NY 10010.

Where this book is distributed in the UK, Europe and the rest of the world, this is by Palgrave Macmillan, a division of Macmillan Publishers Limited, registered in England, company number 785998, of Houndmills, Basingstoke, Hampshire RG21 6XS.

Palgrave Macmillan is the global academic imprint of the above companies and has companies and representatives throughout the world.

ISBN: 978–0–230–10896–7

Library of Congress Cataloging-in-Publication Data

Halverson, Jeffry R.
Master narratives of Islamist extremism / Jeffry R. Halverson, H. L. Goodall, Jr., and Steven R. Corman.
p. cm.
Includes bibliographical references and index.
ISBN 978–0–230–10896–7 (alk. paper)
1. Islamic fundamentalism. 2. Islam—Historiography. 3. Narrative inquiry (Research method) 4. Jihad. I. Goodall, H. Lloyd. II. Corman, Steven R. III. Title.
BP166.14.F85H35 2010
297.09—dc22

2010025810

A catalogue record of the book is available from the British Library.

Design by MPS Limited, A Macmillan Company

First edition: February 2011

D 10 9 8 7 6 5 4 3 2

Printed in the United States of America.

Contents

List of Figures and Tables vii

Acknowledgments ix

Introduction 1

1 What is a Master Narrative? 11

2 The Pharaoh 27

3 The *Jahiliyyah* 37

4 The Battle of Badr 49

5 The Hypocrites 57

6 The Battle of Khaybar 67

7 The Battle of Karbala 81

8 The *Mahdi* 95

9 The Infidel Invaders 109

10 *Shaytan*'s Handiwork 125

11 1924 137

12 The *Nakba* 149

13 Seventy-Two Virgins 165

14 Master Narratives and Strategic Communication 179

Appendix 207

Notes 209

Bibliography 231

Index 237

List of Figures and Tables

Figure 1.1	Story form	20
Figure 14.1	Vertical integration model	182
Figure 14.2	Relationships among archetypes	189
Figure 14.3	Pork eating crusader patch	197
Table 14.1	Summary of master narrative elements	184
Table 14.2	Analogy counterarguments	198

Acknowledgments

This book represents an important interdisciplinary convergence. The project began when Jeffry R. Halverson, a religious studies scholar with an expertise in Islam, completed his first book, *Theology and Creed in Sunni Islam*, and accepted a postdoctoral appointment with the Consortium for Strategic Communication (CSC) at Arizona State University. Steven Corman and H. L. (Bud) Goodall, Jr. were professors at the Hugh Downs School of Human Communication and founding members of the CSC. Under Corman's leadership, the CSC received funding from the Office of Naval Research (ONR) for a research project entitled "Identifying and Countering Extremist Narratives" (N00014-09-1-0872), which supported the development of this book. As the project commenced, Halverson provided the research team with the textual and historical bases for a series of important narratives that our team began to encounter in transnational Islamist extremist discourse and communications. This was the impetus for identifying and analyzing what we describe as the "master narratives" of Islamist extremism described in this book.

Although three names appear as coauthors on this volume, we have benefited greatly from the encouragement and assistance of a wide variety of scholars, research assistants, as well as members of the military, diplomatic, and intelligence communities, whose first-hand experience in the Muslim world and various conflict zones provided us with important perspectives, examples, and leads. Specifically, our esteemed colleagues at the CSC, namely, Angela Trethewey, Pauline Cheong, Daniel Bernardi, as well as two postdoctoral research fellows, Scott Ruston and Chris Lundry, contributed significantly to the development of the narrative theory described in this book. We would also like to thank our former program manager, Kathy Holladay, our team of research assistants, and the Hugh Downs School of Human Communication at Arizona State University. Special thanks go out to our project officers at the ONR for supporting our research, Ivy Estabrooke and Gary Kollmorgen. Thanks are also due to several others, including our ASU colleague Mark R. Woodward, Jarrett Brachman of North Dakota State University, Lt. Col. Reed Sawyer of the Combating Terrorism Center at West Point, and Brooke Goldstein of the Hudson Institute, all of whom provided early encouragement and first-hand expertise of terrorist networks and recruitment strategies. Lastly, we thank our families and friends for their support and patience.

Introduction

This book is about the ideological functions of master narratives that exist in Muslim societies and culture and how these narratives are exploited and employed specifically by Islamist extremists. We provide a detailed analysis of the historical origins, components, and manifestations of more than a dozen master narratives employed by extremists in their ideological rhetoric, propaganda videos, and public statements. The material presented in this book is based on the premise that narratives are powerful resources for defining cultures and framing actions, and it is particularly important to understand how they operate if we hope to understand and counter them. In other words, narratives are essential to understanding Islamist extremism in the "war of ideas."

Since this book is about *narrative*, it is important to explain what we mean by this contested term. In conventional usage, the term is not very clearly defined and often used interchangeably with *story*. For example, Casebeer and Russell claim that "the attacks of September 11th form part of a narrative—or a story—for the American public that shall exist in some form forever."[1] In this book, we take a different approach, defining narrative as a *system of stories*. A narrative is not a single story, but a collection of stories, and a collection is systematic because the stories are components that relate to one another with coherent themes, forming a whole that is greater than the sum of its parts.

Readers in the United States (and elsewhere too) will recognize the American narrative, consisting of sequential interrelated stories about life in colonial times, the Revolutionary War, the founding of the country, the Civil War, the Great Depression, and so forth. This narrative tells people what it means to be American (and how to act like one) through stories that convey a shared struggle of one people (from many places) and express the ideals of that group, such as liberty, individualism, and self-reliance. Likewise, the sacred texts of Islam, namely, the Qur'an, Hadith, and *Seerah* (hagiography) of the Prophet Muhammad, contain a collection of related stories that tell Muslims how they should lead their lives on the path of God (*fi sabil Allah*) and who they are as a nation of believers (*ummah*).

The sacred texts of Islam are a major reference source for this book. We believe that most readers are already familiar with the Qur'an, Hadith, and the story of Muhammad's life, but it is likely that others are not. Accordingly, a description of these sources is provided here, and we also encourage those interested in further study to consult a text such as Akbar S. Ahmed's *Islam Today: A Short Introduction to the Muslim World* or other similar academic works.[2]

The Qur'an (meaning, literally, "the recitation") is the most sacred text of Islam. Muslims believe that the Qur'an is the divinely preserved Speech of God and the final revelation of God (*Allah*) to humanity. It was miraculously dictated through the angel Gabriel (*Jibreel*) to Muhammad ibn 'Abdullah (570–632 CE) over a period of some twenty-two years in the Hijaz region of Arabia. As the recipient of the Qur'an, Muhammad is regarded as the last of a series of prophets that also includes Noah, Abraham, Moses, and Jesus. The Qur'an consists of 114 *surahs* (chapters) that can be classified as either Meccan or Medinan, depending on where in Arabia Muhammad resided when he received the revelations. The *surahs* of the Qur'an do not appear chronologically in the text; rather they are arranged roughly from longest to shortest. As such, the literary structure of the Qur'an is unique. It does not convey linear "historical" narratives the way the Torah or the Gospels often do. Rather, it references or recounts elements (or fragments) of narratives, many of which can also be found in the Torah or the New Testament, to support and illustrate different messages for the reader. As such, understanding the coherence of Qur'anic narratives can be a difficult task and we have attended to this matter with great care.

If it is not already apparent, the familiar description of the Qur'an in the West as the "Muslim Bible" is tremendously misleading. On a structural level, readers familiar with the Christian Bible will recall that it begins with the words of the Book of Genesis describing the beginning of time and creation, stating: "In the beginning, when God created the heavens and the earth." The entire text then comes to an end with the Book of Revelation, which discusses the dramatic events of the end of the world and the Final Judgment of humanity before God. In between, the stories of the Hebrew Prophets and the Christian Messiah, Jesus, are told as linear narratives. In the case of Jesus, the New Testament provides readers with four different linear narratives, two of which begin with his birth and end with his death and resurrection. So, despite the existence of the Psalms, Proverbs, and other wisdom literature in the text, the Hebrew and Christian scriptures established a linear third-person precedent in the Abrahamic tradition of sacred texts. It is a precedent that one must largely discard when approaching the text of the Qur'an, despite the overlap with the Bible in terms of themes and content. The Qur'an begins with the words: "In the name of God, most gracious, most merciful, all praise belongs to God, the lord of all the worlds." The entire text concludes with the one hundred and fourteenth chapter, *al-Nas,* which is actually a six-verse appeal to *Allah* for protection against evil. Therefore, if we wish to read the Qur'an's account of the prophets, let us take the prophet Jesus for example, we must collect verses from a dozen different *surahs* throughout the text, then attempt to organize those verses independently into some semblance of a cohesive narrative. As stated previously, the Qur'an does not exist as a pseudo-historical record relating the life of Muhammad or any of the earlier prophets, it reads like a transcript, similar to a sermon, of *Allah* speaking to Muhammad, the Muslims, or humanity in general, in a one-sided conversation that invokes narratives to illustrate points and imperatives being conveyed to the audience. As the Qur'an states: "We relate unto you [Muhammad] the best of stories in what We reveal to you from this Qur'an" (12:3).

The fact that the text was originally oral, and even in written form is still intended for audible recitation (as the name "al-Qur'an" itself indicates), has implications for our understanding of how messages are communicated by Islamist extremists as well. In fact, the pious ideal among Muslims is to dispense with the written text altogether and commit the entirety of the Qur'an to memory. Such believers earn the title of *hafiz* (for a man) or *hafizah* (for a woman). For example, President Obama's appointed envoy to the Organization of the Islamic Conference, Rashad Hussain, is a *hafiz al-Qur'an* and Obama emphasized this point when his appointment was announced. Therefore, the ability to quote extensively from the Qur'an by memory creates an aura of knowledge and piety in a speaker and establishes a hierarchical position that situates the speaker apart from (or above) the audience on the basis of his or her knowledge of the sacred text, infusing or encoding his or her words with transcendent authority. Indeed, this applies even though 80 percent of the world's Muslims are not Arabs and typically do not understand Arabic. The mere sound of the Qur'an's Arabic verses is sacred, thus the widespread phonetic memorization, and carries persuasive power. This brings us to one of the most important aspects of the oral text, namely, the style of the language and its beauty.

Muslims refer to this as the *i'jaz al-Qur'an,* the unmatchable beauty of the Qur'an's sacred Arabic language, and it carries profound persuasive power that often surpasses the content or apparent meanings of the text being conveyed. As such, references to the Qur'an in persuasive messages may be made in abundance, even when the relevance of the references to the larger message may only be marginal. As the noted historian of religion

Bruce Lincoln has stated: "Religious discourse can recode virtually any content as sacred, ranging from the high-minded and progressive to the murderous, oppressive, and banal, for it is not any specific orientation that distinguishes religion, but rather its metadiscursive capacity to frame the way any content will be received and regarded."[3] This is to say that there are other factors at play when an extremist statement is dressed in Qur'anic verses. In fact, in many instances, and perhaps limited by the particular aesthetic choices of its literary style, the Qur'an provides very little narrative content. One such example is the story of David and Goliath (*Da'ud* and *Jalut*), which is related in *surah* two, *al-Baqarah*, verse 251: "By *Allah*'s Will they routed them and David killed Goliath and *Allah* gave him power and wisdom and taught him whatever else He willed." No more details are offered in the entire text than that and this is not at all unusual for the Qur'an. In most cases, the text assumes a tremendous amount of prior or existing knowledge in its audience, unlike the more detailed accounts of the Hebrew Bible. As such, the narratives often exist in fragmentary forms.

In order for analysts to construct narratives, they must begin with these nonlinear narrative fragments and then rely on a wide range of exegetical materials and supplemental sources, including *tafsir* and Hadith. Compilations of certain Islamic narratives do exist, such as Ibn Kathir's fourteenth-century text, *Stories of the Prophets*, but one must not mistake those accounts as universally authoritative, unlike the content of the Qur'an. Instead, one must bring into consideration a full range of materials. The Hadith (*ahadith*) is a supplemental body of literature that contains the collected reports of the sayings and deeds of the Prophet Muhammad and his companions (*sahabah*). The Hadith is the principal source for the determination of the Sunnah, or exemplary behavior of the Prophet that Muslims should piously emulate. The Hadith began as thousands of oral traditions passed down over the years following the Prophet's death. However, in time, these traditions were eventually recorded, analyzed, and gathered into different collections in the eighth and ninth centuries (CE). The most authoritative collections of Hadith are those attributed to the ninth-century scholars Muhammad ibn Ismail al-Bukhari (d. 870 CE) and Muslim ibn Hajjaj (d. 875 CE). Due to their origins as oral traditions, the Hadith contain not only the content (*matn*) of the stories proper, but also chains of transmission (*isnad*) that list the individuals that relayed them over the years since the time of the Prophet in the seventh century (as a means of authentication). Although often the subject of debate and dispute among Muslims, these traditions are an important source of religious knowledge that ideally allows Muslims to understand the revelations of the Qur'an as they were interpreted by the Prophet during his lifetime. Accordingly, they play an important role in the interpretive and religious sciences of Islamic thought, including jurisprudence (*fiqh*), and provide essential guidance for how Muslims should live their lives and understand the world around them.

Sunni Islam has six authoritative different *hadith* collections, most notably *Sahih Bukhari* and *Sahih Muslim*, as well as numerous popular collections like the *Musnad* of Ahmed Ibn Hanbal, which is the source of the infamous seventy-two virgins story. The Hadith, as well as hagiographies of the Prophet Muhammad like that of Ibn Hisham, are used by exegetes or interpreters of the Qur'an for the composition of *tafsir*, or exegetical commentary. In countries where students do not know Arabic, commentaries (and instructors) in local languages are often the primary channel through which Muslims understand or interpret the sacred words of the Qur'an. Translation of the Qur'an is sometimes discouraged in the Muslim world, and even when used these translations are treated as interpretations rather than translations per se, because *Allah*'s Speech in Arabic is absolute. This realm of interpretation or hermeneutics is where ideas can be debated and where the invocation of narratives can be contested. This is also the realm where the complexities of Qur'anic abrogation are explored, but this topic is most important for matters of Islamic jurisprudence (*fiqh*) and less so pertinent for narrative analysis.

Qur'anic commentaries are integral sources for the details of many narratives not found in the Qur'an, especially about the life of Muhammad. For instance, *surah* 105, *al-Fil,* contains five verses referring to *Allah*'s defeat of the people of the elephant. Without the assistance of Muslim commentaries and supplemental materials, the reader would have no idea what this *surah* is referring to; indeed the reader might even mistakenly assume that it refers to an event or battle during Muhammad's mission. In reality, this *surah* actually refers to an Arab legend that is reported to have taken place during the year of Muhammad's birth around 570 CE. The story goes that a Christian king in Yemen named Abraha was jealous of the pilgrims attracted to the Ka'aba shrine in Mecca, so he built a massive church in Sana'a, and then sent out his army, led by a war elephant to destroy the Ka'aba in Mecca. However, when the army approached, the elephant knelt down in the direction of the Ka'aba and refused to go any further. A swarm of birds then took to the air and pelted the army with stones, causing them to flee and return to Yemen. This story conveys God's miraculous intervention to protect the sacred shrine in Mecca, known to Muslims as the House of God. Commentaries can also carry with them sectarian viewpoints. For example, the *tafsir* of al-Tabari is that of a Sunni historian, az-Zamakshari's *tafsir* is Mu'tazilite, al-Kashi's *tafsir* is Twelver-Shi'ite, al-Kashani's *tafsir* that of a pantheistic Sufi, and Fakhr ad-Din al-Razi's is that of an Ash'arite Sunni theologian. In terms of Islamist extremism, the massive *tafsir* of the Sunni Islamist Sayyid Qutb, entitled *Fi Zilal al-Qur'an,* has proven to be particularly popular.

Of course, throughout this process, the narrative analyst must be very careful not to erroneously reformulate any of the narratives being invoked beyond unavoidable levels. For instance, while analyzing a Qur'anic narrative invoked by Usama Bin Laden, the analyst is justified in looking at the commentary of Qutb, al-Tabari, and Ibn Kathir, but not al-Kashi or al-Kashani. The analyst should also be attentive to uncommon or isolated details at odds with other accounts. In the absence of any single official authority in Sunni Islam akin to the Vatican, it is typically better to talk about dominant versus minority opinions of interpretation, rather than conclusive positions or answers. One must also avoid making assumptions about Islamic beliefs and stories based on the significant overlap with Judaism or Christianity. For example, the Qur'an tells the story of *Allah*'s order to Abraham to sacrifice his son (without naming the son), but unlike the Bible, Muslim exegetes identify the son as Ishmael, the firstborn son, instead of Isaac. The narrative analyst of the Qur'an must therefore be well-grounded in Islamic sacred texts and exegesis to perform this task effectively, which inevitably points to the need for interdisciplinary research, much like the team of coauthors represented in this volume. All of the selections from the Qur'an related in this book are translated from the original Arabic by Jeffry R. Halverson.

This book is a study of how master narratives are invoked specifically by Islamist extremists and how they employ them for ideological ends. As such, the reader is reminded that the ideological understandings of these narratives do not represent the world's 1.5 billion Muslims as a whole. Rather, by "extremists" (a contested term) we are referring to those political actors who seek to impose an Islamist ideology through physical intimidation, coercion, and revolutionary violence against any state or civilian targets that do not share the same vision of the "true" path of Islam, which is typically ultraconservative or puritanical in nature. As such, this book is not concerned with Islamists as a whole, many of which pursue ideological aims through political participation and social activism rather than violence (e.g., Turkey's Justice and Development Party, Morocco's Justice and Charity Party, et cetera). It should furthermore go without saying that this book is not interested in secular-nationalist or leftist movements operating in Muslim societies around the world, even violent revolutionary groups like the Kurdish Parti Karkerani Kurdistan (PKK). Lastly, the reader should also note that most of the narratives contained in this book—such as the

Pharaoh or Badr master narratives—are well-known and treasured by Muslims throughout the world, but the meanings and political implications of these narratives for the vast majority of the world's Muslims do indeed differ substantially from those of the extremists discussed in this book.

Structure of the Book

We begin in Chapter 1 by explaining what we mean by the term "master narrative." Briefly put, it is a narrative that is deeply embedded in a culture, provides a pattern for cultural life and social structure, and creates a framework for communication about what people are expected to do in certain situations. Like all narratives, master narratives have components like story forms and archetypes that can be used to understand their structure. On the basis of these ideas we outline a method for analyzing master narratives that is applied throughout the rest of the book.

Chapters 2 through 13 describe and analyze a series of master narratives employed by Islamist extremists. These master narratives were identified through a comprehensive study of hundreds of extremist statements, texts, web sites, and online media, produced in multiple languages. The master narratives that appeared most frequently in those materials have been included here. However, the selected narratives do not represent a definitive collection of all possible master narratives employed by Islamist extremists. Rather, Islamist extremists selectively use certain master narratives that connect or resonate within a set of cultural and historical circumstances. As circumstances change and develop, new master narratives will inevitably be invoked and developed for dissemination. The master narratives explored here are nevertheless deeply informative and significant selections that outline the current communication of Islamist extremist ideologies. The majority of these narratives are based on Islam's sacred texts, namely, the Qur'an, Hadith, and the *Seerah* of the Prophet, but chapters 9, 11, and 12 are based on later historical narratives, and a range of historical sources were consulted to relate the normative features of those narratives. The specific master narratives included in this book are the following:

- **Chapter 2: The Pharaoh**. The arrogant tyrant rejects the Word of God revealed by His prophet, the tyrant is punished, and his body is preserved as a divine warning for future nations to submit to God's Will.
- **Chapter 3: The *Jahiliyyah***. The Muslim world has regressed to a state of ignorance, barbarism, and polytheism, akin to the pagan society that existed in Arabia before the coming of Islam and its leaders are apostates to be defeated by a vanguard of believers.

- **Chapter 4: The Battle of Badr**. Despite seemingly impossible odds, the early Muslims defeat a much larger and better-equipped army of unbelievers from Mecca through the strength of their convictions and the help of God and His angels on the battlefield.
- **Chapter 5: The Hypocrites**. After migrating from Mecca, Islam is threatened by a nefarious group in Medina who profess to be Muslims publicly but privately do not believe, and use Islam for political expediency as they await the defeat of the Muslims in their conflict with Mecca.
- **Chapter 6: The Battle of Khaybar**. Amidst a pagan siege on Medina, the early Muslims accuse Jewish tribes of breaking an alliance with them, known as the Constitution of Medina, in their conflict with the city of Mecca and punish them for treason.
- **Chapter 7: The Battle of Karbala**. Imam Husayn's martyrdom at Karbala teaches Shi'ite Muslims to see the world as a place where the wicked and corrupt reign, and conclude that it is better to die than to live under tyranny.
- **Chapter 8: The *Mahdi***. In Twelver Shi'ism, "the Hidden One" will reappear as a messianic savior to usher in an era of justice before the Day of Judgment. In Sunni Islam, Muslims believe that a just and righteous leader will emerge at the end of time to guide the world.
- **Chapter 9: The Infidel Invaders**. The Crusader master narrative recounts the occupation of Muslim lands and holy places by Western Christians in order to exploit, subjugate, and desecrate them. Likewise, the Tatar master narrative recounts how Hulagu Khan destroyed the Muslim capital of Baghdad and executed the Caliph during the ensuing massacre. The Mongols (Tatars) later converted to Islam, but ruled according to the *Yasa* (Mongol law) rather than Islamic law drawing their identity as Muslims into question.
- **Chapter 10: *Shaytan*'s Handiwork**. The Qur'an warns believers that alcohol, gambling, and other vices are snares that *Shaytan* (Satan) uses to lead people astray from Islam and send them to Hell.
- **Chapter 11: 1924**. The founding of the secular republic of Turkey and the abolition of the Ottoman Caliphate in 1924 by Atatürk, who is secretly Jewish, is part of a conspiracy by the West and the Zionists to destroy Islam and its power.
- **Chapter 12: The *Nakba***. The establishment of the state of Israel in sacred Palestine and the loss of *al-Quds* (Jerusalem) is a catastrophe, or *nakba*, for the Arab and Islamic world that must be rectified.
- **Chapter 13: Seventy-Two Virgins**. The Qur'anic term *hur al-ayn*, or Houris, is interpreted as dark-eyed maidens who will serve as the

companions of martyrs in paradise as a reward for their righteous sacrifice in the jihad against the infidels.

In the final chapter of the book, Chapter 14, we consider the implications of the master narratives for strategic communication by extremists and those opposing them. Drawing on David Betz's idea of vertical integration,[4] we show how the master narratives create a rhetorical vision containing a stock of story forms, archetypes, and emotional responses that can be used in new narratives. At the other end of the vertical integration hierarchy, the master narratives serve as resources for strategic rhetoric that attempts to persuade audiences to align their personal narratives in the service of three goals that we call the three "R's" of Islamist extremism. As we show, they overwhelmingly rely on analogical reasoning and other similarity-based arguments to relate stories of the master narratives to contemporary events. On the basis of this analysis, we offer five strategies for countering Islamist extremists' use of the master narratives.

CHAPTER 1

What is a Master Narrative?

As noted in the introduction, the term "narrative" is not very clearly defined and it is often used interchangeably with *story*. However, we contend that it is important to make a pragmatic distinction between *narrative* and *story*. We do so because in our analysis of Islamist extremist communications, we have found a useful structural relationship among three types of accounts: stories, narratives, and master narratives. We begin this chapter by defining those terms and elaborating on their structural relationship.

Our exploration of narrative will begin with a story. In 1980 Carl Sagan (d. 1996) had a television show called *Cosmos*. Each episode began with a voice-over telling the audience that the cosmos is made of "billions and billions of stars." From a scientific perspective, this is certainly true. But it wasn't the science of those billions and billions of stars that made Carl Sagan into a household name; it was the narrative about the cosmos that Sagan wove out of individual stories. By connecting those stories over time, he provided "the big picture of the cosmos," which included a narrative of where human beings came from; where we might be going; how stars, planets, black holes, and quarks were organized; all the way down to the story about where human beings fit into the whole of it, and included a message about the singular uniqueness of the "blue planet."

Today we can think about Islamist extremist stories and narratives in much the same way, as well as their relationship to what we call "master narratives." We begin with the fact that what most of us think of as "Islamist extremism" consists of narratives and stories. Academics can offer a technical definition, such as the one articulated by Jeffry R. Halverson in his book *Theology and Creed in Sunni Islam*,[1] but in terms of a popular discourse the phenomenon is generally understood in terms of a mosaic of stories and narratives (e.g., September 11 attacks). When the stories and narratives of Islamist extremism are further linked to culturally embedded master narratives, they reveal a great deal about how members of such extremist groups think about where they came from and where they might be going, how they should be organized, what goals they should pursue in light of what they believe, and what makes them (as "true" followers of the Prophet Muhammad) unique.

Without those connections among stories, narratives, and master narratives, Muslims, like all of the many peoples of the world, would not have a systematic understanding of their tribal histories, lands, states, or nations. Nor would individual believers have a compelling sense of personal purpose that connects an individual "star" with the narratives of the broader community (*ummah*), and their individual stories and collective narratives to the master narratives of an Islamic "cosmos."

Narratives and stories are important because without them language is just a sequence of sounds, little more useful than crude grunts and gestures were to the first homo sapiens. Our ability to make language meaningful is the work of storytelling, an ability that allows us to recognize and make meaningful patterns of words, phrases, and inflections; to make and recognize common story forms and archetypes; and to be responsive to those patterns when they are communicated to us in fragments.

If one were to say "America," what would the average American see? Perhaps some vision of a land of opportunity, the Pilgrim Story, the Civil War, or maybe the flag ("Old Glory"). The same basic pattern recognition that allows hundreds of millions of American individuals to hear in one word, or one story, or one narrative, the whole of American history and culture is evidence of the transhistorical and deeply culturally embedded nature of the American *master narrative.* Our understanding of ourselves, as Americans—who we are, what we are here for, what makes us unique, and so on—is entirely bound up in the narratives we grow up hearing and the stories we connect to them. As the philosopher Alastair MacIntyre put it: "I can only answer the question 'What am I to do?' if I can answer the prior question 'Of what story or stories do I find myself a part?'"[2]

The question "What am I to do?" is of critical importance. What we are interested in analyzing is the cultural work done by narratives of a particular kind—extremist narratives—not so much because we want to be able to define what an extremist narrative "is" (although that is part of it) but rather because as communication and culture scholars, we want to know what work those narratives "do" and how they do it. Whether it is out on the streets of Baghdad, or on the airwaves of Singapore, or through the cell phone texts and tweets of Cairo or Casablanca, these narratives are important sociopolitical forces in our interconnected world.

Our research on Islamist master narratives began with two seemingly simple questions: First, what is so compelling about al-Qaeda's narrative? And second, why is it that Bin Laden and other extremists keep repeating it? In order to answer those questions, we had to pay careful attention to what was being said and repeated, as well as to what linkages and connections were being made within what was being repeated.[3]

From those initial questions came others. We sought to understand the appeal and utility of storylines that suggest that the world is corrupt and that the nations of the Arab and Muslim world have fallen from the path of "true" Islam. We wanted to investigate the basis for notions that the Muslim world exists in a state of ignorance (*jahiliyyah*) like that which existed on the Arabian Peninsula at the time of Islam's birth, or how otherwise ordinary law-abiding Muslims identify with movements that define all "apostate" leaders of Arab and Muslim nations as enemies of God. Finally, we sought to understand the appeal and utility of extremist narratives that define the West, and particularly the United States, as an enemy (the archetypal Crusader) that can only be eradicated by a military jihad, and that serve as a means of recruitment into an ideological alliance that promotes the love of death and the inevitability of victory through martyrdom.

In the end, the reason the narratives of al-Qaeda and other Islamist extremists carry such potency is because they possess an internal coherence for their intended audiences that connects them to grand, deeply culturally embedded, views of history—to master narratives—that Muslim audiences, in broad terms, readily understand, identify with, or feel little need to question. As an exercise in transhistorical pattern recognition, those narratives, and their connection to master narratives, contain powerful persuasive messages that not only resonate or "ring true," but also compel a certain level of ideological identification, behavior, and actions.

We will begin to understand how those extremist stories, narratives, and master narratives work with a review of our terminology and definitions.

Definitions

A story is *a particular sequence of related events that are situated in the past and recounted for rhetorical/ideological purposes*. Events are composed of multiple elements, including actors, times, and other entities (such as *Allah*, angels, the *ummah*, and "the West"), which relate to one another through actions that occur. The term "story" is often used in a colloquial sense to refer to a wide range of resources ranging from official and unofficial news stories to family stories to online postings and blogs. Stories can emanate from a variety of places and serve a variety of purposes, however, they all share a similar structural integrity: a sequence of related events situated in the past that is recounted for a rhetorical or ideological reason.

A narrative is a *coherent system of interrelated and sequentially organized stories that share a common rhetorical desire to resolve a conflict by establishing audience expectations according to the known trajectories of its literary and rhetorical form.* Not all conflicts are resolved, but the desire to do so drives the trajectory of the story form, much as a goal drives a course of action. These conflicts furthermore play out through the actions of protagonists and antagonists in the narrative. Later on, we will explain how narratives are related to the resolution of conflict, but for now let us consider this brief illustration by way of a question: Why is the United States of America engaged in a global counterterrorism campaign?

There are obviously many ways to answer this question, and each narrative possesses its own ideological or rhetorical purpose. Moreover, each narrative—each way of answering the question—depends on an assemblage of smaller stories, each one containing some element, event, or meaning that is assumed to support the overall narrative. In this way, the individual stories serve as units of proof in support of a narrative that is itself employed to accomplish a particular goal.

Finally, and most important for this book, a master narrative is *a transhistorical narrative that is deeply embedded in a particular culture.* By "transhistorical" we do not mean that master narratives are "born" as such. In fact, they "grow up" to attain that stature over time through repetition and reverence within a particular culture. In addition, by "culture" we are referring to an interrelated set of shared characteristics or qualities claimed by an ethnic, social, or religious group to which human beings collectively identify. We have identified thirteen master narratives (divided into twelve chapters) that dominate the present extremist landscape that exists within contemporary Muslim culture and the subsequent chapters explain each of them in exhaustive historical and scriptural detail. Admittedly, the notion of a singular or monolithic "Muslim culture" can be highly problematic, however it is one that is readily employed by anyone who uses the term "Islam" in the singular. Indeed, in the strictest sense, there are undoubtedly a variety of cultures that exist among the hundreds of millions of individuals who identify themselves as Muslims, just as we may speak of multiple "Islams" in the world by pointing to the enormous variety of beliefs and practices among professing Muslims. That said, a singular "Muslim culture" is certainly discernable for our purposes through the same shared elements that allow us to speak of "Islam" in the singular pragmatic sense, including shared sacred texts, rituals, institutions, historical experiences (or memories), festivals, and even language, among others. As such, those shared cultural elements allow us to discuss Islamists in Indonesia and Islamists in Morocco as participants in a shared "culture" possessing master narratives.

Before we move on to an explanation of those master narratives, we must spend a little more narrative space on the reasons why these stories, narratives, and master narratives are so important to our understanding of Islamist extremism. As we have pointed out, our concept springs from the nature of human beings to interpret the world around them through stories, ranging from the most abstract ideas of good and evil, to the use of those ideas to structure relations between humans, to the use of communication to conduct those relationships. By organizing the world in this way, the stories that comprise the narratives that are linked to transhistorical master narratives create not only a sense of coherence but moreover a preferred trajectory for future actions and events that move listeners from desire (which is always rooted in a perceived conflict) to the hope for satisfaction of that desire.

After explaining this framework, we will examine the key features of master narratives, namely, story forms and archetypes. We will then discuss some likely criticism of this scheme by postmodernist scholars in the field. Finally, we conclude this introduction by describing a scheme for analyzing master narratives that we apply in the remaining chapters of the book.

Humans as Storytellers

A master narrative is (as we have defined it above) a transhistorical narrative that is deeply embedded in a particular culture. Why should we focus on them? Answering that question requires us to ask and answer some related ones. First, how do people make sense of the events of everyday life? Second, how do people connect new information to existing information? Third, how do people justify resulting actions? And fourth, where do people want to be in the future and what are they working toward? These questions provide a useful framework for our exploration of the role of master narratives in understanding and countering the rhetoric of Islamist extremists.

We answer these questions by considering three seemingly disparate things, namely, Star Wars, spiders, and Adolf Hitler. This will move us from the "big picture" of cultural narratives to the intermediate level that examines how social organization and order emerge from those cultural narratives, and, finally, to a "ground-level" look at how the two phenomena create a framework for particular kinds of communication.

Star Wars: Good and Evil

A long time ago in a galaxy far, far away, there was a battle between good and evil. In the climax of the story, the hero Luke Skywalker battled his evil father, Darth Vader of the tyrannical Empire. Luke and his noble companions, Han Solo and Chewbacca, destroyed the powerful Death Star, which was poised to definitively crush the freedom-fighter rebel insurrection against the Empire. With the battle won by the heroes, freedom is restored to the galaxy and everyone lives happily ever after.

Star Wars worked as a narrative because it tapped into existing narratives and easily recognizable story forms that are deeply embedded in American culture. Whether the characters are Skywalker and Vader, David and Goliath, Muhammad and the Meccans, or the gunslingers and bandits in *The Magnificent Seven,* good triumphs over evil and restores order to the world, even against seemingly impossible odds. As Joseph Campbell famously conveyed in *The Power of Myth,* such narratives include historical accounts accepted as fundamental answers to fundamental questions; from founding myths about "where we came from" and our "special status" in relation to a divine or cosmic force, to historical parables and precedents used to underscore everyday principles of truth, justice, mercy, and "our" way of life.[4]

As narrative theorist Walter Fisher has observed, cultural beings are best understood as *homo narrans,* or humans as storytellers.[5] Viewed from this perspective, cultures are collections of key stories that are passed along to each new generation to which each subsequent generation adds new material. These stories teach us how to identify our historical enemies and what might be done to defeat them. Much of Campbell's life work on narratives was occupied with the *archetype* (a term we discuss below) of the hero in conflict with a powerful "other." This is a fundamental cultural contest that establishes core principles, including the nature of good versus evil; right versus wrong; and appropriate versus inappropriate dress, deportment, speech, and demeanor. From such narratives, cultures define and inscribe archetypal heroes with the virtues or (as Campbell put it) "masks" of a deity, while using or appropriating those cultural narratives to inspire, direct, and inform every aspect of an ideal life.

How do we make sense of the events of everyday life? How do we connect new information to existing patterns of meaning? How do we justify our resulting actions? And how do we explain where we want to be in the future and what we are working toward? According to Campbell, the answer is *through mythic narratives.* These are fundamental historical artifacts that lie so deeply in our culture that they cannot be separated from it, our personal understanding of who we are, or who we are in relation to what we consider to be transcendent. These narratives are not just abstract systems of stories that are told around campfires or other social gatherings. They are fundamental ways of understanding how we behave together with other human beings.

From Myths to Spiders

Though humans and spiders diverged on the evolutionary path millions of years ago, something they still hold in common is the ability to construct the environments in which they operate. This fact was not lost on the German sociologist Max Weber, who explained the political and economic work of human beings by comparing them to spiders. Humans, as the anthropologist Clifford Geertz (working from Weber) phrased it, are "suspended in webs of significance that we ourselves have spun."[6] Viewed through this metaphor, the political, ideological, and economic life in all cultures is organized by narrative patterns—what Weber called "ideal types" (*idealtypus)*—that provide the "charismatic, traditional (or bureaucratic), and legal" basis for a social order.[7] According to Weber, the authority for all rational action is drawn from the master narratives that represent and evoke these ideal types. Here we see the connection to Fisher's *homo narrans* and Campbell's cultural myths: These powerful narratives provide every society with its own sense of rationality, particularly the rationality that says what counts as truth in arguments in the public sphere.

To show how this schema works, Weber unpacked two intertwined cultural narratives, the *Protestant ethic* and the *spirit of capitalism.* He contended that these two narratives have historically defined Americans' beliefs about how hard work and the accumulation of capital are related to an ironic Biblical view of the good life that warrants entrance into Heaven. This is "ironic" because the Biblical account of the life of Jesus of Nazareth strongly emphasizes selflessly working for social justice and giving away capital to the poor—values that are quite the opposite of those that drive American industry and the work of the faithful under the Protestant ethic.

Yet the apparent contradiction between the Biblical narrative and the interpreted meaning is not surprising. Cultural narratives and powerful tribal or national interpretations of them are constructed out of symbols, particularly in the form of language. Symbols are necessarily ambiguous and subject to local interpretations for meaning. There is, as the Christian story of St. Thomas suggests, room for doubt in this narrative world of mythic, or textual, certainty.[8] We see these same kinds of internal contradictions between verses from the Qur'an that prohibit killing innocents and the diverging interpretations of those verses by al-Qaeda, or any of the extremist groups that identify with them.

Thus, how do we make sense of the events of everyday life, even when events may appear contradictory? How do we connect new information to existing patterns of meaning, or reconcile contradictory information to those patterns of meaning? How do we justify our resulting actions, regardless? And how do we explain where we want to be in the future and what we are working toward? The answer is that we connect events, new information, or actions to our understanding of existing cultural narratives, or what we call master narratives. Weber showed us that these master narratives define and defend principles of a particular (e.g., divinely sanctioned) social order. A social order does not just appear out of nowhere. It is actively constructed and shaped by people as they communicate with each other, arguing that some ways of behaving and relating to one another are preferable to others, often by being encoded with transcendent status. Next we turn to a literary critic who explains how master narratives shape communication for ideological ends.

Hitler the Storyteller

Kenneth Burke (d. 1993) offers a third path into our narrative framework. Burke was a rogue literary critic most interested in the social and political work accomplished by the rhetoric of stories. He provided us with a detailed account and illustration of how narratives "work" to bring about social and political ends. He began his career as a critic with an analysis of extremist ideological texts—those that defined communism, capitalism, and socialism. But he is probably best known for his 1939 essay, *The Rhetoric of Hitler's Battle*, an interpretive rhetorical reading of Adolf Hitler's narrative manifesto, *Mein Kampf* ("My Struggle").

In that essay, Burke outlined a theory of narrative form as *symbolic action*—as communication. He discerned that for Hitler, symbolic action was rooted in the standard storytelling device of defining a common enemy, in this case "the Jews." Through a recounting of his personal experiences and anecdotes, Hitler used his allegations against Jews to create *identification* among sympathetic readers. His argument was that Germans have an "inborn dignity" sullied by "others" not of their own race. Only a *symbolic rebirth* that rids their land of the influences of these "others" (particularly in the finance industry) can lead to a utopian society founded, once again, on (mythic) Aryan principles. This narrative and its political or ideological end even shares some similarities with the narratives conveyed by Usama bin Laden and other extremists who call for the "purification" of Muslim societies through the establishment of the "Islamic state," or the Caliphate, by ridding the Muslim world of the negative influence of "others" (including, once again, the Jews) who do not share "true" Islam and its cultural values.

For Burke, all symbolic action depends on story form, because "form *is* the appeal."[9] By "form" Burke means an *identifiable pattern* that is born out of a *desire to resolve a conflict* and ends in *satisfaction* of that original desire. For example, Hitler's dream of a utopian Aryan society establishes a desire that can only be satisfied by ridding Germany of the common enemy that is keeping the country from being the ideal. Hitler symbolically constructed the Jews as the common (racial) enemy, the evil "other," against which the true racial Aryans (the heroes responsible for realizing the utopian Aryan narrative) must fight. If the audience does what Hitler says, the Germans will restore racial purity and financial order and a utopian society will come to fruition. Anything less than a narrative trajectory that ends with the symbolic (if not actual) elimination of Jews from Germany would be, for Hitler and his followers, a failure to satisfy completion of the form.

The rhetorical organization of the narrative is based on a belief that the present is defined by chaos, that the very soul, as well as the land and property and government of the German people, was tainted by powerful bankers and Jews and immigrants, and that if readers/listeners learned to identify with the personal experiences of the storyteller (i.e., Hitler), they, too would see themselves as having a place in this fight.

Indeed it was their duty or sacred honor to help the leader once again purify the German race by ridding it of these evil influences, and once again establish the Aryan supremacy that was God's will. Consider this well-known passage from volume one, chapter eight of *Mein Kampf*:

> What we have to fight for is the necessary security for the existence and increase of our race and people, the subsistence of its children and the maintenance of our racial stock unmixed, the freedom and independence of the Fatherland; so that our people may be enabled to fulfill the mission assigned to it by the Creator.[10]

Figure 1.1 below depicts visually the idea of symbolic story form. Desire to resolve a conflict creates a narrative trajectory composed of participants, actions, and events that can only be satisfied by the resolution of the original conflict. This depiction of a symbolic form is progressive in that each account or story in *Mein Kampf* leads the reader from identification with

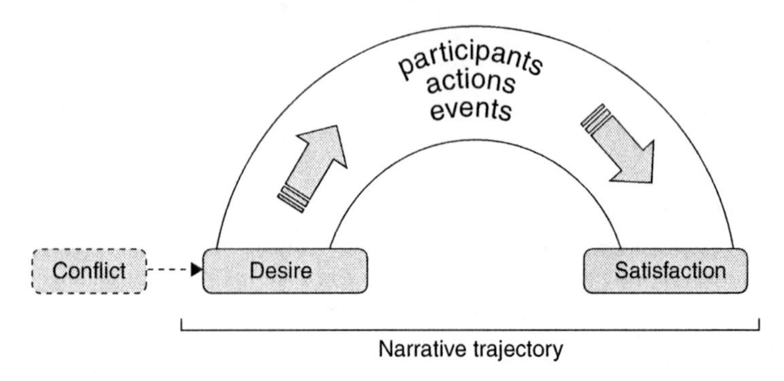

Figure 1.1 Story form

the narrator and his experiences to a shared perception about how the conflict must be resolved through a battle designed to rid Germany of outsiders who prevent it from reaching its full (mythic) potential. From the time of its original publication to its cult status among racialist groups today, *Mein Kampf* represented a master narrative against which ordinary German citizens were asked to measure their everyday experiences, frame any new information that they received, and justify their individual and collective actions.

Burke's ideas about the relationship between narrative form and political or ideological action are useful for three reasons. First, they allow us to understand how many *story forms* follow the same narrative trajectories and can therefore be understood in relation to a master narrative. Second, they point out the singularly important role of archetypes as sources of cultural information relevant to the parsing of stories, narratives, and master narratives. Third, they show us how the abstract ideas of myth and social order can inform real, everyday attempts to persuade others to accept a given point of view.

Stories and Their Forms

Master narratives contain distinct *story forms.* This means that each one of them displays a distinct pattern that can be understood as the desire to satisfy or accomplish the preferred political or ideological end of a conflict. Story forms are *standard patterns on which stories may be based, defining the typical characters, their actions, and sequences of events in a story.* For example, a "rags to riches" story involves a protagonist who goes from poverty to prosperity, only to suffer a setback at the hands of an antagonist, which must be overcome in order to restore his or her success.

It is important to note here that while all story forms have a preferred outcome—the satisfaction of the desire rooted in conflict—that these desired endings *do not always occur.* In fact, the allure of a preferred ending is a powerful inducement to do whatever work is required to bring it about. For Islamist extremists, the reinstatement of the Caliphate, the implementation of *shari'ah* law, or the expulsion of the "Crusaders" from their lands, forms a powerful source of narrative satisfaction despite the fact that those hoped-for-events have not occurred.

With that in mind, it is easy to see the work of symbolic framing devices in many stories or narratives that follow the same basic pattern. For example, Hitler's account of his experiences that comprises *Mein Kampf* consists of a series of interconnected stories. Those stories, when read as an example of a *Deliverance* story form, provide a way to understand how to "read" or interpret the conflict and its intended outcome. The result is that readers perceive the conflict, or Hitler's "heroic struggle" to save the nation, as a battle waged between a heroic Aryan leader (himself, and, by extension, his loyal readers and followers) and—as he portrayed them—the powerful Jews and their allies.

In form, as well as content, this is a typical narrative pattern for a Deliverance form in which the intervention of (in this case) a deity, allows for order to finally be restored. For Hitler, that order—that rational, idealized, if mythic, order—was captured in the ideal Aryan state. In Chapter 4, we will show how another Deliverance tale, rooted in a conflict between the Prophet Muhammad and a powerful pagan "other," follows the same story form and narrative trajectory. In the story of the Prophet's confrontation with the pagans of Mecca, divine intervention satisfies the desire for divine sovereignty over an ignorant pagan society or state. The struggle between good and evil that it constructs has been used—and is still used—to justify a variety of political actions by Islamist extremists.

Archetypes

Archetypes are *standard characters that one might expect to find in a story.* They unlock motives and operate as "shorthand terms for situations" in which characters might find themselves. All archetypes are tied to story forms, but not all characters in stories are necessarily archetypes.

Examples of archetypes that we have seen thus far are those of the prophet and pagan. In Islamist extremist propaganda, the term "Crusader" is often used as an archetype that calls forth a particular story form and character. This archetype calls forth a foreign Christian occupier who unjustly invades and occupies Muslim lands for profit, plunder, and the imposition of his religion or ideology. When an extremist uses this archetype, he also invokes an overarching narrative that binds this story form, this pattern, to a larger historical and political end—the reestablishment of Islamic authority over the land.

Archetypes may also be expressed in narrative fragments, in which part of a story or a title or an icon is utilized to evoke an entire master narrative. For example, Shi'ite Muslims often refer to "Karbala," a tragic battle that occurred in 680 CE, in order to evoke a much longer narrative about a historical event that helped define competing religious identities and worldviews that remain with us today.

As much as archetypes capture the essence of a story form, they also obscure points of possible departure. Calling American and allied forces "Crusaders" distorts the mission of coalition forces in Iraq and Afghanistan and does not make narrative space for the good work being done by those troops and contractors in rebuilding infrastructure, schools, and mosques. But that is, of course, the power of the archetype. It not only encapsulates an entire story form, but also obscures or distorts details that may make that story form less complete or compelling.

This is particularly true when archetypes are placed in binary oppositions, such as that between the Prophet and the pagans of Mecca. As H. L. Goodall Jr. has argued:

> The result is a radical fundamentalism made to legitimize a narrative of holy war through extreme bifurcation of the known world into two, and only two, camps—one made up of true believers and an "other" of infidels; one made up of "us" and another made up of "them;" Jihadists versus Crusaders. This unfortunate and unrealistic bifurcation serves to simplify a complex world that is otherwise threatening, unknown, ambiguous, different, and often unfair, so much so that it becomes the duty of all true believers—or all of "us," whichever "us" you be—to rid the world of "them"—by force, a force, itself extreme, that often means a truck bomb when it doesn't mean a flurry of bullets and hand grenades, purposefully targeted at civilians.[11]

As we will argue in the final chapter of the book, finding new ternary ways to transcend these binary oppositions is one important step in countering extremist narratives. Another possible point of departure is located in postmodern challenges to modernist thinking.

Enter the Postmodernists

Through MacIntyre, Fisher, Campbell, Weber, and Burke, we have thus far come to understand master narratives as powerful resources for motivating actions. We appreciate that narratives are key to understanding how cultures organize themselves as well as how cultures deploy narratives to inspire a connection between individual and group experiences to historical stories that embody precedents, values, and principles. Through Burke, we also see exactly how the inner workings of cultural narratives help accomplish communicative ends.

By now some readers may ask why we are relying on elements of modernist notions of narrative. After all, haven't scholars moved beyond modernist conceptions like "master narratives" in our understanding of the circulation and work of narratives within cultures? Our answer is "yes," but there is a caveat.

While postmodern theories may well represent attractive resources for how we might learn to *counter* extremist arguments (in the same ways that postmodern theories provide rich textual resources to counter modernist conceptions of narrative) it is vital to remember that Islamist extremists emphasize the articulation of traditional "transcendent" values derived from a "grand" or authoritative text. These master narratives are thoroughly "modern" (in the macro sense) and their ideological uses are definitely "modernist." Therefore, on a pragmatic level, modernist conceptions of narrative offer important opportunities to approach an understanding of how these master narratives achieve political and ideological ends for extremists. Countering those narratives, however, is likely to require a more postmodernist campaign.

Furthermore, just because postmodern theories have supplanted some modernist traditions of criticism and vehicles for interpretation among academics does not mean that postmodern cultures have been successful in supplanting traditional ones, particularly those Islamic cultures that are heavily reliant on traditional religious authority and enduring narrative practices that proscribe cultural life. As the poet Octavio Paz once expressed it, ours is a "plural present."[12] We live in a world that is neither modern nor postmodern, but instead in a world whose evolution is still underway and where those two ways of knowing and being in the world do, in fact, coexist. Paz's characterization of the "plural present" seems abundantly meaningful as a way of engaging extremist Islamic narratives as modern texts as well as challenging them. But we are getting ahead of our story. Before we begin to challenge these narratives, we must first labor to understand them.

From Narratives to Master Narratives

To review: A narrative, then, is *a coherent system of stories that share a common rhetorical desire to resolve a conflict by establishing audience expectations according to the known trajectories of its literary and rhetorical form.* A master narrative is *a transhistorical narrative that is deeply embedded in a particular culture.* All master narratives are narratives, but not all narratives are master narratives. This complex definition of two of our key terms and how they relate to one another requires some further unpacking.

Fisher defines two tests of narrative validity or rationality. One is *narrative probability*, or whether the narrative "hangs together," meaning it is coherent and makes sense. If a narrative is created out of a collection of stories, some of which show that God cares if humanity believes in Him, and others that show He couldn't care less, it would not be consistent or make sense.

To be coherent, a collection of stories must be *systematic.* In other words, the stories must relate to one another in consistent ways, and carry a common theme. They must form a structure where one story reinforces, elaborates, or combines with another so that the whole is greater than the sum of the parts. In later chapters, we show how many of the master narratives of Islamist extremism originate in the stories of the sacred texts, and then resurface as they are applied to contemporary situations. They form the basis for analogies that allow their audiences to understand what is happening now in their terms.

Fisher's second test of validity is *narrative fidelity*, or whether the narrative relates to the reality of the world as the audience understands it. According to Burke, this happens when a narrative taps a shared desire among audience members to resolve an archetypical conflict. Despite important cultural differences, all human beings share basic desires for survival, security, safety, happiness, freedom, prosperity, and so on. They also face common situations where fulfillment of these desires is threatened.

Narratives make sense of these situations by establishing archetypical characters, relationships, and standard actions that rationalize these threats. For example, natural disasters can be explained as the action of a deity to punish sinners who have angered him. War can be explained as an attempt by a villain (or villainous group) to exploit, humiliate, or eliminate an innocent and heroic population. By framing negative events in this way, a narrator makes sense of them. But without a framing narrative—in this case a master narrative—the ability to recognize a common pattern and to derive a common meaning for it would be impossible. There would be, to paraphrase Burke, "no thisness of that, no thatness of this." The event would be essentially incoherent because there would be no plausible way to connect it to those patterns of meanings that define our myths, our senses of social order, or give purpose to our lives.

Narratives not only hang together and make sense of the world. As we discussed above, they also create expectations for what is likely to happen and what the audience is expected to do about it. If a villain is threatening to exploit or humiliate an innocent and heroic population through war, members of that population are not expected to sit back passively and let events unfold. They know from other stories that are part of the narrative that if they do, the villain will probably succeed and they will likely be killed, subjugated, or enslaved. The known trajectory of the story form is that the population fights back in an attempt to repel the villain. It spares no effort in doing so and individual members make sacrifices of their lives if necessary to protect the group. Having been given a narrative framework, the audience simply knows—without being told—what is likely to happen and what actions they are supposed to take.

This last characteristic distinguishes master narratives from other narratives. Narratives might meet the above characteristics without being deeply embedded in a culture. As mentioned previously, people apply the term "culture" to just about any social collective. So an organization such as a business, church, or university, can often be said to have its own "culture," as is also the case with a family, a city, or a region. If we fix our attention on a tribe, then it is possible that particular families that belong to it could have narratives, but these would not be master narratives for the tribe unless they were shared among all (or most) families that make up the tribe. Even then, it might not be deeply embedded. For that to happen it must demonstrate historical persistence and be institutionalized. To borrow from sociologist Anthony Giddens, this means that the narrative must be deeply layered in a social system so that it is "chronically reproduced," told again and again over time, and extremely resistant to change.[13] Some narratives may simply be too new or too insignificant for this to develop.

To relate our distinction to American culture within the general context of a global "war on terror" requires looking no further back than to the tragic events of September 11, 2001. At the time the attacks occurred that date was not yet fixed as a narrative nor was a story form, derived from a conflict between Islamist extremists and the United States, yet developed. There was no "end point" or satisfaction yet in sight. For the first few days at least, "9-11" was a collection of stories told about the events. Only over time has "9-11" grown to become a master narrative for Americans, and indeed, possibly for the world.

A Method for Understanding Master Narratives

Our definition and the components described above form the basis of our methodology for analyzing master narratives and understanding how they operate. Specifically, our analysis is attentive to the following questions:

- What are the stories and how are they systematically related?
  - What stories make up the narrative?
  - How do they relate to one another to create coherence?
  - What are the archetypes, and how do they relate to one another?
- What is the trajectory of the story form?
  - To what desire(s) of the audience does the narrative appeal?
  - What is the end state conveyed by the narrative for satisfaction of the desire?
  - What is the narrative path that leads from desire to satisfaction?
- How are the narratives used by speakers to create ideological preferences for courses of action and expectations for what is to be done?
- What evidence is there that the narrative is deeply embedded within a culture?

We contend, as Burke put it, that "form *is* the appeal," and because typical story forms are identified by applying known master narrative templates, that each one of these questions affords potential opportunities for not only understanding the ideological and motivational sense-making work that master narratives perform within a culture, but that they also afford new opportunities for countering them.

CHAPTER 2

The Pharaoh

The Greek historian Herodotus (d. ca. 420 BCE) wrote that the ancient Egyptians were "religious to a higher degree than any other people."[1] The culture that Herodotus observed along the Nile extended into every aspect of life, including the institution of kingship. The Pharaohs were believed to be divine kings who served as intermediaries between humanity and the gods. They organized the universe to make it habitable and protected human civilization from the malevolent forces of chaos, the god of which was Set (arguably the prototype for Satan). Even time was measured by the reign of the Pharaohs, a chronological framework that spans some three thousand years.

The grandeur of the Pharaonic culture was elegantly expressed in its art, most notably by the reliefs that still decorate the monumental walls and pillars of Egypt's ancient stone temples and tombs. Pharaonic statuary, in particular, had propagandistic, religious, commemorative, magical, and decorative functions, and it was believed that the statues were endowed with life when ritually consecrated.[2] The Egyptian emphasis on depicting the divine in two and three dimensional forms or cult objects lies in stark contrast to the iconoclasm that would later develop in the Abrahamic traditions of Judaism and Islam. Scholars, however, have observed certain continuities between Pharaonic religion and Christianity, facilitated by the shared doctrines of divine incarnation and trinitarianism (both common elements in Pharaonic religion). For instance, the iconic image of Isis and the infant Horus is thought to be the precursor to popular depictions of Mary and the infant Jesus throughout Christendom.

According to the Torah of Judaism, which was written well after the reign of the monotheistic "heretic" Pharaoh, Akhenaten (r. 1372–1355 BCE), a child of the nomadic Hebrews named Moses was raised as an Egyptian prince. As he grew older, Moses discovered his Hebrew roots and encountered the god of his ancestors, Yahweh, in the desert (i.e., the story of the burning bush). From then on, Moses assumed the mantle of Yahweh's chosen prophet and returned to the court of the Pharaoh on Yahweh's behalf, urging him to free the Hebrew people under threat of divine retribution. Pharaoh refused to allow the Hebrews to leave and he was drowned in the sea by Yahweh as punishment for his arrogance. There is no historical or archeological evidence for the existence of Moses or the enslavement of the Hebrews. Furthermore, the Torah does not identify the Pharaoh in the story by name. But when the religion of Islam arose in the seventh century among the Semitic Arab tribes living adjacent to Egypt in the Hijaz (western Arabia), the Torah narrative of Moses and the Pharaoh found new life in an Arabic sacred text, the Qur'an. It is believed that the Qur'an was the first to introduce the figure of the Pharaoh into Arabic literature.[3] The Arabic term for Pharaoh in the Qur'an, *fir'aun*, even gave rise to a verb, *tafar'ana*, meaning to "behave like a hardened tyrant."[4]

The Pharaoh Master Narrative in the Qur'an

The arrogant and obstinate tyrant, the Pharaoh, is arguably the most prominent narrative archetype in the Qur'an. His confrontation with Moses is referenced more than any other narrative in the text, which we should note is *not* an account of Muhammad's life. The conflict between Pharaoh and the great prophet Moses (*Musa*) is repeatedly referenced in the Qur'an's nonlinear, sermon-like, literary structure.

As was the case in the Torah, the Pharaoh of Moses is not identified by name in the Qur'an, but Muslims commonly believe that he was Ramses II (d. ca. 1213 BCE). The Pharaoh is the Qur'anic personification of human arrogance, disobedience, pride, and self-deification. He is an authoritarian and rules his dominion with an iron fist, obsessed with its illusions of power and wealth. He is, in short, the prototypical fallen man seduced by the temporal world; a world that the Qur'an contends is nothing more than a trial in preparation for the life to come. As the famous Sunni exegete Ibn Kathir (d. 1373 CE) once wrote: "Pharaoh and his court were intoxicated with pride of race and material civilization."[5] Ultimately, Pharaoh's destruction is ensured by his own stubbornness and refusal to submit to the Will of *Allah*, despite all the clear signs and miracles that are presented to him by the prophet. This seems to be a departure from the Torah narrative, which explains that Yahweh hardened Pharaoh's heart to make him impervious to the miracles and message of Moses, thus granting Yahweh the opportunity to demonstrate His devastating power to all nations by destroying him (see Exodus 7:3–5).

When Moses is sent to Pharaoh, he is accompanied by his brother Aaron (*Harun*) due to Moses' speech impediment. Aaron, like Moses, is recognized as a prophet in Islam. The Qur'an tells us that Moses implored his Lord: "My brother Aaron is more eloquent than me in speech, so send him with me as a helper to support me, for verily I fear that they will accuse me of lying" (28:34). The deity granted Moses' request and the two prophets traveled together to confront the Pharaoh and demand the release of *Bani Isra'il* (the Hebrews) in the name of the One True God and Lord of the Worlds (*rabbil-'alameen*). The Pharaoh responded by asking: "And what is the 'Lord of the Worlds'? . . . If you take any god other than me I will put you in prison." (26:29) Pharaoh thereafter accused Moses of madness, sorcery, and spreading lies among the people. Ibn Kathir relates in his commentary that "Moses stirred up the wrath of Pharaoh both by putting forward the name of the One True God against Pharaoh's pretended godhead, and by suggesting that any man of sound judgment would understand *Allah*'s majesty."[6]

Thereafter Pharaoh challenged Moses to show him some clear proof of the truth of his message. So Moses cast down his walking staff and it became a living serpent in front of the entire royal court. But still Pharaoh refused to believe. He challenged Moses to a contest against the magicians (or high priests) of Egypt. The parties agreed and the magicians made their staffs and ropes appear as if they were alive. But *Allah* assured Moses not to worry, telling him: "Cast forth what is in your right hand! It will quickly overtake what they fake, for verily what they fake is a magician's trick and the magician will not prosper where he is going" (20:69). The Qur'an further tells us that the magicians were so bewildered by Moses' miraculous display that they threw themselves down in prostration and declared their belief in the god of Moses and Aaron (see 20:70). Ibn Kathir writes that "they [i.e., the magicians] turned back on their past life of false worship and oppression of the weak and confessed their belief in the One True God."[7] Enraged, Pharaoh accused the magicians of conspiring with Moses against him and had the magicians executed (making them into martyrs).

As time passed, Pharaoh grew even more severe and stubborn in his opposition to Moses, but tradition tells us that his wife, known as Asiya (although not named in the Qur'an), accepted his message of monotheism. The Qur'an states: "And God sets forth as an example to those that believe, the wife of Pharaoh (*Imrati Fir'aun*)" (60:11). For her steadfast piety, Asiya is traditionally regarded as one of the best women in Islam alongside figures such as Mary, the mother of the great prophet Jesus (*'Issa*). Unlike the account given in the Torah, the Qur'an relates that Moses was adopted as an infant by Asiya, the wife of Pharaoh, instead of Pharaoh's daughter (Exodus 2:5). Thus, she had a special motherly relationship with the great prophet. Mothers are highly revered in Islam. Incidentally, Khadijah (mother of Fatima) and Fatima (mother of Hasan and Husayn) are also regarded among the best women in Islam. Islamic tradition concludes Asiya's story by telling us that she was tortured and martyred for her beliefs by her husband the Pharaoh when she refused to abandon her monotheism and return to the false polytheism of Egypt.

The Qur'an's narrative emphasizes the materialism and arrogance of the Pharaoh by employing the Torah's story of the Tower of Babel (Genesis 11:3–9), which is a previously unrelated narrative set in Persia. In it, the Pharaoh commands one of his ministers, Haman, to build him a tower to the heavens so that he might see the god of Moses. The Qur'an states: "And Pharaoh said: 'Oh Haman! Build for me a lofty tower so that I might reach the means; the means to reach the heavens and ascend to see the god of Moses for verily I believe he is a liar!'" (40:36–37). Commenting on this verse, Ibn Kathir remarks that "Pharaoh, in the arrogance of his materialism, thinks of the kingdom of heaven like a kingdom on earth; he thinks of spiritual things in terms of palaces and ladders."[8]

Pharaoh is guilty of equating himself, a mere mortal creation, and his human will and whims with that of the supreme deity, the One True God. So misguided is the Pharaoh that he cannot even distinguish the divine (eternal and uncreated) from the material (temporal and created), as indicated by his foolish command to build a tower up to heaven to look at the god of Moses. The Qur'an tells us that the One God of Moses is beyond finite form and incomparable to anything in creation. "He does not beget, nor is He begotten, and there is nothing comparable to Him" (112:3–4).

In keeping with the Torah narrative, the Qur'an relates that Moses threatened Pharaoh with divine retribution for his disobedience in the form of a series of plagues and disasters. Ibn Kathir lists these seven disasters as drought, crop failure, disease, locusts, lice, frogs, and water turning to blood.[9] When the disasters took place, the Egyptians pleaded with Moses to intercede for them. The Qur'an states: "And when the divine punishment falls on them, they say: 'Oh Moses! Call on your Lord for us, by what He committed to you; for if you remove from us the punishment, then we will believe in you and send you off with *Bani Isra'il*'" (7:134–135). But each time the disasters ended, Pharaoh and his people treacherously reverted to their old ways in defiance of the divine will. The Qur'an states: "And We [i.e., *Allah*] did not show them a sign that was not greater than its predecessor, so We overtook them with punishments so that they might return (to obedience) . . . But when We removed from them the punishment, behold they relapsed (into disobedience), and Pharaoh declared to his people: 'Oh people! Does not the kingdom of Egypt belong to me?'" (43:48–51).

Notably absent from the Qur'anic narrative is the killing of the firstborn sons of Egypt, which is the climatic event in the Torah that allows the Exodus to take place (see Exodus 11:1–12:3).

The Qur'an, again in its nonlinear structure, picks up the narrative with Pharaoh in pursuit of Moses and the Hebrews. The deity, *Allah*, commands Moses to lead his people out of Egypt in the cover of night and head toward the sea to the east. Pharaoh is enraged by their escape and leads his soldiers out across the desert to catch them. When Pharaoh's army reaches them, the Hebrews fear they'll be captured or killed. The deity orders Moses to strike his staff against the sea. As the Qur'an relates: "And We revealed to Moses: 'Strike your staff against the sea.' And it divided, and the separated parts were like a great soaring mountain" (26:63). When the Egyptians pursued the Hebrews across the miraculous path through the sea, *Allah* released the waters and drowned the Egyptians.

As Pharaoh struggled in the water and realized his own frail mortality, he cried out with his final breaths that he accepts the god of Moses as the One True Lord. The Qur'an relates: "[Pharaoh] said: 'I believe there is no deity except the God of *Bani Isra'il* and verily I am among those who submit [i.e., *al-muslimeen*]!' . . . [And *Allah* said:] 'Today We will save your body so that you will be a Sign to whomever comes after you! For verily many people are heedless of Our Signs'" (10:90–92). One obscure Muslim legend even adds that the angel Gabriel (*Jibreel*) pushed Pharaoh down into the water to hasten his death for fear that *Allah* would mercifully forgive him and spare his life. However, this is not a normative element of the master narrative.

The Qur'an's account of Pharaoh's death and the preservation of his body led to the development of a fascinating folk practice in modern Egypt, where the mummified remains of Ramses II sit in a room on display at Cairo's Egyptian Museum in Tahrir Square. Unlike the other royal mummies kept in the special climate-controlled room, the remarkably preserved remains of Ramses are regarded as a Sign to all believers of the horrible fate that awaits those who reject God's Will. When a Muslim gazes on the face of Ramses II, he or she sees the face of the tyrant that was salvaged from the sea as a Sign and a warning for all nations. "Did you see *Fir'aun*?" is a question a visitor may well encounter on the streets of Cairo. The practice is probably rather unsettling to Egyptian politicians who fail to satisfy the expectations of Egypt's highly religious population.

The Pharaoh Master Narrative in Extremist Discourse

Conflicts between state regimes and political rebels have been a major force in shaping modern Islamic history, especially after the withdrawal of the colonial powers in the middle of the twentieth century. Independence movements throughout the Muslim world ushered in vigorous debates that exposed the inherent tensions between newly constructed national identities (e.g., Saudi Arabian, Pakistani) and traditional religious and tribal-ethnic ones.

Those debates extended into the arena of politics and legislation, as the systems of government and sources of law for the new nation-states had to be formulated. In most cases, the colonial powers imposed their own designs (often secular monarchies), but once the colonizers withdrew the indigenous masses inevitably sought to exercise their own political will. This often took the form of military revolutions, as was the case in Egypt (1952), Libya (1969), Iraq (1958), Syria (1949), Lebanon (1952), Pakistan (1958), Bangladesh (1971), and Algeria's bloody struggle against colonial France that achieved independence in 1962.

The segments of Muslim societies that emphasized above all else their religious identity and supported an "Islamic" system of governance, rather than the dominant nationalist and secular ideologies of the day (favored by many of the revolutionaries), are known as "Islamists." As stated in the introduction to this volume, Islamists are not at all a monolith. However, in their most radical "jihadist" or extremist form, the Islamists adopted the same violent revolutionary strategies that nationalists had done before them, including the early Zionists that established the state of Israel in 1948.

For Islamist extremists, the master narrative of the Pharaoh vividly reflected their own struggles against rulers and state regimes deemed to be irreligious, anti-Islamic, or even atheistic. Their deployment of the master narrative is far-reaching and can be found in extremist literature and media from as far away as Indonesia. But one of the earliest and most shocking modern extremist invocations of the master narrative appeared in the land where it was originally set, the land of Egypt.

On October 6, 1981, President Anwar Sadat was reviewing a military parade commemorating Egypt's 'victorious' campaign in the 1973 Yom Kippur War. Four years prior, Sadat initiated peace negotiations with Israel by visiting Jerusalem with the encouragement of U.S. President Jimmy Carter. The peace treaty was enormously controversial and made Egypt the first Arab state to recognize Israel. Sadat's autocratic regime was terribly unpopular in Egypt and its notorious prisons were full of political dissidents and critics ranging from secular-liberal intellectuals to the senior leadership of the Muslim Brotherhood. As the military parade passed by the reviewing stands on a comfortable October afternoon, television cameras broadcast the events across the region. A truck turned out of the procession and came to a stop. Four soldiers exited the vehicle. They rushed toward the reviewing stands and Sadat stood up to salute them. The soldiers drew their weapons and opened fire. The four men were members of a small Islamist extremist group known as *Tanzim al-Jihad.* As Lieutenant Khalid al-Islambouli, the leader of the plot, finished firing his weapon at Sadat, he cried out: "I have killed the Pharaoh!" Sadat was shot thirty-seven times. Thereafter, videotapes of the bloody televised spectacle fetched huge prices on the black market and it remains readily accessible online today.[10]

Sadat had attempted to brand himself as the "believing President" after he succeeded the Pan-Arab socialist, Gamal Abdel-Nasser (d. 1970). He released Islamist activists from prison to help him neutralize Nasserists and other Leftist factions in Egypt. He also amended the Egyptian constitution in 1980 to emphasize Islamic law (*shari'ah*) as the principal source of legislation. But despite these overtures, serious social and economic turmoil at home and abroad fostered considerable instability and enmity toward the state regime. Sadat, whose rule was a military dictatorship, resorted to brutal crackdowns and police sweeps to suppress his critics, which included many of the same Islamists he had freed and sought to appease. To the extremists, he was an arrogant tyrant that persecuted the believers and prevented the establishment of the Islamic state that *Allah* demanded. Sadat had also done the unthinkable by recognizing the "Zionist entity" of Israel, which even secular Arab states like Syria or Iraq had refused to do.

The Pharaoh designation is not reserved only for the rulers of Muslim countries. Any political ruler deemed to be hostile to Islam is a worthy Pharaoh to be opposed. One of the most hated modern political leaders in the Muslim world is the former Israeli general and Prime Minister, Ariel Sharon. To many Muslims, Sharon is the "butcher of Sabra and Shatila"; a reference to the horrific massacre of Palestinian refugees by Israeli-backed Christian militias in Lebanon in 1982. Sharon was Israel's Minister of Defense at the time, but was forced to resign after details of the tragedy came to light. In the following years, he maintained aggressive right-wing political positions that denied Palestinians the right to a state of their own, regularly stating that Jordan is the state for Palestinians.

In September of 2000, Sharon enraged Arabs and Muslims with a provocative stunt in which he toured the *al-Aqsa* Mosque complex, known as the Noble Sanctuary to Muslims and Temple Mount to Jews, along with hundreds of Israeli security guards and affirmed Israeli sovereignty over the contested holy site. When the people of Israel democratically elected Ariel Sharon as the Likud Party candidate for Prime Minister shortly thereafter, it sent shock waves throughout the Muslim world. Over the years, however, Sharon moderated some of his right-wing positions and moved increasingly toward a pragmatic centrism, even leaving the Likud Party to organize a new political party called Kadima. He ordered the withdrawal of all Israeli troops from the Gaza strip, but maintained a militarized border. The move enraged right-wing Israelis, especially religious Jews who believed Gaza was given to them by Yahweh, and Arabs for turning Gaza into "the world's largest prison."

When Sharon suddenly had a stroke and fell into a coma in January of 2006, Islamist extremists (as well as Jewish extremists) attributed his fate to divine retribution. Soon a doctored image began to appear on Islamist web sites depicting Ariel Sharon lying in a hospital bed in a vegetative state. Beside the image of Sharon was a photograph of the mummified remains of Ramses II and a verse from the Qur'an in Arabic across the top, reading: "Today We will save your body so that you will be a Sign to whomever comes after you! For verily many people are heedless of Our Signs" (Qur'an 10:91–92).

The special position of the United States as a world superpower, and its controversial foreign policies, has made the U.S. president a popular target of the Pharaoh narrative, especially during the administration of George W. Bush (2000–2008). The Saudi extremist, Usama Bin Laden, referred to President Bush as "the pharaoh of the century" in an al-Qaeda audio statement released in November of 2002.[11] More recently, in the thirty-seventh issue of the Taliban's online Arabic language magazine *Al-Sumud*, published in the summer of 2009, an article stated:

> Little Bush came and brought with him Hollywood, as well as television stations, to brainwash the heads and fool the minds. He reminded us of the Pharaoh and his people, who represented evil and non-belief. The mujahidin reminded us of Moses (peace be upon him) and his people.[12]

But this hostile designation is not restricted to Bush or U.S. presidents. It has been deployed to refer to Western leaders as a whole as well. In the January 2009 issue of the online English language extremist publication, *Islamist Magazine*, an article entitled "The Propaganda War: War of Words" stated: "Pharaoh (*Fir'aun*), much like western rulers today, murdered and oppressed the believers for their religion and then claimed that Moses was a liar, lunatic, and sorcerer; that he and Aaron were conspiring to terrorize the Egyptian people and brainwash them into leaving their beliefs and values for a backwards ideology."[13] In another online extremist treatise produced in South Africa, entitled "Rejecting the *Taghout* (False Idols)," the author "Shaykh Faisal" writes that "the Pharaoh of Egypt killed children in a desperate attempt to hang on to power. Today we see the pharaohs of the 21st century killing Muslim children in occupied Muslim lands in a desperate bid to hang on to power." In these schemes, not only is the leadership of the West situated in the role of the Pharaoh, but the extremists claim for themselves the archetypal role of the prophet (Moses), or the agent of the deity, to deliver pious warnings and divine retribution.

Analysis of the Pharaoh Master Narrative

As we have seen, the Pharaoh narrative relates a story form of a conflict with God, or between a mortal and an immortal. It begins with an assertion of divine sovereignty (*hakimiyyah*) over creation. The deity, *Allah*, reveals Himself and commissions Moses to serve as His prophet (the agent of the deity or immortal) and exercise His Will. The conflict that produces the story form is one of human arrogance, manifested in the archetype of the powerful (but mortal) Pharaoh who claims sovereignty over the land and its people for himself. As a result of Pharaoh's false-consciousness, which will ultimately lead to his own destruction, Moses' people, the *Bani Isra'il*, suffer enslavement to an oppressive social order.

The narrative trajectory consists of a progressive series of individual stories that further reveal Pharaoh's growing arrogance as Moses presents him with seemingly undeniable Signs of the deity. Throughout these individual stories, Pharaoh refuses to relinquish his arrogant desire to claim the role of the deity for himself. His misguided choices bring destruction on his lands and his people in the form of plagues and disasters. Finally, when the god of Moses commands the *Bani Isra'il* to leave the land of oppression and enslavement (Egypt), Pharaoh sets out to preserve the false social order and destroy them. Assuring his own destruction, the immortal deity destroys the mortal Pharaoh in the sea as an assertion of divine sovereignty. The narrative arch thus completed, this narrative is satisfied by a warning (or a Sign) preserved through Pharaoh's body, that human beings must remember their proper place in the order of creation, regardless of their wealth, armies, and grand civilizations.

The stories that comprise the master narrative of the Pharaoh and Moses meet our criterion for "transhistorical" importance within a culture. The Pharaoh, as the tyrant, is a powerful narrative archetype readily understood by Muslims across the world. Its prominence in the text of the Qur'an has ensured its longevity and continued dissemination. But the enduring political turmoil and tensions across much of the postcolonial Muslim world has also ensured a particularly virulent appropriation of the archetype. Many state regimes remain highly susceptible to polemical designations and associations that invoke the tyrannical Pharaoh. This is most visibly apparent in countries where democratic institutions do not exist. However, more alarmingly, this also applies to any country where governments adhere to largely secular (or insufficiently "Islamic") platforms, even if the governments enjoy popular support.

More broadly, extremists are radically exclusionary with regards to those they accept as "legitimate" Muslims. For instance, an extremist treatise disseminated online, entitled *Lahbat al-Fira'una* ("Game of the Pharaohs"), is a harsh rebuke of the Saudi royal family and religious establishment, advising its readers to "Sharpen [your] blade and punish the [idolaters] by his skinning and butchering them, a just recompense, and the recompense is according to the action committed."[14] This means that virtually anyone with political authority outside of their own immediate fold may well be designated as a Pharaoh to be fought and opposed. In its most virulent form, such as in the case of Anwar Sadat, the Pharaoh master narrative can be mobilized as a framework for violent revolutionary action, including assassinations or other terrorist attacks. In so doing, the extremists are claiming a prophetic role as *Allah*'s agents on Earth, creating death and destruction as a Sign for all the nations of the world.

CHAPTER 3

The *Jahiliyyah*

Religions often articulate worldviews that sharply contrast a morally corrupt social order with a purer, if utopian, counterpart. In the Abrahamic tradition, the time of corruption is contrasted with a time when an agent of God, or prophet, arrived (or will arrive) to lead the people into a new era of righteousness or guidance. For instance, in Christianity, the world was corrupted by the primordial parents of humanity, Adam and Eve, who sinned in the blissful Garden of Eden and corrupted the world and their countless human descendents (i.e., Original Sin). This world of imperfection and sin will one day be perfected when Jesus Christ, who was sacrificed to redeem humanity from Original Sin, returns to the world and ushers in the eternal Kingdom of Heaven.

In Islamic thought, particularly within Sunni Islam, the Prophet Muhammad emerged in a time of corruption and ignorance to deliver the final divine message (the Qur'an), overturn the old pagan order in Arabia, and bring about a utopian social order based on *Allah*'s Will. This past age of ignorance and corruption is known in Islam as the *jahiliyyah*, or the "Age of Ignorance."

The *Jahiliyyah* Master Narrative

Before the Prophet Muhammad began his religious mission in the seventh century (CE), the arid land of Arabia was dominated by polytheistic animism with only small pockets of Jews, Christians, and Zoroastrians. The pre-Islamic era is traditionally depicted in Muslim sources as a time of cruel barbarism and ignorance of *Allah*, known as *jahiliyyah* ("ignorance"). The Arab tribes, both the settled city-dwellers and nomadic herders (Bedouin), venerated a range of spirits (*jinn*) and deities (*alihat*) that inhabited sacred idols, objects, and the landscape of the natural world. The Arabs honored kinship, courage, and martial prowess, and zealously adhered to their ancestral customs. A handful of small cities, such as Mecca, housed important animist shrines where devotees petitioned particular deities through sacrifices and other rituals.

The principal shrine in Mecca was a fifty-foot-tall stone structure that still stands there today, known as the *Ka'aba* ("Cube"). Muslims believe that the shrine was originally built by the prophet Abraham (*Ibrahim*) and his first-born son Ishmael (*Ismail*), but over the centuries human beings went astray and corrupted the shrine for pagan worship. Tradition says that the precincts of the *Ka'aba* sanctuary (*haram*) housed some 360 deities at the time of Muhammad's birth in 570 CE. At the time, the city was controlled by wealthy traders from the Quraysh tribe. References to the Quraysh can be found in the Qur'an, such as this verse from *surah* 106: "By the bonds of the Quraysh, their bonds to travel in winter and summer; let them worship the Lord of this House [i.e., the *Ka'aba*]; He that satisfies their hunger and shields them from fear" (106:1–4). But the animist and merchant society controlled by the Quraysh was a harsh and unforgiving one, which explains in part the emergence of Islam as a radical restructuring of the existing social order and a reaction to its serious socioeconomic shortcomings.

The nineteenth century British anthropologist E. B. Tylor derived the term "animism" from the Latin *anima*, meaning "spirit." In his 1871 work, *Primitive Culture*, Tylor defined animism as a belief in spiritual beings that inhabit the known world. At the heart of Arabian animism was a large contingent of no less than twenty-five deities. At the head of this group was a distant creator deity, *Allah* ("the God"). The name is likely a cognate of the Hebrew *Eloah* (pl. *Elohim*) and Aramaic *Alaha,* given that Arabic is a closely related Semitic language to both Hebrew and Aramaic. In cultic practice, *Allah* was generally passed over in favor of lesser, more personalized or specialized deities, such as the goddesses *al-Uzzah*, *al-Manat*, and *al-Lat.*

These three goddesses were called the "daughters" of *Allah* and reportedly worshipped by the Arabs for the purpose of intercession with the distant high god. The deity *al-Lat* was a sun goddess whose main shrine was located in the city of Ta'if to the east of Mecca; a town ruled by the Thaqif tribe where Muhammad was stoned and nearly killed when he preached his monotheistic message there in 619 CE. The shrine of *al-Uzzah* was in Nakhlah to the south, and Manat's shrine was located in Qudayd on the Red Sea.[1]

Other prominent deities included *Hubal*, a moon god of Mesopotamian origin that was worshipped by the Quraysh at the *Ka'aba*. According to a ninth century (CE) treatise by Hisham ibn al-Kalbi, there were seven divination arrows stationed in front of the idol of *Hubal* that were consulted by the Arabs for a myriad of occasions.[2] The Prophet Muhammad reportedly smashed the idol of *Hubal* when he conquered Mecca in 630 CE and cleansed the *Ka'aba* shrine for iconoclastic, monotheistic veneration of *Allah* alone. The worship of the animist deities during the age of *jahiliyyah* is also evident in the recorded names of the ancient Arabs, such as 'Abd al-Shams ("Servant of the Sun") or Muhammad's ancestor 'Abd al-Manaf ("Servant of the goddess Manaf"). These names were banned under Islam.

The deities of the pre-Islamic Arabs were said to possess powers that could influence nature and the immediate world wherein the tribes struggled to survive. For example, they could assist a barren woman in having a son, or bring rain to a farm besieged by drought. But they were not supreme universal deities in the way that Judaism or Islam envisioned the One God of Abraham. In fact, the Arabs did not even believe in the idea of an afterlife or Day of Judgment.

The idea of the resurrection of the body articulated by Muhammad repulsed the animist Arabs and they mocked him for it. This is evident in several verses of the Qur'an, such as: "And among His Signs is that you see the earth barren, and when We send rain down it bursts with life and grows; truly, He that revives the barren earth can also raise the dead! Truly He has power over all things" (41:39). For the animist Arabs, their actions in life had no consequences for an eternal afterlife. Death was the end of the individual, but the continuity of the tribe remained.

The Arabs did not share a single codified moral code or law either. Rather, they each adhered to their own tribal customs and judgments of their chieftains. The honor, prosperity, and survival of the tribe remained the most important concern in a region where resources were extremely scarce. This harsh order is evident in the tribal blood feuds and tradition of *ghazi* raids that plagued the tribal societies of Arabia for generations. It also meant that any individuals or families that did not belong to a tribe to protect or defend their interests risked being cast to the margins of society, robbed of their property, or even being killed with impunity.

Most of Muhammad's early followers were from the disenfranchised segment of Arabian society. The *ummah* that the Prophet Muhammad proposed was a community based on shared faith that anyone could join, rather than an exclusionary group based on tribal kinship and bloodlines. The Qur'an leveled a similar charge against Judaism because of its traditional emphasis on ethnicity as the defining basis for membership (although conversion is still practiced). Overall, the monotheism (*tawhid*) that Islam articulated was the core component of Muhammad's new social order, as it unified all ritual and worship activities toward a single deity shared by all people.

The Qur'an issued a strong moral critique of ancient Arab society. It condemned many of the practices and socioeconomic inequalities that have since become synonymous with the *jahiliyyah* in Islamic thought. There are an abundance of examples that can be discussed here. One of the most commonly cited examples is the practice of female infanticide. Despite their worship of female deities, the animist Arabs were patriarchal, practiced unrestricted polygamy, and strongly favored sons over daughters. Female infants were sometimes buried alive in the desert. In other cases daughters were sold for a profit as concubines and slaves. The practice of female infanticide is referred to in the Qur'an, such as this verse evoking the Day of Judgment: "And when the female infant, buried alive, is asked for what crime she was killed . . . Each soul will know what it has done" (81:8–9, 14). Another verse states: "Do not kill your children in fear of want, We will provide for them and you; verily killing them is a great sin" (17:31). Islam abolished the practice of female infanticide and Muhammad raised four daughters, the most famous of whom is Fatimah az-Zahra (d. 632 CE).

Another condemned pre-Islamic (*jahili*) practice regarding women relates to the marriage dowry. The Arabs traditionally gave the marriage dowry to a woman's father or other male guardian (e.g., brother), as a price for the woman. Thus, women were property and could be bought and sold. Islam reformed the practice and the dowry was given directly to the bride. Muslim women also retained exclusive rights to the dowry, even from their husbands. These Islamic reforms, along with many others, are points that Muslims commonly reference when they assert that Islam improved the status of women, gave women rights, and affirmed their equality with men. A few contemporary scholars, particularly feminists, have challenged the historicity of such accounts, even suggesting that Muhammad imposed the oppressive patriarchal order of the Abrahamic tradition (i.e., Judeo-Christian) onto the Arabs, resulting in a regression of rights.[3] However, such revisionist views remain highly contentious and take us away from our purpose in this chapter, which is to present the dominant historical narrative in Islamic thought.

The violence associated with the *jahiliyyah* period is depicted through Muslim accounts of corpse mutilation, abuse and torture of captives, and indiscriminate killing. There is certainly a polemical slant to such accounts. However, this is the *jahiliyyah* as it exists in Islamic thought and discourse. For example, it is reported that the body of the Prophet Muhammad's favorite uncle, Hamza ibn 'Abdel-Muttalib (d. 625 CE), was horrifically mutilated by the *jahili* Arabs after the Battle of Uhud. The animist women of Mecca reportedly wore severed body parts (e.g., ears) around their necks and danced around the mutilated corpses of the Muslims to celebrate the pagan victory. The Prophet Muhammad forbade mutilating corpses, even those of the pagan animists.

Other accounts report the torture of early Muslims, such as Bilal, Yassir, or Sumayyah, by the animists of Mecca. The violent barbarism of the Arab animists portrayed in the Muslim sources may have some veracity if the content of the Torah is any indication of ancient Near Eastern tribal conduct. The Israelites are repeatedly commanded by Yahweh to commit brutal atrocities against their tribal opponents, including the slaughter of women and children (e.g., Numbers 31, Deuteronomy 2–3) and mutilation of corpses (e.g., Samuel 18:27).

The time of Islam's birth was dominated by a series of wars between the two superpowers of the ancient Near East, the Byzantine and Sasanian empires. The Byzantine Empire (ca. 395–1453 CE), the Christian successor of the Roman Empire, ruled over Eastern Europe, Anatolia, Syria, Palestine, Egypt, and parts of North Africa. The Zoroastrian Sasanian Empire (224 BCE–651 CE) ruled over what are now Iran, Iraq, Kuwait, Azerbaijan, Turkmenistan, Afghanistan, and other parts of neighboring territories. However, periods of ascendency and decline caused serious fluctuations in the borders and territories under the control of both empires. Arabia, meanwhile, remained largely independent of the two powers, although pockets of the peninsula (especially along the coasts) were controlled by the empires at different time periods.

The war between the Byzantines and Sasanians meant that more trade routes were diverted south through Arabia, including the Qurayshi trading city of Mecca. The presence of the *Ka'aba* shrine had already made it a center of trade because the Arab tribes were forbidden to fight within its sacred precincts, thus facilitating a safe atmosphere for trade. But the diversion of northern trade routes brought in a new level of wealth, which the leaders of the Quraysh enjoyed. The wealth of Mecca led to economic disparities and a competitive materialism developed among the tribes, including usury.

The Qur'an harshly condemns the decadence of the time and the suffering of the poor, declaring: "Woe to every backbiter and slanderer! He that gathers wealth and hoards it, thinking that his wealth is eternal! Nay, he will be thrown into the *Hutama* (the Fire of Hell)!" (109:1–4). A tradition from the Hadith relates that a companion of the Prophet said to the leaders of the Quraysh: "Inform those who hoard wealth, that a stone will be heated in the Hell-fire and will be put on their chests till it comes out from the bones of their shoulders and then put on the bones of their shoulders till it comes through their chests."[4]

Muhammad banned usury (see, e.g., Qur'an 3:130) and prescribed obligatory alms, the *zakat*, that "purified" wealth through distribution to the poor and needy, especially widows and orphans. Muhammad's message thus threatened the economic hierarchy of Mecca, including his call for an end to the worship of the pagan deities that people (and their money) came to honor from throughout the region. The animists of Mecca did not know that Muhammad's religion would one day bring millions of people from throughout the world to visit the sacred precincts of Mecca.

In the traditional Muslim view of history, the time of *jahiliyyah* came to a close with the establishment of Islam in Arabia by the Prophet Muhammad. His prophethood was the culmination and completion ("Seal of the Prophets") of a long line of prophets (*anbiyya*) and messengers (*rusul*) going back to the primordial father of humanity, Adam. Islamic tradition suggests that there have been some 124,000 prophets and messengers throughout history. When each of those prophets died, their people and nations inevitably went astray. Thus, the Seal of the Prophets was called by *Allah* to deliver the sacred Qur'an, a divinely preserved revelation (*wahy*) to guide humanity forward until the Day of Judgment. The *jahiliyyah* thus came to a close with this revelation and the establishment of the Muslim community in Medina.

But the concept of *jahiliyyah* has remained a fixture of Islamic thought. Practices or ideas deemed to be un-Islamic can be rebuked by mere association with the pre-Islamic age of ignorance. For example, tradition says that the decadent *jahili* Quraysh used to wear long robes that dragged along on the ground, therefore devout Muslim men will avoid any similar behavior and wear pants that end high on the upper ankle. Sunni Muslims may argue that the practice of temporary marriage (*mutah*) is *jahili* and forbidden (Shi'ite Muslims disagree). Other Muslims, particularly Wahhabites or Salafis, may rebuke the popular practice of saint (*wali*) veneration by likening it to the idolatrous polytheism of the *jahiliyyah*. However, the idea that entire Muslim societies have experienced a reversion to a state of *jahiliyyah* is a modern innovation without orthodox precedent.

The *Jahiliyyah* Master Narrative in Extremist Discourse

During the last decade of his life, the Egyptian Islamist ideologue Sayyid Qutb (d. 1966) diagnosed the ills of the modern Muslim world as symptoms of a global reversion to a state of *jahiliyyah*. In his view, Muslim societies had abandoned the divine guidance of the Qur'an in favor of foreign atheistic (or self-deifying) systems created by mere men, such as nationalism, socialism, or communism. In the absence of God's sovereignty (*hakimiyyah*) on earth, the most deviant and barbaric qualities of humanity emerged and shaped entire societies. The result was a self-indulgent, individualistic, crime-infested, and oppressive social order ruled by tyrants who brutally abuse their subjects and unjustly govern according to their own whims and self-interests. The immediate reference point for Qutb's observations was the regime of Gamal 'Abdel-Nasser (d. 1970) in Egypt. Qutb briefly held close ties to Nasser's revolutionary regime before Qutb's imprisonment in 1954. His articulation of this new age of *jahiliyyah* was most famously articulated in his radical treatise, *Ma'alim fi'l-Tariq* ("Milestones"), which was written during his imprisonment and published in 1965 prior to his execution.

The savagery that Qutb and his fellow inmates suffered in Nasser's prisons, including the murder of over twenty Muslim Brothers in their cells in 1957, led him to conclude that the Egyptian regime and its fervent supporters were not Muslims at all. Rather, they were *apostates*; "Muslim" in name only. Qutb articulated the heretical doctrine of *takfir* ("excommunication") associated with the ancient Kharijite (*khawarij*) sect and medieval Hanbalite jurist, Ahmed ibn Taymiyyah (d. 1328 CE). By contrast, orthodox Sunni Islam advocates the view that anyone who professes to be a Muslim should be accepted as a Muslim. Only God can judge the sincerity in people's hearts or judge their shortcomings.

But proponents of *takfir*, which includes most extremists, claim the right to decide who *is* or *is not* a Muslim, typically by judging outward behavior. For example, Ahmed ibn Taymiyyah deemed that anyone who does not rule according to Islamic law (*shari'ah*) is an unbeliever and must be fought. He denounced the converted Mongols of his time who ruled by the *Yasa* (customary Mongol law) rather than *shari'ah*, and called for a military jihad against them (see Chapter 9). Likewise, for Qutb, the remedy was clear: the implementation of an Islamic system based on *shari'ah* and an all-out war on the forces of *jahiliyyah*.

Qutb's *Milestones* was a radical departure from the more moderate and traditional ideas of his earlier works. His prior contention that Islam was a comprehensive, all-encompassing way of life was amplified to a radical degree and colored by venomous denunciations of all "man-made systems" that had usurped the sovereignty of God from the world. Qutb declared that the Muslim community, even Islam as a whole, vanished from existence centuries ago, at the moment the laws of God were suspended on earth.[5] Human civilization, after a momentary interruption in the seventh century (CE), reverted to a state of total ignorance, formulated degenerate false systems, and suffered from a disease that only the medicine of the Qur'an could cure.

Qutb applied this "new" state of ignorance (*jahiliyyah*) to "all existing so-called Muslim societies," stating:[6]

> If we look at the sources and foundations of modern ways of living, it becomes clear that the whole world is steeped in *jahiliyyah*, and all the

> marvelous material comforts and high-level inventions do not diminish this ignorance. This *jahiliyyah* is based on rebellion against God's sovereignty on earth. It transfers to man one of the greatest attributes of God, namely sovereignty, and makes some men lords over others. It is now not in that simple and primitive form of the ancient *jahiliyyah*, but takes the form of claiming that the right to create values, to legislate rules of collective behavior, and to choose any way of life rests with men, without regard for what God has prescribed. The result of this rebellion against his authority of God is the oppression of His creatures. Thus the humiliation of the common man under the communist systems and the exploitation of individuals and nations due to greed for wealth and imperialism under the capitalist systems are but a corollary of rebellion against God's authority and the denial of the dignity of man given to him by God.[7]

The principle of God's sovereignty (*hakimiyyah*), which Qutb borrowed from the writings of the Pakistani Islamist Abu 'Ala Mawdudi (d. 1979), became the principal ideological basis for his vision of the "Islamic state." Qutb interpreted verses of the Qur'an focused on *al-hakimiyyah* (5:44–45, 47) by altering the meaning of the verb *yahkumu* from "judge" to "rule," and thereby sanctioned action to dismiss a ruler who failed to apply the divine law.[8]

Qutb's political ideology was deeply tied to an idealized conception of Medina during the time of the Prophet and his companions (*sahabah*), which, for ease of reference, we will call the Medinan paradigm. "At one time, this Message [i.e., Islam] created a generation, the generation of the companions of the Prophet," he wrote, "[who are] without comparison in the history of Islam, even the history of man."[9] As Qutb saw it, the companions of the Prophet were limited to only one source of guidance, the Qur'an, despite being surrounded by the cultures and civilizations of the Byzantines, Persians (Sasanians), Jews, Syrian Christians, and many others. "Their training was to be based on the method prescribed by God," Qutb wrote, "Who gave the Qur'an, purified from the influence of all other sources."[10]

But later generations were influenced by foreign ideas, such as Greek philosophy, creating a "mixed source" and "the like of this generation [i.e., the *sahabah*] never arose again."[11] The highly flawed assumptions of this claim aside,[12] it reveals Qutb's belief that the decline of Islam was due to the loss of the Qur'an as the sole source of guidance and basis for all action. The modern onslaught of *jahiliyyah* forces in the world thus included any society in which "people's beliefs and ideas, habits and art, rules and laws," even things considered to be a part of Islamic culture or Islamic thought, dictate the affairs and actions of human beings.[13] Such constructions, in his view, are not only illegitimate rivals to the Qur'an, or at least sources of "mixing," but a form of the gravest sin, *shirk* ("idolatry").

To turn to any source other than the Qur'an as a basis for a system of governance, law, or anything else, is no different than worshipping *Hubal* or *Manat.* He states: "We must also free ourselves from the clutches of *jahili* society, *jahili* concepts, *jahili* traditions and *jahili* leadership. Our mission is not to compromise with the practices of *jahili* society, nor can we be loyal to it."[14]

Qutb wrote that the world needs "a Muslim community to come into existence which believes that 'there is no deity except God,' which commits itself to obey none but God, denying all other authority, and which challenges the legality of any law which is not based on this belief."[15] He identified this Muslim community as an Islamic "vanguard" that would set out to "revive Islam" and "then [keep] walking on the path, marching through the vast ocean of *jahiliyyah* which has encompassed the entire world."[16] Qutb's idea of a revolutionary vanguard to lead the struggle for a new social order clearly echoes the Marxist treatises of Lenin (d. 1924) and Trotsky (d. 1940). For Qutb, Islam is not only a system of worship, thought, or theology, but a living social system that must be realized through action.

The process toward this realization is a gradual one, beginning with belief and evolving into a "living reality" that "challenges [and struggles against] *jahiliyyah* both in theory and in practice."[17] Qutb's call for a struggle against the "treacherous tactics" of the forces of *jahiliyyah* has been a source of alarm for many, including the Egyptian government, and a major inspiration for Islamist extremists, such as Ayman al-Zawahiri. Qutb never explicitly called for acts of terror against state regimes in *Milestones*; however, there are numerous passages that call for an armed struggle (*jihad*) and clearly reflect his negative experiences with the Nasser regime. He writes:

> [The *jahiliyyah*] is always ready and alive to defend its existence consciously or unconsciously. It crushes all elements which seem to be dangerous to its personality. When *jahiliyyah* takes the form, not of 'theory' but of an active movement in this fashion, then any attempt to abolish this *jahiliyyah* . . . which presents Islam merely as a theory is [useless] . . . *Jahiliyyah* controls the practical world . . . In this situation, mere theoretical efforts to fight it cannot even be equal, much less superior to it. When the purpose is to abolish the existing [*jahili*] system, and to replace it with a new system . . . then it stands to reason that this new system should also come onto the battlefield as an organized movement and a viable group. It should come into the battlefield with the determination that its strategy, its social organization, and the relationship between its individuals should be firmer and more powerful than the existing *jahili* system.[18]

The responsibility for this armed struggle falls to the "vanguard." This vanguard would then separate itself from *jahili* society and mobilize under "a new leadership" that Qutb compared to the Prophet after the *hijra* ("migration") to Medina in 622 CE. This singular concept provided the ideological foundation for the formation of al-Qaeda. Indeed, it is generally believed that Usama bin Laden was a student of Qutb's brother, Muhammad Qutb, in Saudi Arabia, a man who himself produced many writings reiterating the views of his martyred sibling.

For Sayyid Qutb, any society where one group holds authority over another subservient group is considered "backward" and represents *jahili* society.[19] Authority, in this scheme, belongs to God alone. A state that forms around the sovereignty of God, through the implementation of God's law, may take various forms in its material and organizational structure, but its principles and values are eternal and unchangeable.[20] Qutb lists these principles as: "The worship of God alone, the foundation of human relationships on the belief in the Oneness of God, the supremacy of the humanity of man over material things, the development of human values and the control of animalistic desires, respect for the family, the assumption of being representative of God on earth according to His guidance and instruction, and in all affairs of this viceregency the rule of God's law (*shari'ah*) and the way prescribed by Him."[21]

Qutb's perception of the "Islamic state" as the rule of God through a government based on the *shari'ah*, which is responsible for regulating human affairs and harmonizing them with the order of the universe, led him to the view that rulers are servants of the divine law as well.[22] Qutb's conception of *shari'ah* as the foundation of his entire construction of the "Islamic state" is thus essential. He defined his unique understanding of *shari'ah* as "everything legislated by God for ordering man's life; it includes the principles of belief, principles of administration and justice, principles of morality and human relationships, and principles of knowledge."[23] As such, the *shari'ah* is not limited to mere legal injunctions as traditional definitions would have it, but includes all aspects of life, the sciences, and the arts, as well as political, economic, and social affairs, all in correlation with complete submission to God alone.[24]

For Qutb, the *shari'ah* also formed the basis of citizenship, nationhood, and family ties, in contrast to racial tribalism of the *jahiliyyah*. He writes: "A Muslim has no country except that part of the earth where the *shari'ah* of God is established and human relationships are based on the foundation of relationship with God; a Muslim has no nationality except his belief, which makes him a member of the Muslim community in *Dar al-Islam* ("land of Islam"); a Muslim has no relatives except those who share the belief in God . . . A Muslim has no relationship with his mother, father, brother, wife and other family members, except through their relationship with the Creator, and then they are also joined by blood."[25] This is the radical transnational vision espoused by al-Qaeda and other like-minded extremists.

When the Egyptian extremist Muhammad 'Abdel-Salam al-Faraj (d. 1982) later penned his treatise, *al-Faridah al-Ghaybah* ("The Neglected Duty"), he reflected the ideology of Sayyid Qutb and cited various Qur'anic verses and hadiths to support his positions. Citing one hadith in particular, he contended that it is obligatory upon every Muslim to establish the "Islamic state," for to die in its absence is equivalent to dying in the days of the *jahiliyyah.*

Analysis of the *Jahiliyyah* Master Narrative

The *Jahiliyyah* master narrative describes a world in turmoil and ignorance, despite the efforts of thousands of prophets and messengers in the past. The merciful deity, *Allah*, intervenes and commissions a new prophet to bring guidance to the world and establish a righteous social order. The prophet plays out a *deliverance* story form where he faces violent resistance to his mission on behalf of the deity. Only a select few accept his message and follow him into exile (in Medina). Faced with annihilation and the extinction of the divine message, the archetypal prophet leads his followers into a struggle against the infidel forces of the *jahiliyyah*. Ultimately, he is victorious. The prophet destroys the false idols of the *jahiliyyah* and purifies the sacred *Ka'aba* shrine for monotheistic veneration of the one true deity, *Allah*, God of Abraham. Thereafter, the *jahiliyyah* is vanquished from the world and a grand civilization based on the deity's revealed message (i.e., the Qur'an) thrives and stretches across the earth.

The extremist variant of the *jahiliyyah* master narrative, as articulated principally by Sayyid Qutb, evolved in response to the decline of Islamic civilization, the onset of European colonial domination, and the adoption of foreign ideologies. For extremists, the emergence of the utopian social order (i.e., the "Islamic state") was only temporary. It began to wane after the time of the Prophet's companions (*sahabah*). Over the centuries, the pure guidance of Islam was contaminated by "mixing" with other systems of thought, such as Greek philosophy. Meanwhile, the forces of *jahiliyyah* persevered and surged forward.

By the time of Europe's emergence as a global colonial power, the Muslim world was weak, divided, and backward. It was easily occupied by the forces of the *jahiliyyah*. These forces, rebelling against divine sovereignty, seduced even those that called themselves Muslims. Societies that professed outwardly to be "Muslim" were, in fact, not Muslim at all and had fully reverted to a state of ignorance. Thus, it is the responsibility of a special vanguard, like the prophet and his companions, to lead the struggle (jihad) against the forces of *jahiliyyah* and restore divine sovereignty on earth. This is the struggle that many extremists claim to be undertaking today.

The "desire" for a perfect society can only be narratively satisfied by the restoration of a righteous, utopian state. This overarching structure is supported by examples drawn from a particular interpretation of history. The story form is primarily one of deliverance, where people are delivered from a world of corruption by Muhammad (or even Qutb or Usama bin Laden), who overcomes overwhelming obstacles and political and/or military opposition to carry out *Allah*'s Will on earth.

The prophet in these stories is the binary enemy of ignorance, and he is (or will be) assisted in his time of need by divine intervention, thus underscoring the idea that even the weak, the under-resourced, the poor, and the abject among us can win great victories if guided by righteousness. *Allah* is always on their side. Furthermore, because in this heroic story the "set-up" is the idea that this struggle against ignorance is a sacred battle, martyrdom is expected and praised, the final satisfaction of a righteous life.

CHAPTER 4

The Battle of Badr

The stories and myths of ancient civilizations are rife with tales of great and epic battles. In many cultures, even the gods themselves took part in military confrontations. The chief deity of the pre-Christian Norsemen, Odin, rode a horse, wore battle armor, and carried a spear. When the Norse achieved victories in battle, they attributed those victories to Odin. Norse warriors who died bravely in battle also joined Odin in Valhalla, the great golden hall of the next world.

Islamic history also has its great battle stories and archetypal champions. Arguably the most famous of these battles is the Battle of Badr, which took place at an oasis southwest of Medina in 624 CE. On this occasion, the Prophet Muhammad led a small and ill-equipped army of some three hundred Muslim believers against a superior army of one thousand pagan (animist) warriors from the city of Mecca. Miraculously, Muhammad's small army of believers defeated the pagans (and their false gods) with the aid of *Allah* and His angels.

At its core, the Battle of Badr master narrative tells the story of the weak triumphing over the mighty through divine favor or decree. It shares the same story form as the Biblical narrative of David and Goliath, a story that is briefly told in the Qur'an (see 2:251). The Badr master narrative asserts that the power of the deity is greater than any earthly power through the story of a miraculous victory. The righteous that fight for the sake of the deity, despite all the odds against them, can defeat those that fight for any other cause, be it nation, race, false beliefs, booty, or brute conquest. The Battle of Badr also fundamentally altered the nature of communal identity among the Muslims.

The Battle of Badr Master Narrative

In the year 622 CE, the Prophet Muhammad and approximately one hundred of his followers fled violent persecution in Mecca and settled in the city of Yathrib (Medina) situated to the north. This pivotal event in Islamic history is known as the *hijra*, or "migration," and it marks the start of year one in the Islamic calendar. The Muslims, group by group, fled Mecca hastily to undertake the arduous journey through the harsh Arabian desert to Medina. They took with them only what they could carry on their backs and those of their camels or horses, and left their homes behind. Mecca, as we discussed in Chapter 3, was a merchant city that benefited from the existence of a major religious shrine, the *Ka'aba*. It was not an agricultural settlement. In fact, it had insufficient water supplies (only the well of Zamzam) to sustain farming.

Medina, however, was just the opposite. It was an oasis settlement with a thriving agricultural industry (e.g., date palm trees) and a diverse tribal population that included a substantial number of Jews. The Muslim migrants from Mecca, known as the *Muhajirun*, arrived at Medina without homes, jobs, or the skills to work in its main industry, agriculture. But there was still one traditional method of revenue left open to the migrants—*ghazi* raids. The Muslims were within the traditional cultural norms of Arabia by launching raids against pagan caravans for booty. Furthermore, when the Muslims left Mecca, they left behind any goods that they were unable to carry. Those goods were confiscated by the pagans, and some of those goods were sent off on the seasonal trade caravans to Syria and other markets. The loss of the property belonging to the *Muhajirun* meant that *ghazi* raids against the Quraysh were a given. A series of minor skirmishes subsequently ensued in 623 CE.

These *ghazi* raids were morally justified by a new revelation from *Allah* granting the Muslims permission to fight against the pagan Meccans for the first time. The revelation is preserved as *surah* 22:39 and states: "Permission [to fight] is given to those who are attacked, because they are oppressed and verily God is powerful in His support; those who have been expelled from their homes without right, only because they say our Lord is God (*Allah*)."

Planning a major raid against the Quraysh in 624 CE, Muhammad sent two scouts north to al-Hawra where they awaited the Meccan caravan for several days. When the Meccan caravan was sighted, the scouts returned to Medina and Muhammad rallied the Muslims to ride out against it. The scouts reported that the caravan carried some fifty thousand gold dinars and it was guarded by forty armed men.[1] A full-scale battle was not anticipated, only a *ghazi* raid to capture the wealth of the pagan caravan. The Muslim force of approximately three hundred poorly equipped fighters consisted of some eighty *Muhajirun*, sixty tribesmen from the Medinese 'Aws tribe, and one hundred and seventy tribesmen from the Medinese Khazraj tribe, with only two horses and some seventy camels.[2]

The Meccan caravan, led by Abu Sufyan (d. 650 CE), dispatched his own scouts who reported that the Muslims had mobilized. He immediately sent a messenger to Mecca to call for reinforcements. Shocked by the news, the Quraysh quickly organized an army of some 1,300 well-equipped warriors with one hundred horsemen and many more camels.

In the meantime, Abu Sufyan successfully guided the Meccan caravan away from danger and evaded the Muslims by traveling along the coast of the Red Sea. He sent word to the approaching Qurayshi army that the caravan was safe and they could return to Mecca. The Banu Zahrah clan agreed and returned, but the rest of the Meccan forces remained.[3] The Meccan army had one thousand warriors remaining in force. Muslim scouts reported to Muhammad that the Meccans had set up encampments and the Muslims feared that the pagans intended to attack Medina. Muhammad consulted with his men, especially the Medinese converts, and they responded with a pledge of obedience to follow him into battle.

The Muslims marched toward a group of wells at the oasis of Badr, which was the only water source in the area. They fortified one well for themselves and destroyed the other wells to deprive the advancing Meccans of water.[4] The next morning, Muhammad organized the Muslim ranks and awaited the enemy. The fighting began with three duels between champions on both sides. The Muslims put forth Ubaidah ibn al-Harith (d. 624 CE), Hamza ibn 'Abdel-Muttalib (d. 625 CE), and 'Ali ibn Abu Talib (d. 661 CE). Both Hamza and 'Ali (major heroes in Islam) quickly defeated their opponents, however, Ubaidah, although victorious, was mortally wounded. It was a humiliating start for the Meccans, who were vastly overconfident in their ability to quickly defeat the weaker Muslims.

As the battle shifted to full-scale combat, the Muslims prayed to *Allah* for divine assistance. The Muslim warriors assumed defensive combat positions, while the Prophet remained in constant prayer. *Allah* responded by sending down angels from heaven to join the Muslims in battle. As the Qur'an states: "I will reinforce you with a thousand angels following in ranks" (8:9).

It is also reported in the Hadith of *Sahih Bukhari* that the Prophet Muhammad looked out over the Battle of Badr and, upon seeing the angels, said: "This is Gabriel holding the head of his horse and equipped with arms for the battle."[5] The Prophet expressed great joy at this news, and, encouraged by Gabriel, he cast a handful of dirt at the Meccans and cursed them with confusion. As the Qur'an relates: "For it was not you that fought them, but *Allah* that fought them; and you did not throw, but *Allah* threw . . . *Allah* weakens the plots of the unbelievers" (8:17–18). Thereafter, the Muslims pushed forward in battle toward victory. Islamic tradition even relates that Satan (*al-Shaytan*) took the form of a tribesman among the Meccan forces, but he retreated at the sight of God's angels joining the struggle.

As the battle turned decidedly in favor of the Muslims, many of the Meccans began to retreat, but some remained. Among the holdouts was Abu Jahl ("Father of Ignorance"), who was one of the worst enemies of Islam. Abu Jahl was a prominent leader of the Makhzum clan, and regularly denounced the Prophet as a *jinn*-possessed poet and sorcerer. The Qur'an references these attacks with verses such as: "And what you fail to see is that this is truly the word of a noble messenger; it is not the word of a poet, little is what you believe! And it is not the word of a diviner!" (59:40–43).

His real name was 'Amr ibn Hisham, known among his tribesmen as Abu al-Hakam ("Father of Wisdom"), but he is immortalized in the Muslim accounts under his pejorative title. It was Abu Jahl who famously insulted and reviled the Prophet at the *Ka'aba* in the early days of Islam, only to be struck by the bow of the enraged Hamza, who declared his adherence to his nephew's religion there on the spot.[6]

Now Abu Jahl faced Muhammad and the Muslims on the battlefield. Still seated on his horse, he was confronted by two young members of the *Ansar* (Medinese converts to Islam). Despite their inexperience in battle, the two youths rushed toward Abu Jahl and struck him with their swords. Later on, a companion of the Prophet, 'Abdullah ibn Masud, found Abu Jahl on the ground taking his last breaths and addressed him saying: "See how *Allah* has disgraced you?"[7] He then beheaded Abu Jahl. When the Prophet Muhammad observed the corpse of Abu Jahl after the battle, he reportedly stated: "This is the Pharaoh of this nation" (see Chapter 2).[8]

The victory of the Muslims was a shocking and shameful blow to the Meccans. Tradition reports that fourteen Muslims were killed in the battle, while seventy Meccans were killed and seventy were taken captive by the Muslims.[9] The bodies of the Meccans were thrown into a pit at Badr, and these bodies included those of many of the most prominent leaders of the Quraysh (e.g., Abu Jahl). Two of the seventy captives were reportedly executed, including 'Uqbah ibn Abu Muait who had strangled and abused the Prophet in Mecca.[10]

Back at Medina, there was extreme anxiety, including unfounded rumors of Muhammad's death, followed by elated joy at the news of the Muslim victory. Those reluctant to embrace Muhammad now accepted his message, and the Bedouin tribes took notice of the new Muslim power in the region. The crushing defeat of the Meccans not only affirmed Muhammad's capability as a leader and commander, but bolstered the claims of his prophetic message. *Allah* had defeated the army of the false (or simply inferior) pagan deities. It was a tremendous confirmation of Islam.

The Badr Master Narrative in Extremist Discourse

The Battle of Badr narrative tells the story of a pivotal turn in the course of Islamic history and it serves as a powerful lesson for all Muslims to be firm in their faith through trials and adversity, even in the face of seemingly impossible odds or certain death. As the Qur'an states: "For *Allah* helped you at Badr, when you were weak; so fear *Allah*, perhaps you will be thankful" (3:123). Another verse from the Qur'an states: "There was a Sign for you in the two armies that met [at Badr]; one fighting on the path of *Allah*, and the other ungrateful, seeing with their own eyes twice their number; for *Allah* aids with His support whomsoever He wills, and verily there is a lesson in this for those who see" (3:13).

The Badr narrative has certainly resonated with modern extremists who find themselves faced with vastly superior opponents that possess advanced weaponry. One of the most important examples is the Afghan Mujahideen who defeated the mighty Soviet Army in a brutal ten-year conflict during the height of the Cold War. The war in Afghanistan from 1979–1989 is widely regarded as the birthplace of the transnational jihadist movement active in the world today.

The chief ideologue and coordinator of the jihadist movement in Afghanistan was a Palestinian Islamist, 'Abdullah Yusuf Azzam (d. 1989), who received a doctorate in Islamic jurisprudence (*fiqh*) at al-Azhar University in Egypt. He later served on the faculty of Abdel-Aziz University in Jeddah, Saudi Arabia, where one of his students was a young Usama bin Laden.[11] In 1979, the year of the Soviet invasion, he traveled to Pakistan to teach at the International Islamic University in Islamabad, but he resigned from his post and devoted himself to the *jihad* in Afghanistan instead.[12]

Usama bin Laden, as we know, later followed his teacher to the front of the *jihad*. Bin Laden stated in 1998 that "the Islamic jihad in Afghanistan did not benefit from anyone as much as it benefited from Shaykh 'Abdullah Azzam."[13] In an elaborate *fatwa* ("legal ruling"), entitled *Defense of Muslim Lands*, Azzam put forth the case that fighting against the unbelievers (i.e., Communists) in Afghanistan was a duty incumbent on all believers around the world, even if their governments opposed it.

The conflict was not framed in the nationalist terms that dominated approaches to the conflict in sacred Palestine at the time (the PLO was secular). Rather, the Afghan jihad transcended the "false" nationalist categories that divided the besieged Muslim *ummah*, just as the warriors of Badr transcended their old tribal allegiances, even fighting against their own tribes and family members.

Later on, the Egyptian Islamist Ayman al-Zawahiri, who knew Azzam during his time in Cairo, argued that it was forbidden for Muslims to show any amity toward unbelievers, even from among their own families. He invoked the Battle of Badr as proof, stating: "The verse containing God Almighty's words 'even though they were their fathers' was revealed after Abu 'Ubaidah killed his own father during the Battle of Badr, 'or their sons' refers to Abu Bakr al-Siddiq's killing of his own son, 'Abd al-Rahman, 'or their brothers' refers to Mus'ab Bin Umayr's killing of his brother Ubayd Bin Umayr on the same day, 'or their kindred' refers to Umar's killing of a blood relative on that day also, and to the fact that Hamza, 'Ali, and Ubaydah Bin al-Harith killed Atabah, Shaybah, and al-Walid Bin Atabah on that day. But God knows best."[14]

In a book written by Azzam in the 1980s, entitled *Signs of Ar-Rahman in the Jihad of Afghanistan*, he recounted dozens of miracles that were alleged to have occurred among the Mujahideen, compiled as part of his vast international recruiting efforts. Azzam envisioned the jihad in Afghanistan as the gathering point of Qutb's vanguard against the *jahiliyyah* forces in the world (see Chapter 3).[15] Many of the stories in his book bear a striking resemblance to traditional accounts of the Battle of Badr. Azzam related several tales of miraculous victories that feature small groups of ill-equipped Mujahideen defeating much larger and well-armed Soviet battalions. He also recounts stories where angels fight alongside the Mujahideen in battle, saving them from seemingly inescapable defeat.

For instance, Azzam wrote that in 1980: "A large battalion came from Russia; consisting of seventy tanks and some regiments, covered by twelve planes. The Mujahideen were only one hundred and fifteen in number. A fierce battle ensued. Eventually the enemy was defeated. We had destroyed thirteen tanks. From amongst us only four were blessed with martyrdom."[16] In another more elaborate account, Azzam relates that

> [Arsalaan said:] The [Soviet] tanks attacked us and they were about one hundred and twenty in number. They were assisted by mortar and many aircrafts. Our provisions were exhausted. We were convinced of being captured. We sought protection from *Allah* by means of *Du'a* [prayer]. All of a sudden, bullets and shells rained upon the Communists from all directions. They were defeated. There was no one on the battlefield besides us. He said: 'They were the *Mala'ikah* (angels).' Arsalaan also narrated to me: 'We attacked the Communists at a place called Arjoon and we killed five hundred

> and captured eighty-three.' We said to them: 'Why is it that you people were defeated, whereas you people killed only one martyr?' The prisoner said: 'You people were riding on horses, and when we shot at them they ran away and we could not hit them with bullets.' It is established from the Qur'an that the *Mala'ikah* (angels) descended on the occasion of Badr.[17]

The story form evident in these miracle reports (which structurally resemble the Hadith) is clearly derived from the Battle of Badr master narrative. Azzam reports these tales concisely and needs not rely on extraneous details to explain or prove their validity either, as the miracles already "fit" the expectations of his audience based on their prior knowledge of the Badr master narrative.

Yet another story recounting the participation of angels in the Afghan jihad relates: "Muhammad Yasir reported to me: When the communists entered a town with their tanks, they enquired where the 'stables for the horses of the Muslim brothers' were. The people were surprised since they did not ride horses. They then realized that these were the horses of the angels."[18]

On February 15, 1989, the Soviet Union announced the withdrawal of the last remaining Soviet troops from Afghanistan. By that time, more than one million Afghanis were killed, more than five million were displaced, and approximately fifteen thousand Soviet troops had been killed.[19] The numbers of wounded civilians and fighters on both sides were enormous. Later that year, 'Abdullah Azzam was killed by a mysterious car bombing in Peshawar, Pakistan.[20] Thereafter, Ayman al-Zawahiri and Usama bin Laden assumed the leadership of organizing the "Afghan Arab" volunteers, or what eventually became al-Qaeda ("The Base").

According to Olivier Roy, Bin Laden and his followers formulated a new foundation narrative for al-Qaeda to "enhance their own legitimacy and belittle the role of 'Abdullah Azzam."[21] This narrative is known as the Battle of Jaji (located near the Pakistan border), and it relates events that occurred in the summer of 1987 when Soviet troops stormed Bin Laden's *al-Masada* compound of caves and tunnels. Despite allegedly being vastly outnumbered by well armed Soviet troops, the small contingent of Mujahideen succeeded in defeating the Soviets and defending the compound. Many of al-Qaeda's founding figures, including al-Zawahiri, participated in the pivotal battle, and it was Usama Bin Laden's first combat (he was wounded during the battle).[22]

The Battle of Jaji narrative repeats the same basic story form found in the Badr master narrative, as well as Azzam's miracle reports from the battlefield. Indeed, Badr has remained a normative reference point for al-Qaeda's vision of its military operations up to the present. For instance, during an interview in 1998, later broadcast by al-Jazeera television after the attacks of September 11, 2001, Usama bin Laden stated:

> In the Holy Qur'an, *Surat al-Anfal*, God says, addressing his prophet, may the peace and blessings of God be upon him, and the Battle of Badr fighters, who were among the most righteous, may God rest their souls in peace: 'Just as thy Lord ordered thee out of thy house in truth, even though a party among the believers disliked it. Disputing with thee concerning the truth after it was made manifest, as if they were being driven to death and they (actually) saw it.' If this description had applied to the Battle of Badr fighters, the most righteous ones, it is only natural to apply to us as well."[23]

Analysis of the Badr Master Narrative

The Battle of Badr master narrative echoes the familiar core message of David and Goliath (see 1 Samuel 17:1–54) and countless other similar tales of achieving victory in a battle or conflict against all odds. It invokes the story form of deliverance, specifically a miraculous victory by *Allah*, and proposes that righteousness, not strength of arms or material resources, is the key to success and victory, both in this life and the next. When Muslim believers are confronted by an aggressive unbelieving foe or enemy of overwhelming strength and military capabilities, like the fearsome giant of the pagan Philistines (Goliath), the righteous believers must trust in the truth of their convictions, namely, the supreme power of the One True God (*Allah*). Any power can be defeated through faith in *Allah*, be it the pagans of ancient Mecca or the Soviet Red Army, regardless of bombs, bullets, or swords.

The decline of Islamic civilization in the eighteenth century and the defeat of Arab nationalism in the Six-Day War (see Chapter 12) created the conditions for Islamist extremists to treat the Badr master narrative with special reverence. The military power of the great Muslim empires had faded and the nations of the Muslim world were left militarily weak in the face of European ascendency and colonialism. The responsibility of the so-called jihad against the infidel powers thus fell to individuals coming together for the fight, despite all the disadvantages against them. The Badr master narrative and its outcome provides the core persuasive rallying cry for the vanguard to act and persevere in the face of certain death (i.e., martyrdom), framing the conflict in terms of many victorious Muslim conflicts that came before.

CHAPTER 5

The Hypocrites

The Qur'an makes many references to *al-Munafiqin*, or "the Hypocrites," including the title of a *surah* (number sixty-three). The term has become prominent in Islamist extremist discourses. Aside from traditionally denoting a particular group in a specific time period, the master narrative of the Hypocrites contains a ruse story form where the true identity of an individual or group is hidden for the sake of worldly ends. It differs from a betrayal story form (see Chapter 6) in that a ruse story depicts an individual or group that is insincere and opportunistic, rather than being outright treasonous. But like a betrayal story, the motives, plots, and ploys of the imposters in the ruse story are foiled by archetypal heroes in the narrative.

In the Torah, we find the story of the prophet Moses and the Israelites (Hebrews). In Chapter 32 of the Book of Exodus, Moses returns from atop Mt. Sinai to find that a group of Israelites has persuaded the other Israelites to construct a blasphemous idol of a golden calf. Although they were members of the community themselves, these dissidents doubted the prophet Moses and questioned him throughout the story of the Exodus. They followed Moses out of bondage in Egypt only to complain and criticize Moses once they were free. So when Moses discovered that these imposters had built an idol for worship in place of Yahweh, he called on the true believers among the Israelites to eliminate the imposters from their midst:

> [Moses] cried: "Whoever is for the Lord, let him come to me!" All the Levites then rallied to him, and he told them: "Thus says the Lord, the God of Israel: Put your sword on your hip, every one of you! Now go up and down the camp, from gate to gate, and slay your own kinsmen, your friends and neighbors! The Levites carried out the command of Moses, and on that day there fell about three thousand of the people.[1]

We can see that the above passage does not tell the story of a treacherous outsider, or a member of a group switching sides to join an opposing force against the group. Moses explicitly orders them to kill their own kinsmen, friends, and neighbors. The imposters, or "hypocrites," are insincere insiders who go along with the group when it benefits them, but are quick to disrupt it for their own benefit when it suits them. They can appear outwardly to be the most pious in the community, as if wearing righteous masks, but when Moses goes up the mountain, or they retire behind the closed doors of Medina, or even into the secret recesses of their hearts, there is no sincerity in their words or actions. Thus the hypocrite is a danger to the true believers unlike any other because the hypocrites represent a profound danger within the group. For Islamist extremists, the Hypocrites master narrative fits perfectly into their struggles against their fellow Muslims, or the so-called near enemy.

The Hypocrites of Medina

The Medinese Muslim community that developed after the *hijra* in 622 CE consisted of three primary groups. The first group was the *Muhajirun*, or the Muslim migrants who accepted Islam in Mecca and fled with Muhammad to Medina. They were a small group of no more than one hundred individuals. The second group was the much larger *Ansar*, or the Medinese Muslim converts or "helpers" of the Meccan migrants. The third group was the *Munafiqun*, or "the Hypocrites," who came from among the Medinese converts (the *Ansar*) but only pretended to be Muslims for the sake of political expediency. They did not actually believe in *Allah* or His Messenger.

In Mecca, the Muslims were a small, persecuted minority and there was no advantage to joining their ranks, unless a person was entirely tribeless or a slave. But in Medina, the Prophet Muhammad was a statesman, arbitrator, and military commander with resources and power—being a Muslim in Medina had certain advantages. As the Qur'an describes the Hypocrites:

> And from the people there are those that say "We believe in *Allah* and the Last Day," but they do not believe; they seek to deceive *Allah* and those that believe, but they do not deceive anyone except themselves, yet do not realize it. . . And when it is said to them: "Do not bring about destruction on the earth," they say: "We are peacemakers!" But they are the destructive ones, even though they do not realize it. . . And when they meet those that believe they say to them: "We believe!" But when they are alone with their evil ones (*shaytans*) they say: "Truly we are with you! We were only pretending in jest." (2:8–16)

Numerous other passages from the Qur'an describe the Hypocrites as liars, cowards, perverse, blind, deaf, diseased, foolish, and bound for the lowest depths of Hell (see, e.g., 4:145, 2:17–18, 59:11–14). And yet, the Qur'an does not identify any of the Hypocrites by name. In fact, Muhammad tolerated their existence among the believers at the same time the Qur'an chastised their deviant conduct.

Eventually, the Qur'an called for open conflict or warfare against them, but that call appears to be historically specific because the passages suggest that the Hypocrites forged an alliance with the Meccan pagans. Verses 9:73 and 66:9 state: "Oh Prophet! Struggle against the disbelievers (*kuffar*) and hypocrites (*munafiqin*), and stand firm against them, and their abode is Hell, an evil refuge" (9:73). It goes on to refer to their participation in a plot against the Muslims, apparently during a raid on Tabuk in 630 CE, and welcomes their repentance (see 9:74). But broadly speaking, the Hypocrites remained accepted (or tolerated) members of the community. For further analysis, let us look at the complex example of the so-called arch-hypocrite of Medina.

The historical figure most often associated with the Hypocrites is 'Abdallah ibn Ubayy ibn Salul (d. 631 CE), an Arab chieftain of the Khazraj tribe in Medina. His tribe is notable because six men from the Khazraj were the first to accept Islam in Medina.[2] Prior to the arrival of Muhammad and the *Muhajirun* in Medina, Ibn Ubayy was the leading candidate for ruler or king of the city.[3] As such, he had obvious reservations about Islam's political ascent after Muhammad's arrival. Like most of the animist Arabs from the Khazraj and 'Aws in Medina, Ibn Ubayy accepted Islam, but he did so reluctantly and seems to have only been a nominal Muslim. His son ('Abdallah) and daughter (Jamilah), however, were reportedly zealous devotees of Muhammad and Islam. Thus, even his own family had abandoned their old tribal ties in favor of the Prophet.

Ibn Ubayy, as a general policy, sought to avoid open confrontation, but four notable events are highlighted in the Muslim sources. His tribe, the Khazraj, had been close allies with some of the Jews in Medina, especially the Bani Qaynuqa tribe. When conflict broke out between the Muslims and the Bani Qaynuqa (see Chapter 6), Ibn Ubayy interceded on their behalf and reportedly issued a veiled threat to Muhammad that such conflicts go in cycles.[4] "Ibn Ubayy was different from the majority of lukewarm or insincere converts [i.e., Hypocrites] by reason of his far-reaching influence, which made him all the more dangerous."[5] He could present serious difficulties to Muhammad by disrupting crucial tribal alliances that still formed the core of the community he was leading. The next incident involving Ibn Ubayy was more ominous, for it directly endangered the survival of both Muhammad and Islam as a whole.

The Battle of Uhud in 625 CE is the most famous Muslim defeat during Muhammad's lifetime. Prior to that battle, Muhammad consulted with his followers and the elders of the city to agree on a strategy to confront the Meccan army advancing on Medina. Ibn Ubayy initially supported Muhammad's plan to remain in the city's fortifications as a defensive tactic against the vastly superior force of the Meccans. This was the dominant view among the older generation of the Muslims, but the youths were eager to face the Meccans in direct combat.[6]

Muhammad changed his mind in response to the youths and decided to lead the Muslim army out to encamp at Mount Uhud and face the Meccans directly. This plan was rejected by Ibn Ubayy, and he rebelled against Muhammad's leadership en route to Uhud by returning to Medina with three hundred warriors, approximately one-third of the Muslim army.[7]

After the Muslim loss at Uhud, Ibn Ubayy seized the opportunity to more actively undermine Muhammad's leadership. Both Muhammad's strategic wisdom and his claims to prophethood were called into question. The next Friday, during the weekly congregational prayer in the *masjid* (mosque), Ibn Ubayy was rebuked and told to remain seated by others in attendance, leading him to depart in a huff without praying.[8]

When the conflict with the Jews of the Bani Nadir (see Chapter 6) came to a head, Ibn Ubayy encouraged the Jews not to submit to exile and instead resist the Muslims. They were reportedly preparing to leave peacefully when Ibn Ubayy intervened and made promises of support and reinforcements that never materialized. As one modern Muslim account relates: "The chief of the hypocrites, 'Abdallah ibn Ubayy, urged the Jews not to pay heed to the Prophet's words and to stay in their habitations, offering to run to their support with two thousand of his followers, and assuring them of help to come from the Qurayzah tribe and former allies, the Bani Ghatfan . . . [he] failed to keep his promise of support."[9] This account then invokes a Qur'anic verse comparing Ibn Ubayy's lies to those of Satan. The verse states: "[He is] like Satan, when he says to man: 'Reject God'; and then when man disbelieves, Satan says: 'I am free from you, for I fear God, the Lord of all the worlds!'" (59:16).

Later on, Ibn Ubayy continued to use his influence to undermine Muhammad and the Muslims, again without actively waging any direct battle of arms. During the scandal involving 'Aisha bint Abu Bakr, a prominent wife of the Prophet, Ibn Ubayy spread slanderous and very serious accusations of infidelity about her.

The incident began when the Muslims were returning from a military expedition against the Bani Mustaliq tribe. 'Aisha had accompanied her husband, the Prophet, on the journey. When the caravan stopped to camp, 'Aisha went off to answer the call of nature. However, when 'Aisha returned she noticed that her necklace was missing and she went back to look for it. Thinking that she had returned, the Muslim caravan departed without her. Left in the desert alone, she waited until another Muslim riding behind the rest of the caravan, Safwan bin Mu'attal, found her and brought her back to the caravan atop his camel. When 'Aisha caught up to the caravan with Safwan, the Hypocrites, including Ibn Ubayy, began to spread rumors that she had been engaged in illicit sexual activity with Safwan—a very serious accusation.

Some of Muhammad's companions (*sahabah*) believed the allegations were true and advised him to divorce 'Aisha. Although still hesitant to condemn her, the Prophet's behavior nevertheless grew cold and distant toward her. In response, she left to stay at her father's home for a time. Finally, after several weeks of great sorrow, 'Aisha was cleared of the malicious charges against her by a revelation from *Allah*. As the Qur'an states:

> Why did the believers, male and female, when they heard of the alleged affair, not keep goodness in their minds and say: 'This is an obvious lie.' . . . And you said things that you had no knowledge about; and you think it is a small matter, but it is a serious matter with *Allah* . . . Verily those that love to spread scandal among the believers will have a terrible punishment in this life and the next, for *Allah* knows and you know not (24:12–19).

The main perpetrators of the slander campaign against 'Aisha were flogged with eighty stripes in accordance with the law set down in the Qur'an. It states: "Those who launch a charge against chaste women, and do not produce four witnesses [to support their charges], flog them with eighty stripes and do not accept them as witnesses thereafter, for they are transgressors" (24:4). Ibn Ubayy, however, escaped this punishment. One Muslim account of the events speculates that he was spared his punishment either for the sake of communal harmony among the tribal factions in Medina or because corporal punishment would have nullified the far more severe punishment awaiting him in the afterlife.[10]

The Hypocrites, as previously mentioned, were generally tolerated, despite their machinations, both indirect and direct, against Muhammad and Islam. In fact, the Muslim sources indicate that Ibn Ubayy grew largely inactive in these efforts after 628 CE. Perhaps he simply came to accept Islam's ascent and abandoned his political ambitions. Most striking of all is the fact that when Ibn Ubayy, one of Muhammad's most bitter enemies, died of an illness in Medina in 631 CE, it was the Prophet Muhammad who led his funeral service and prayed over his grave. Thus, Ibn Ubayy retained his status as a Muslim to the end, because Muslims do not offer prayers over the graves of their pagan enemies. Yet, this fact has not prevented Muslim sources from conveying their intense dislike of Ibn Ubayy over the centuries. The story of the *Munafiqin* in Medina, preserved by numerous references in the Qur'an and Hadith, continues to remain relevant in modern Islamist discourses, especially among those extremists caught in a struggle against fellow Muslims.

The Hypocrites Master Narrative in Extremist Discourse

The Egyptian extremist, Ayman al-Zawahiri, in his ideological writings, posited the existence of two principle adversaries in the Islamist struggle for the establishment of the so-called Islamic state. These two adversaries are identified as the "near enemy" and the "far enemy." The former is the central concern of this chapter. It describes the regimes of the Arab and Muslim worlds, such as al-Zawahiri's own homeland of Egypt, and their associated entities and agencies, such as their militaries and police forces. The designation of "hypocrites" is commonly used by extremists to refer to any professing Muslims who do not advocate Islamist extremism, even other Islamists who might support political pacifism or compromise with existing state regimes (e.g., the Muslim Brotherhood). This is apparent in numerous statements and ideological writings from extremists that we will examine in greater detail.

A revealing statement regarding extremist usage of the Hypocrites master narrative was made in a speech by an al-Qaeda affiliate in Yemen and posted as an online video on December 23, 2009. We should note that two days later, on Christmas day, a Nigerian extremist named Umar Farouk 'Abdulmutallab, who apparently trained for his mission in Yemen, attempted to blow himself up on a flight en route to Detroit from Amsterdam. The al-Qaeda video, disseminated on a known extremist web site, called for revenge against the United States and its agents in response to the Abyan air raid that targeted extremist preacher, Anwar al-Awlaki. It stated:

> O servants of God, we inform you that the enemy of Muslims is an external enemy and a domestic one. The external enemy is the Jews and the Christians, whereas the domestic enemy is the hypocrites, who seized power in the country; and thus, corrupted both the country and the people.[11]

The domestic enemy, or near enemy, is identified in this al-Qaeda statement as the "hypocrites" (*munafiqin*). The "hypocrites" are further identified in the statement as the people who "seized power in the country," referring to state regimes (often authoritarian) who are considered illegitimate and that have "corrupted" the people and led them astray from "true" Islam. Given that this message originated from Yemen, the specific regime being described is the government of 'Ali 'Abdallah Saleh. President Saleh has held office in Yemen since 1978, when he came to power through a military coup. He is considered an ally of the United States in the global "War on Terror."

Across the sea to the south of Yemen sits Somalia, which has struggled through a civil war between various tribal warlords and (more recently) Islamist factions, including the al-Qaeda affiliate group called *al-Shabab*, for some twenty years. No central government has existed in Somalia since 1991, allowing new Islamist groups, like *al-Shabab*, to enter into the lawless political vacuum by promising order and security. On December 18, 2009, a forum member on an extremist web site posted a statement by al-Qaeda's Abu Muhammad al-Maqdisi, entitled "Khaybar Khaybar, O Jews, the Army of Muhammad will Return," addressing the conflict in Somalia and invoking the Hypocrites master narrative. It stated:

> News from Somalia and messages from the Mujahidin brothers give us some good news after the other, and inform us that they apply Islamic *shari'ah* as far as they can in the Islamic provinces. There is no doubt that the implementation of *shari'ah* was not an easy thing in the view of the opinion of the scholars of flattery and hypocrisy for the West. Those hypocrites wait for the permission of the United Nations to implement the rulings of the Qur'an. In spite of obstructing the path of God by the scholars of dissuasion, and in spite of all the obstacles, God has enabled our brothers there to apply all the orders of almighty God, Exalted be He, in God's land. There are judges who enforce God's *shari'ah* in every province. This has led to the disappearance of most of the vices, which indecent people used to commit openly and in public.[12]

In the statement by al-Maqdisi, the "hypocrites" designation refers to Muslim scholars (*ulama*). It specifically refers to those that have failed to oppose state regimes that do not implement the Islamist vision of *shari'ah* or the "Islamic state." Historically, the vast majority of Islamist extremist leaders and ideologues have not been members of the *ulama*, but "laity" who have challenged the traditional interpretive authority of the *ulama*. In many countries, including Egypt, Morocco, and others, the *ulama* are employees of the state and risk their privileged positions if they speak out against government policies.

Other prominent targets for the "hypocrite" label are the security forces of the "enemy" state regimes. After all, they are the armed enforcers of the governments at war with the extremists. In Iraq, where the creation of a new national state government has proved to be a precarious task, extremists have actively targeted security agencies and recruits applying for employment with such agencies. The same situation can be found in Afghanistan, where the establishment of a centralized state government has proven to be even more challenging.

The extremist web site, Al-Fallujah Islamic Forums, frequently reports news of casualties from extremist attacks in Iraq and Afghanistan. For example, one such statement from 2008 refers to members of the Afghan "puppet police" as "hypocrite terrorists," stating:

> Wednesday 17-12-2008, Mujahideen of the Islamic Emirate of Afghanistan ambushed a joint convoy of American terrorists and its puppet police in Wazikhoa district of Paktika province, in the ambush Mujahideen destroyed one American invaders army tank and one vehicle of puppet police but the number of *kafir* [i.e., infidel] and *munafiq* [i.e., hypocrite] terrorists killed or wounded could not be confirmed. Reported by Zabihullah Mujahid.[13]

The above statement was made by Sunni Islamist extremists. However, the Qur'anic basis of the Hypocrites master narrative means that it can be utilized across sectarian lines. Thus, we also find its usage in the Twelver Shi'ite state of the Islamic Republic of Iran. In this case, however, the master narrative is being deployed by state-run media in support of the ruling state regime and against political dissidents, such as pro-democracy protesters, who advocate government reform.

On December 22, 2009, amidst ongoing protests following the controversial reelection of Iranian President Mahmoud Ahmadinejad, the Tehran Fars News Agency reported that a large group of people started to gather outside the house of the late Imam Ruhullah Khomeini in Qom "in protest to insults against Islamic Iran's sanctities" and added that protestors were chanting slogans in support of the current supreme leader, Ayatollah Ali Khamenei.[14] The News Agency further stated that the gathering was a protest against "the hypocrites" who "insulted Islamic Iran's sanctities on the sidelines of the funeral procession for Hoseyn Ali Montazeri" on December 21, 2009.[15]

As we can see, the Iranian government's use of the master narrative is an inversion of the examples cited previously. The state regime, in this case, claims the mantle of religion and seeks to portray critics of the regime as "fake Muslims" bent on attacking Islam. This functions in the same way as when Sunni Islamist extremists (claiming the mantle of religion) deploy it against the governments of Egypt, Pakistan, or Afghanistan, among others.

Judging by the evidence, the Hypocrites master narrative has a broad range of applications. In another interesting deployment of the master narrative, a forum participant on an extremist web site assailed numerous Muslim charities as "hypocrites." The giving of alms, or *zakat*, is one of the five pillars of Islam, so charities serve an important role in distributing obligatory contributions for Muslims around the world. The forum poster stated:

> Dear beloved, I am so much confused concerning the behaviors of those who pretend belonging to Islam, and collect money under the title of Islam. In fact, they are hypocrite thieves, who look for their personal profit and for the satisfaction of the oppressors. The existing Islamic institutions are only designated for relief work in the first place and none of them dare publicly call for Islam. The ignorance, greed and inexperience of those people in the banking issues, their use of wrong means in transferring money, as well as their use of the banks that are subject to the rules of the oppressors caused the closing of institutions, even those destined to charity and relief for the benefit of the orphans and widows.[16]

In the above instance, as well as those previously cited, the utilization of the Hypocrites master narrative reflects a tactical, exclusionary assertion that there are enemies "in our midst" (among the Muslims) and provides fodder for both conspiracy theories and internal acts of violence. In the absence of an "official" centralized religious institution in Islam (e.g., Vatican) to dictate who *is* or *is not* a member of the Muslim community, ruse stories can be particularly important because they allow individuals to articulate a separate identity within a community that may otherwise be ambiguous and better facilitate the usage of binary ideological constructions.

Analysis of the Hypocrites Master Narrative

The Hypocrites master narrative of Muhammad's internal enemies in the nascent Muslim city-state of Medina is one rich with numerous implications and ties to other narratives included in this book. The ruse story form is less common than those found in the other master narratives presented here, such as the victorious battle against impossible odds (e.g., Badr) or the tyrannical ruler destroyed for his wickedness (e.g., Pharaoh). Nevertheless, the Hypocrites master narrative and the imposter archetype have proven to have wide applicability and deep resonance among Islamist extremists, particularly when they speak out against "apostate regimes," as well as when they wish to persuade listeners to their mode of thought.

Traditionally, Muslim scholars have frowned upon the emergence of sects or denominations within the *ummah* on the basis of ideals conveyed in the Qur'an and Hadith. Aside from the obvious Sunni-Shi'ite split, sectarian factions do indeed exist in the Muslim world, even though denominationalism runs contrary to Muslim sensitivity to such divisions within the community. The absence of a centralized authority in Islam has also complicated these matters further. Thus, the Hypocrites master narrative, through its archetypal imposter and ruse story form, provides a framework for extremists to differentiate one faction of Muslims from another in a manner that is readily understood in a religious tradition where "orthodoxy" and "heresy" remain highly ambiguous.

CHAPTER 6

The Battle of Khaybar

Treachery and betrayal are common motifs in the narratives of many cultures. In the Gospels, we read that one of Jesus' twelve disciples, Judas Iscariot, betrayed him and led the Romans to his location at Gethsemane where he was arrested and ultimately crucified at Golgatha (see, e.g., Matthew 26). Overcome by his guilt, Judas reportedly committed suicide. In Christian thought, Judas is the archetypal betrayer or traitor. His name has become synonymous with treachery. In the United States, the archetypal traitor is Benedict Arnold, who unsuccessfully conspired with the British Empire against the American colonies during the Revolutionary War. He lived out the rest of his life in exile.

In Islamic thought, the Battle of Khaybar (629 CE) is a tale of treachery and the dire consequences of plotting against *Allah* and His Prophet. However, as discussed below, the role of the traitor is assumed by an entire group, rather than a single individual, and that group (tribe) was Jewish, not Muslim. The Khaybar master narrative thus condemns an entire group as inherently treacherous; it is the same group condemned in the narratives of the New Testament prior to the advent of Islam.

Early Christian Anti-Semitism and the Charge of Deicide

A great deal of attention was given to Mel Gibson's controversial 2004 film *The Passion of the Christ* for its portrayal of Jews in the religious narrative of Jesus' arrest, trial, and execution. Much of what the film's critics found offensive, however, was taken directly from the four canonical Gospels of the New Testament and not from Gibson's own prejudicial views. Looking past the fact that Jesus was a Jew, the Gospel of Mark, written by a Greek gentile after the disastrous Roman-Jewish War (66–70 CE), portrayed the crucifixion of Jesus as a Jewish plot that Pilate only reluctantly accepted when a Jewish mob threatened to rebel, crying out "crucify him!"[1]

To emphasize the point, Mark's gospel further relates that Pilate gave the crowd a choice to free a notorious criminal named Barabbas or free Jesus, but the Jews chose the wretched Barabbas (see Mark 15:6–15). Mark's gospel also depicts the Jewish leadership (e.g., the Pharisees) as the deniers and persecutors of Christ, whereas a Roman soldier is the first to recognize his true nature (see Mark 15:39).

Much of this material was repeated in the Gospel of Matthew. For instance, Jesus declares that the Jewish Pharisees, the historical precursor to Rabbinic Judaism, are "serpents" and a "brood of vipers" that are "filled with hypocrisy and evildoing" (Matthew 23:28–33). But the most infamous passage in Matthew's gospel is the declaration made by a Jewish mob to an "innocent" Pilate, proclaiming: "His [i.e., Jesus'] blood be upon us and upon our children!" (27:25). This passage from the Passion narrative has historically been used by Christians to justify the perpetual collective guilt of the Jews and helped to produce centuries of persecution and genocide in Europe and Russia.

Other writings contained in the New Testament, including the Gospels of Luke and John, continue the themes put forth by Mark and Matthew. In the Gospel of John, Jesus replies to a group of Jews who reject him by stating: "You belong to your father the Devil and you willingly carry out your father's desires" (John 8:44). The Book of Acts furthermore recalls the persecution and murder of early Christians (e.g., St. Stephen) by Jews, including Saul of Tarsus (St. Paul). The eschatological Book of Revelation twice refers to the Jews that makeup a "synagogue of Satan" (2:9, 3:9) and the epistles of Paul rebuke the Jews as adversaries of Christ. For example, Paul's First Letter to the Thessalonians states: "For you suffer the same things from your compatriots as they did from the Jews, who killed both the Lord Jesus and the prophets and persecuted us; they do not please God, and are opposed to everyone, trying to prevent us from speaking to Gentiles that they may be saved, thus constantly filling up the measure of their sins; but the wrath of God has finally begun to come upon them" (2:14–16). Such passages, we should note, fail to mention the role of the Romans in the crucifixion and place the blame for Jesus' death (i.e., the crime of deicide) exclusively upon the Jews.

By the time the Bible was canonized in the fourth century CE, those narratives were firmly entrenched in the writings and teachings of the Church patriarchs and theologians. St. Augustine (d. 430 CE) decreed that all Jews were responsible for killing Christ, but should be treated like Cain, that is, not murdered but made to suffer as living witnesses to their "crime."[2] Thus, St. Augustine called all Jews "Cains," St. Jerome (d. 420 CE) saw all Jews as "Judases," St. John Chrysostom (d. 407 CE) regarded all Jews as useless animals fit for slaughter, and St. Ambrose (d. 397 CE) wrote about the "stiff-necked Jewish people whose ears listen but do not hear, whose eyes look but do not see."[3] The Jews hence formed the archetypal evildoers and devotees of the Anti-Christ in Christian thought, especially in eschatology, and this remained the dominant view by the time of Islam's emergence in the Middle East in the seventh century (CE).

When the Arab Muslims expanded beyond the Arabian Peninsula in the years immediately following the Prophet Muhammad's death in 632 CE, much of the conquered lands to the north and west, including Palestine, were part of the Christian Byzantine Empire. The lands that the Muslims encountered during those crucial formative years were rife with the Biblical Passion narrative of the Jews acting as the treacherous "killers of Christ." For the new Muslim arrivals, the resistance that Muhammad's prophetic mission had reportedly found among the Jewish tribes of Arabia, such as the Bani Nadir, seemed to fit into a well-established pattern, as did their alleged effort to kill Muhammad in Medina. Those notions are preserved in the complex master narrative of the Battle of Khaybar.

The Jews and the Constitution of Medina

After the *hijra* in 622 CE, Muhammad and the *Muhajirun* (Muslim migrants) from Mecca settled in Medina, known at the time as the oasis town of Yathrib (see Chapter 4). Muhammad, now as a political leader (i.e., chieftain), formed an alliance between the different tribes that inhabited the town, including the three leading Jewish tribes of Bani Qaynuqa, Bani Nadir, and Bani Qurayza. The Jews of Medina and the surrounding area, in contrast to other Greek or Aramaic-speaking Jews in the Middle East, spoke Arabic and kept Arabic names. Scholars disagree over whether they were Judaized Arabs or Arabized Jews, perhaps even refugees from the Roman occupation to the north. Regardless, the resulting contractual agreement affirming mutual rights and protection between the Muslims, Jews, and Arab tribes ('Aws and Khazraj) in Medina is known as the "Constitution of Medina." It states:

> To the Jew who follows us belong help and equality. He shall not be wronged nor shall his enemies be aided. . . . The Jews shall contribute to the cost of war so long as they are fighting alongside the believers. The Jews of the Bani 'Awf are one community with the believers (the Jews have their religion and the Muslims have theirs), their freedmen and their persons except those who behave unjustly and sinfully, for they hurt but themselves and their families. The same applies to the Jews of the [other tribes] . . . Loyalty is a protection against treachery. . . . None of them shall go out to war save the permission of Muhammad, but he shall not be prevented from taking revenge for a wound. . . . The Jews must bear their expenses and the Muslims their

> expenses. Each must help the other against anyone who attacks the people of this document. They must seek mutual advice and consultation, and loyalty is a protection against treachery . . . Yathrib [i.e., Medina] shall be a sanctuary for the people of this document . . . The contracting parties are bound to help one another against any attack on Yathrib.[4]

The ensuing military conflict between the Muslims and the Meccans (see Chapter 4) put the articles of the Constitution of Medina to the test. The first blow to the alliance came from the Bani Qaynuqa, which was the least formidable of the three major Jewish tribes in Medina.

The story goes that one day, a Muslim woman was horribly insulted in the market by a Jewish merchant from the Bani Qaynuqa. Overhearing the exchange, a nearby Muslim man from the *Ansar* came to the aid of the woman and a fight broke out between the Muslim man and the Jewish merchant. The merchant was killed in the scuffle, and then a group of other Jews in the market avenged the merchant by killing the Muslim that had come to aid the insulted woman. Apparently, rather than following the terms of the Constitution and agreeing to arbitration, the Bani Qaynuqa withdrew to their fortified settlements, stocked them with provisions, and summoned their old tribal allies to defend them.[5] Obviously the Jews of the Bani Qaynuqa expected the Muslims to act in accordance with the old Arab tribal system of honor, revenge, and blood feuds. But when they finally surrendered after weeks in their fortifications, Muhammad banished them to Syria for breaking the terms of the Constitution of Medina.

The next blow to the alliance came from the Bani Nadir. Tensions with the tribe had already started when the Jewish chieftain and belligerent poet, Ka'b ibn al-Ashraf, was assassinated by a group of Muslims after the Battle of Badr in 624 CE. However, the dissolution of the Medinan alliance, due to another alleged act of treason, did not occur until after the Battle of Uhud in 625 CE.

The story goes that a Jewish woman from the Bani Nadir invited Muhammad and some of his followers to her home for a feast with the intention of poisoning him. The timing of the alleged plot is particularly significant, because after the Muslim defeat at Uhud, he was perceived to be weak, and several tribes, such as the Bani Asad, saw an opportunity to strike against Muhammad's *ummah* in Medina.[6] When Muhammad arrived at the woman's home, he reportedly received a prophetic warning that the meat was poisoned and he abruptly left without explanation. Tradition says that the angel Gabriel had appeared to him and informed him of the plot. Later that evening, a messenger was sent by Muhammad to the Bani Nadir informing them that they had ten days to leave Medina or they would face execution for treason.

The Bani Nadir refused and fortified themselves in their settlements. They reached out to their old Bedouin and Jewish allies (i.e., the Bani Qurayza) and received promises of reinforcements in response should the Muslims besiege them. But as the Muslims launched an attack and the Bani Nadir fired arrows and stones from their fortifications, no reinforcements arrived from their tribal allies and they were left to face Muhammad's army alone.

After several days, the Bani Nadir agreed to surrender to Muhammad. They would be permitted to leave Medina with as much of their property as they could carry on their camels, but could never return to their homes and lucrative date palm trees. The Bani Nadir reportedly made a spectacle of the event by donning their finest clothes and jewels and parading out of the city with musicians playing alongside their caravan of goods. Some of them migrated to Syria and Palestine, but most chose to settle in the town of Khaybar some ninety miles north.

After their expulsion from Medina, a chief from the Bani Nadir named Huyay ibn Akhtab traveled to Mecca to meet with Abu Sufyan and the leaders of the Quraysh. The Jews of the Bani Nadir thereafter formed an alliance with the Quraysh against the Muslims, and pledged to rally the Bedouin of the Najd region for their cause. The Bani Asad joined the alliance, as did a portion of the Bani Sulaym, and the Bani Ghatfan accepted after they were promised half the date harvest of Khaybar.[7]

In 627, shortly after the New Year, the confederates (*al-Ahzab*) marched on Medina with some ten thousand warriors, intent on destroying Muhammad, his followers, and his new religion.[8] Luckily, tribal allies of Muhammad rode toward Medina to inform him of the impending Meccan attack and reached him one week before the confederate force arrived at the city. Muhammad summoned the people of Medina and consulted with his followers. Salman al-Farsi (d. 653 CE) rose and suggested that the Muslims dig a trench around the city to fend off the Meccan cavalry, a strategy used in his homeland of Persia. Muhammad agreed to this unconventional strategy and work immediately began on a series of large trenches running between fortifications and rock formations to create a defensive "wall" around Medina. Muhammad personally helped dig the trench with the other men and boys of the city.

Huyay ibn Akhtab, the chieftain of the Bani Nadir, told the Quraysh that he could convince the Jews of the Bani Qurayza, still in Medina with the Muslims, to join the confederates. The Bani Qurayza's relationship with the Muslims was strained, but they still honored their allegiance to Muhammad and assisted in the construction of the trench around Medina. However, Huyay came to personally meet with the chieftain of the Bani

Qurayza, Ka'b ibn Asad, to persuade him of Muhammad's impending doom at the hands of the Meccan confederacy. Ka'b initially resisted, but ultimately conceded and announced his decision to his tribe. Debate broke out among the Bani Qurayza, but supporters of betraying the alliance with Muhammad won out after the loyalists went out to see the enormous Meccan confederacy of ten thousand warriors encamped around Medina. They were convinced that Muhammad and the Muslims would inevitably be defeated by such a large army. It was decided that it would be in their best interests to join Huyay ibn Akhtab and the confederates against Islam.

News of the Bani Qurayza's betrayal spread quickly to the Muslims. As the Battle of the Trench commenced, the Muslims were forced to not only defend the entire length of the trench at all times, but guard the fortress of the Bani Qurayza as well. The situation was incredibly precarious. As time passed, the trench proved effective. Combat was limited to exchanges of arrows and javelins; only a few confederate warriors were able to breach the trench. The longer the stalemate continued, the more difficult it became for the invading confederate army to sustain itself. The weather grew cold and a fierce storm of torrential rain made conditions very difficult. As the Qur'an relates: "Remember God's grace upon you when the armies came against you and We sent a storm against them and armies that you did not see" (33:9). The confederates also had inadequate provisions to maintain a prolonged assault on the city in the inhospitable desert. Finally, the Meccans and their disgruntled allies ended their siege and withdrew in failure. The number of casualties from the battle was only six Muslims and three confederates.[9]

As the confederate forces returned to Mecca and their settlements, the Bani Qurayza, who had been persuaded by Huyay ibn Akhtab to betray their alliance with Muhammad, was left behind (along with Huyay) to face the Muslims alone. Shortly thereafter, the angel Gabriel appeared to Muhammad and ordered him to besiege the fortress of the Bani Qurayza for their treachery. As a tradition reported in *Sahih Muslim* relates:

> When [Muhammad] returned from the Trench and laid down his arms and took a bath, the angel Gabriel appeared to him and he was removing dust from his hair (as if he had just returned from the battle). [Gabriel] said: "You have laid down arms. By God, we haven't (yet) laid them down. So march against them." The Messenger of *Allah* (may peace be upon him) asked: "Where?" He pointed to Bani Qurayza. So the Messenger of *Allah* (may peace he upon him) fought against them.[10]

A further tradition adds that Gabriel stated: "Verily God in His might and His majesty commands thee, O Muhammad, that thou should go against the sons of Qurayza. I go to them even now, that I may cause their souls to quake."[11] The Muslims, three thousand strong, marched on the fortress of the Bani Qurayza and the siege lasted for some twenty-five days until both sides agreed to negotiate.[12] The next day the Jews surrendered and their fate was left to a member of the 'Aws tribe, who were former allies of the Bani Qurayza, named Sa'd ibn Muadh. As the event is reported in *Sahih Muslim*:

> They surrendered at the command of the Messenger of *Allah* (may peace be upon him), but he referred the decision about them to Sa'd, who said: "I decide about them that those of them who can fight be killed, their women and children taken prisoners and their properties distributed (among the Muslims)."[13]

The judgment of Sa'd was approved by Muhammad, and the men of the tribe were separated from the women and children. The treachery of the Bani Nadir, in the Muslim view, had proved that banishment from Medina was no longer an option. The previously banished Jews of the Bani Nadir had helped plan and carry out the assault by the confederates at the Battle of the Trench. Thus, Sa'd's penalty was strategically necessary, especially in the wake of the narrow victory at the Battle of the Trench.

A new trench was dug in the marketplace of Medina and for hours the men of the Bani Qurayza were beheaded in small groups and cast into the trench as a mass grave. Muslim sources state that between six hundred and seven hundred men from the tribe were executed.[14] Most of the women and children were ransomed by the Bani Nadir in Khaybar, although some, such as Safiyah (d. 670 CE) and Rayhanah (d. ca. 631 CE), remained captive in Medina. This event is alluded to in the Qur'an, which states: "And *Allah* turned back those unbelievers with their rage . . . and brought down those people from the People of the Book [i.e., the Bani Qurayza] from their forts and cast terror into their hearts; a faction you killed and a faction you imprisoned. And He gave you their lands, and their homes, and their wealth" (33:25–27).

The account of the mass execution of the men of the Bani Qurayza and enslavement of the women and children certainly offends our modern sensibilities, especially in a world that has witnessed the horrors of the Holocaust. However, the Bani Qurayza incident should be understood within its seventh-century tribal context, where such reprisals were normative. Furthermore, the punishment of the Bani Qurayza was more lenient than that decreed by

Yahweh against the tribal foes of the prophet Moses and the Israelites in the Torah (see, e.g., Numbers 31).

The Battle of Khaybar

In 628 CE, Muhammad signed a peace treaty with the Quraysh of Mecca known as the treaty of *Hudaybiyyah*. The temporary peace allowed Muhammad to focus his energies elsewhere and he directed his attention to the north toward the Jewish stronghold of the oasis of Khaybar. As one Muslim account describes it, Khaybar is where "they used to hatch their plots, ignite the fire of dissension and allure the Arabs living in the vicinity of Medina to join them with the aim of exterminating the Islamic state [i.e., Medina], or at least inflict heavy losses on the Muslims."[15] It was the Jews of Khaybar, after all, who had convinced the Bani Qurayza to commit the treachery that led to their gruesome end.

The Battle of Khaybar occurred in 629 CE. The Jews of Khaybar were alerted to the impending Muslim attack by their Bedouin allies, and they recruited the Bani Ghatfan of the Najd region to join them against the Muslims by promising half of their crop harvest. The Bani Ghatfan had been a member of the confederates at the Battle of the Trench. Together the Jews of Khaybar and their allies numbered fourteen thousand, thus vastly outnumbering the Muslim force of less than two thousand.[16] Knowing that the Jews and Bedouin awaited his advance, Muhammad led his army to Khaybar, which was a collection of farms and eight fortresses, by cover of night. Miraculously, the Muslims moved in complete silence and not even the birds were disturbed by the force of some fourteen hundred warriors.[17] In the process, they succeeded in evading the Bani Ghatfan and separating them from Khaybar. When the sun rose the following morning, the laborers of Khaybar came out of their forts to work in the farm fields unaware of the Muslim army encamped outside. As *Sahih Bukhari* relates:

> Narrated Anas: The Prophet set out for Khaybar and reached it at night. He used not to attack if he reached the people at night, till the day broke. So, when the day dawned, the Jews came out with their bags and spades. When they saw the Prophet they said: "Muhammad and his army!" The Prophet said: "*Allahu Akbar*! (Allah is Greater) and Khaybar is ruined, for whenever we approach a nation (i.e., enemy to fight) then it will be a miserable morning for those who have been warned."[18]

The different clans of the Jews each holed up in their respective fortresses and did not face the Muslims as a unified force. Muhammad entrusted the banner of the army to 'Ali ibn Abu Talib (d. 661 CE), who faced the leader of the fort of Na'im, named Marhab, in single combat and defeated him. The siege of the fort continued for several days until the inhabitants retreated to the fort of as-Sa'b. The siege of the fort of as-Sa'b lasted for three days and the Muslims acquired both booty and provisions inside.[19] The Muslim attack then moved to the next fort, but the Jews abandoned it and barricaded themselves in the formidable mountain fort of az-Zubair.

The fort of az-Zubair was fed by a water source that allowed people to remain inside for long periods of time. A long siege would be very difficult for the Muslims to sustain. But a Jewish man from one of the other fortresses came to Muhammad and offered to provide him with the secret to az-Zubair in return for the safety of himself, his family, and his processions. Muhammad agreed. The man informed Muhammad about the existence of the water source and how to cut it off. The Jews of az-Zubair were quickly forced out and direct combat ensued. During the fierce fighting, several Muslims and ten Jews were killed.[20] In the mean time, the Bani Ghatfan decided to abandon their alliance with the Bani Nadir and returned to the Najd without explanation.[21]

The siege of Khaybar continued with the fort of 'Abi and then the nearly impregnable an-Nizar. The Muslims succeeded in taking both of the forts, the second through sheer persistence and the use of captured siege equipment (e.g., battering rams) from the other forts. Only three more forts remained in Khaybar after an-Nizar fell to the Muslims, and the Muslim sources differ over whether the remaining forts were taken by force or through negotiations. The dominant view relates that the fort of al-Qamus put forth considerable resistance that lasted for two weeks.[22] Negotiations were finally convened and the inhabitants would be allowed to live in exile if they turned over their arms, wealth, and possessions. When the leaders of the fort attempted to hide some of their goods, they were executed and the rest of the clan was sent off into exile.[23]

After the fort of al-Qamus fell, the two remaining Jewish fortresses immediately surrendered. But the Jews from the forts of al-Wateeh and as-Salalim pleaded with Muhammad to let them stay in Khaybar to maintain their crops. In exchange, they would give half of the yield to the Muslims in tribute and Muhammad could terminate the agreement if he chose to do so. As a tradition in *Sahih Bukhari* relates:

> Narrated 'Abdullah: *Allah*'s Apostle rented the land of Khaybar to the Jews on the condition that they would work on it and cultivate it and take half of its yield.[24]

The remaining Jews of Khaybar thus continued to inhabit the oasis for many years until the second Caliph, Umar al-Khattab (d. 644 CE), apparently accused them of further treachery and rebellion and expelled them from the Hijaz during his reign. Other traditions recorded in the Hadith and hagiographies of the Prophet state that Muhammad had decreed on his deathbed that all Jews and Christians should be expelled from the Hijaz, however, neither he nor his immediate successor, Abu Bakr (d. 634 CE), carried out this plan.

Western scholars and critics have often looked on the Battle of Khaybar, and the events in Medina that precipitated it, with tremendous skepticism and postulated that Muhammad was making political maneuvers to expel the Jews, take their wealth, and ascend to unrivaled political power in Arabia. Another view put forth by Patricia Crone in her controversial book *Hagarism* argues that Islam was originally a Jewish heresy and the tale of Muhammad's conflict with the Jews (as well as the Qur'an itself) is an invention of the eighth century (CE) designed to obscure and differentiate Islam's historical origins from Judaism.[25] But in the Muslim view, the Jewish tribes of the Bani Qaynuqa, Bani Nadir, and Bani Qurayza were guilty of inexcusable treachery that violated the terms of the Constitution of Medina. Worst of all, they had plotted against *Allah* and His Messenger and they received their just recompense.

The Khaybar Master Narrative in Extremist Discourse

Historically, relations between Muslims and Jews have been relatively amicable, especially when compared to Jews and Christians. There are numerous incidents of remarkable coexistence and cooperation between Muslims and Jews, but there have also been tragic incidents of communal violence and intolerance. That said, the events recounted in the Khaybar master narrative have never led to the formulation of a perpetual condemnation of Jews as "Satanic" or "Christ killers" in the same way the Gospel narratives have informed Christian thought over the centuries. The establishment of the state of Israel by Zionists in Palestine in 1948 and the ensuing decades of bloody Arab-Israeli conflict in the Middle East (see Chapter 11), however, brought new relevance to the Khaybar master narrative to modern times, especially among extremist groups in the Middle East.

In Lebanon, conflict between the Twelver Shi'ite-dominated south and the state of Israel has occupied headlines for decades. The most prominent and influential sociopolitical movement among Lebanon's disenfranchised Shi'ite minority is undoubtedly Hezbollah ("The Party of God"). The organization did not formally declare its existence, including its active military wing, until 1985, but its fighters were already active in the early 1980s within various Iranian-backed Lebanese resistance groups.

Some five months before Hezbollah's first "martyrdom operation" in 1982 (see Chapter 7), Israel invaded southern Lebanon and besieged the capital Beirut to annihilate the secular-nationalist Palestine Liberation Organization (PLO) that was based there at the time.[26] The three-month Israeli assault resulted in the death of an estimated fifteen thousand to twenty thousand Palestinians, Lebanese, and Syrians, and some five hundred Israeli soldiers, while injuring many more and destroying enormous amounts of infrastructure.[27]

The ideology of Hezbollah was deeply influenced by the Iranian revolutionary leader, Ayatollah Ruhullah Khomeini (d. 1989), but the devastating war with Israel, as well as Lebanon's internal sectarian tensions, had a direct impact on its formation. It would not be an overstatement to say that the war with Israel significantly defined Hezbollah's nascent identity. As such, invocations of the Khaybar master narrative by Hezbollah's leadership should not surprise observers in the least. Hezbollah has even named one its long-range rockets (developed to target Israel) the Khaybar-1.[28]

During a live speech in Beirut on May 7, 1998, broadcast via *al-Manar* satellite television throughout the region, Hezbollah's Shaykh Sayyed Hassan Nasrallah stated: "When this Muslim nation was small, the Jews were unable to defeat it, and the Jews of Bani Nadir, Bani Qurayza, and Khaybar were forced out of their castles and fortresses."[29] Nasrallah, the secretary general of Hezbollah since 1996, went on to further state:

> But let us return to Khaybar: the army of Muhammad has returned carrying the Message [of Islam], history, religion, and culture, full of resolve and determination, with its leaders being martyrdom-seekers, just like 'Ali and Husayn, may God's peace and prayers be upon them. So wait for the dream of the Khaybarites to collapse, just as Khaybar collapsed.[30]

The Khaybar master narrative invoked in the speech by Nasrallah is explicitly directed toward Israel. The shocking losses that the Arab world experienced in its wars with Israel (e.g., 1967) have contradicted the expected outcome of the Khaybar master narrative. Thus, Nasrallah noted in his speech that "when the Muslim nation was small" it achieved victory against the Jewish tribes, but in the twentieth century, when the Arabs and Muslims numbered in the hundreds of millions, they were defeated. The Khaybar master narrative thus functions as a denunciation of secular-nationalism, both for its divisiveness and its un-Islamic deviations from the *shari'ah*, and as an affirmation that the desire for victory can only be satisfied through returning to Islam. Victory, in their view, will only come when Islam is once again realized in all spheres of Muslim societies, then the fall of the mighty yet temporary "fortresses" of Israel, like Khaybar before it, will only be a matter of time.

In Iraq, the U.S.-led invasion that commenced in 2003 opened new possibilities for extremist groups to operate in the country, including Iranian-backed Shi'ite militias akin to Lebanon's Hezbollah. But Sunni extremists, including groups claiming affiliation with al-Qaeda, also took root in Iraq in the wake of Saddam Hussein's overthrow. Remnants of Pan-Arab nationalist groups (e.g., Baathists) also remained and contributed to a complex array of "resistance" groups operating in the different regions of Iraq. This curious amalgamation of different Islamist extremists with Pan-Arab nationalists became apparent online as well. On November 27, 2009, an Islamist extremist web site posted links to an audio message by the notorious Baathist commander, Izzat Ibrahim al-Duri, entitled "Brothers and Comrades in the Path of Jihad and Liberation." In it, he states:

> When our forefathers stood against the tribes of Bani Qurayza, Bani Nadir, Bani Qaynuqa, and Khaybar when they resisted and waged war against the Message, they were not of Moses' religion, but rather a deviant and oppressive form of that religion created by the Jews (having altered and removed parts of the original religion). Today we stand against the Zionist Jews and the deviant and oppressive crusading Christianity, the banner of which is carried by Bush and his gang. We are not against the religion of Christ (peace be upon him) his people, his scholars, and his followers. Did not the deviant Crusaders, the forefathers of Bush, fight our religion and Arabism according to their warped and repulsive version of religion that is against the nation, its true religion, and its eternal message in the Crusades, as the Jews fought us in Medina and Khaybar?[31]

Al-Duri's invocation of the Khaybar master narrative is deliberately meant to be broad in its appeal, targeting both militant Arab nationalists and Islamist extremists. It is also interlaced with other narratives discussed in this book, namely, the Crusader master narrative (see Chapter 9).

On yet another extremist web site, a forum participant posted a statement of praise and celebration regarding the formation of a group called the "Jerusalem Brigade" in war-torn Somalia. In it, the forum member fantasized about the day a Qutbian Islamist vanguard would overtake the state of Israel. Invoking al-Qaeda's Usama Bin Laden, he states:

> Shaykh Usama Bin Laden will stand and say: "People, mujahidin in the east and the west of the earth, in the name of God, we declare the establishment

> of the righteous Islamic caliphate throughout our Islamic land from the confines of China in the east to Andalusia in the west." Then, the people will exclaim "God is Great" and their voices will resonate and shake the walls "God is Great, God is Great, Khaybar is ruined. With the Qur'an and the gun, we will destroy the Jewish State."[32]

These statements by contemporary extremists invoking the master narrative of the Battle of Khaybar all project the notion of a treacherous Jewish adversary with an innate hatred for Islam and a thirst for political power. But the Jewish tribes of the Khaybar master narrative also represent a superior enemy, wealthier, and having a more powerful military force, than the Muslims. Although the Muslims were smaller in number and lacking in resources, they managed to overcome their treacherous foes through unity, obedience, and the strength of their religious convictions. Thus, the Khaybar master narrative shares certain key elements with the master narrative of the Battle of Badr, including the miraculous participation of angels in the battles. However, history has provided certain convenient parallels for extremists in this case that obviously give the master narrative a very specific application.

Analysis of the Khaybar Master Narrative

The Khaybar master narrative makes use of the betrayal or vengeance story forms. Betrayal is, of course, a precursor to vengeance, so the two forms operate together to produce a narrative trajectory that moves forward from a conflict between Muslims and Jews rooted in oppositional ends. Into this conflict comes an archetype of the trickster or traitor in the form of a Jew, namely, Huyay ibn Akhtab, and the Bani Nadir and Bani Qurayza tribes, who committed treason by violating the covenant of Medina. Through analogy, extremists may frame modern Jews, most obviously Israelis, in terms of distrust, promising peace and reconciliation even though it is a goal that the Jews never want to see fulfilled. Instead, the Jews use their cunning and their powerful allies to further persecute the Palestinians, build new settlements in Palestinian territories, annex the holy city of Jerusalem, and otherwise betray any real sense of cooperation that could lead to peace. It is at this point in the story that the vengeance story form building on the betrayal theme requires a hero to seek justice, either by punishing the traitors/tricksters for their crimes (as the Bani Qurayza were defeated and executed) or, as is the case in the nuclear apocalyptic scenarios invoked among a few extremist groups, remove all of Israel from the map.

The Passion narrative of Christianity shares many of the elements found in the Khaybar master narrative. As discussed earlier, however, it has not historically played out in Muslim culture the same way the "Christ killer" Passion narrative has played out in Christendom. Nevertheless, there are lessons to be observed. The Khaybar master narrative is a means by which contemporary individuals can be framed or envisioned in terms of events that those individuals or communities have absolutely no connection with and ascribed guilt, blame, or stereotypical qualities. Such a master narrative, featuring an archetypal traitor and betrayal story form, not only provides fodder for violent actions but also a degree of persuasive power that discourages those who may otherwise be inclined toward peace and reconciliation.

CHAPTER 7

The Battle of Karbala

Thus far the master narratives we have explored lack any distinctive Islamic sectarian character, even though the extremists we have focused on so far come mostly from within the Sunni branch of Islam (broadly speaking). The Battle of Karbala, however, is a distinctly Shi'ite master narrative. It forms the basis for a decidedly sectarian and dualistic worldview upon which other Shi'ite narratives and master narratives are founded (e.g., *al-Mahdi*). It is also arguably the most vivid and powerful of all the master narratives examined in this book, one that has been expressed continuously over the centuries through elaborate rituals, art, poetry, and dramas. It has also been convincingly argued that the Battle of Karbala master narrative forms the basis for modern Iranian nationalism.[1]

Karbala is a narrative that posits an essential dualism. Historically, dualism has had a prominent place among Near Eastern religions. In ancient Persia (Iran), Zoroastrianism posited the existence of two opposing deities, a god of light (Ahura Mazda) and a god of darkness (Angra Mainyu). The prophet-priest, Zarathustra (d. ca. 600 BCE), taught that the world was a battleground between the forces of light and darkness, good and evil, or life and death. According to Zoroastrianism, Angra Mainyu (or Ahriman) is the source of all death, decay, pollution, and evil. He exists in direct opposition to Ahura Mazda (or Ohrmazd), who is the source of all life, growth, purity, and goodness. The universe is essentially good as a creation of Ahura Mazda, but all malevolent or harmful forces within it, including death, are the machinations of Angra Mainyu.

These two cosmic deities are at battle with one another; Ahura Mazda's army of winged angels struggles with Angra Mainyu's army of demons. Thus, the physical world is a battleground in which people possess free will to make ethical choices and purify themselves from demonic pollution and corruption. Human souls will one day face divine judgment for their actions before Ahura Mazda and enter either paradise or a hellish domain of fire and torment. Death represents the triumph of Angra Mainyu, so corpses are the most dangerous source of pollution. For this reason, Zoroastrians have traditionally placed their dead in a "Tower of Silence," called a *dakhma*, to be consumed by vultures. Otherwise, burial would pollute the earth, submersion would pollute the water, and cremation would pollute the fire (which is a sacred symbol of Ahura Mazda).

The present age of struggle between the forces of good and evil will finally end when a savior, called the *Saoshyant*, comes to lead the final battle against evil and reign over the earth. The *Saoshyant*, tradition says, will be born from a virgin who bathed in a sacred lake that preserves the seed of Zarathustra. In ancient Greek sources, Zoroastrian priests are referred to as *magi*. The Gospel of Matthew (written in Greek) in the Christian New Testament reports that three *magi* travelled from the east to see the infant Jesus, who, according to the Gospel, was born to a virgin (Mary).

Christian Gnosticism, attacked as a heresy by the Roman Church, articulated a dualistic worldview with notable differences from its predecessor, Zoroastrianism. Christian Gnostics posited a dualistic opposition between spirit and matter. While diversity existed within Gnostic thought, the core narrative envisioned the malevolent entrapment of spirit by matter and a future battle between good (the realm of spirit) and evil (the realm of matter) that will finally liberate spirit and restore it to a perfected higher state.[2] The Gnostics believed that Jesus was an emissary of the spirit realm who revealed secret knowledge (*gnosis*) to attain salvation, and Jesus' bodily (i.e., material) form was only an apparition (meaning the crucifixion was an illusion).[3] The physical world, furthermore, was viewed as inherently evil and the creation of a lesser deity (Yahweh of the Old Testament), therefore making life in this world, including sex, something evil to be renounced.[4]

In the third century (CE), Gnostic ideas were further developed by the teachings of the prophet Mani (d. 276 CE). Born into Zoroastrian Persia at the dawn of the Sasanian Empire, Mani was raised as a Christian Gnostic before proclaiming his own prophethood and the advent of a new universal religion, known to us as Manichaeism. Like the Gnostics, Manichaeans believed that the realm of spirit was good and that matter was evil. Arguably, the most famous adherent of Manichaeism was the famous theologian St. Augustine of Hippo (d. 430 CE), who practiced Manichaeism for many years before converting to Christianity around the age of thirty-three. Over the centuries, many Christians have envisioned Satan ("The Devil") as an opposing deity waging war against God and ruling over Hell, ironically the name of a Germanic-Norse underworld and goddess of death, and its evil legions until the *Apocalypse*; which is Greek for "revelation," the concluding book of the New Testament depicting the final battle between good and evil.

The Battle of Karbala Master Narrative

When the Prophet Muhammad died of an illness in Medina in 632 CE, it set off a dispute among his followers that would forever shape the history of Islam. After the early Muslims migrated from Mecca to Medina in 622 CE (i.e., the *hijra*), Muhammad emerged as a statesman, judge, and military commander. Thus, even though he was the "Seal of the Prophets" who marked the end of the prophetic line extending back to Adam, his political office still needed to be filled after his death. Islam created a new *ummah* (community) apart from the tribes of old and it required leadership.

The community had to find a new leader (*imam*) to guide them in an uncertain future. According to the majority view, Muhammad never selected a successor. He also had no sons (all three died as infants). The community had to select a figure from among their elders that they felt had the most outstanding knowledge of Islam, affinity to the Prophet, and trust of the people. The candidate they chose was Abu Bakr (d. 634 CE) and he became the first Caliph (*khalifah*) of Islam. Abu Bakr was Muhammad's best friend, one of the earliest converts to Islam in Mecca, and Muhammad's father-in-law ('Aisha's father). When the Prophet was ill, he also selected Abu Bakr to lead congregational prayers at the mosque in his absence. The majority faction that supported Abu Bakr as Caliph would later be identified as the precursor to the Sunni branch of Islam.

A minority of the community rejected the selection of Abu Bakr and contended that Muhammad's cousin and son-in-law, 'Ali ibn Abu Talib (d. 661 CE), was the Prophet's rightful successor. They argued that the leadership of the *ummah* should stay within the family of the Prophet, or the *Ahl al-Bayt* ("People of the House"). After Abu Bakr died following a short reign, the party of 'Ali, or *Shi'at 'Ali* (the basis for the term Shi'ite), continued to support the candidacy of 'Ali and opposed the selection of the second Caliph, Umar ibn al-Khattab (r. 634–644 CE), and third Caliph, Uthman ibn Affan (r. 644–656 CE).

As the *Shi'a* political movement developed a distinct set of dogmatic formulations over the years, the *Shi'a* promoted the belief that the male descendents of Muhammad, through his son-in-law 'Ali and daughter Fatima, were the infallible divinely ordained leaders of the *ummah* and the definitive interpreters of Islam. In their view, even though God had ended the line of prophets with Muhammad, He, in His infinite mercy, had bestowed the line of Holy Imams upon humanity to continue to provide proper guidance and pious leadership.

However, revelation (*wahy*) did indeed end with the prophets. The Imams ("leaders"), depending on the sectarian doctrine (there are several different branches of Shi'ism), possessed the primordial "light of Muhammad" within them and had almost supernatural abilities. Thus, for the *Shi'a*, the cardinal belief of Islam became faith in and devotion to the Holy Imams, and all those who refused to honor them, including the "Sunni" Muslims, were (generally speaking) unbelievers destined for hellfire (including the usurpers Abu Bakr, Umar, and Uthman).

When 'Ali was killed by a Kharijite Muslim assassin in 661 CE, the *Shi'a* recognized 'Ali's firstborn son, Hassan (d. 670 CE), as the second Imam. Meanwhile, the throne of the Caliphate was assumed by Muawiyyah (d. 680 CE), the Umayyad tribesman of the third Caliph Uthman and son of Abu Sufyan (see Chapter 4). He had opposed 'Ali by force during his troubled Caliphate (r. 656–661 CE) and contended that 'Ali had not brought the assassins of Uthman to justice as he was obligated to do. It is reported in the sayings of the *Nahjul Balagha* that 'Ali stated: "By *Allah*, Muawiyyah is not more cunning than I am, but he deceives and commits evil deeds."[5] The subsequent rise of Muawiyyah to the throne in Damascus began the first caliphal dynasty in Islamic history, known as the Umayyad Caliphate. The Muslim empire expanded and thrived under the Umayyads, but many Muslims opposed their rule.

Unlike the first four Caliphs, venerated by Sunni Muslims as the Rightly Guided Caliphs (*al-Rashidun*), the Umayyads transformed the Caliphate into a hereditary monarchy that enjoyed tremendous material luxuries and crushed all opposition to their reign. The Umayyads envisioned an empire where Arab Muslims ruled as an aristocracy and they discouraged conversion to Islam among their non-Muslim and non-Arab subjects. They even forced new converts to pay the non-Muslim poll tax (*jizya*) that Christians and Jews were obligated to pay. Umayyad courts were also places of luxury, where silk, singing girls, and wine were known to be commonplace. "Pious" was not a term commonly used to describe the Umayyads, aside from the popular Caliph, Umar ibn 'Abdul-Aziz (r. 717–720 CE).

This was the historical setting for the Battle of Karbala, which might be more rightly described as a tragedy rather than a battle. Despite the prosperity of the Muslim empire, which extended from Spain to the Indus River valley, there was widespread opposition to Umayyad rule among the Muslims. The Umayyads faced particularly strong opposition from the

Shi'a, who reviled Muawiyyah as an apostate tyrant who fought against the rightful Imam, 'Ali. When Muawiyyah assumed the Caliphate in 661 CE, he established negotiations with 'Ali's firstborn son, Hassan, who lived in Kufa, Iraq. Hassan pragmatically accepted his terms and relinquished any claims to rule. He lived out the rest of his life quietly in Medina until his death in 670 CE. According to *Shi'a* tradition, Hassan was poisoned by the Umayyads.

Before Muawiyyah's death, he selected his son Yazid (d. 683 CE) to be his successor, which was a controversial political innovation at the time. Yazid proved to be an extremely unpopular ruler. The *Shi'a* in Kufa implored 'Ali's second son (recognized as the third Imam), Husayn, to lead the resistance to Yazid's reign and claim the Caliphate for himself. Unlike his older brother Hassan, Husayn answered their call and rode out from Medina with a small party of family members and supporters toward Kufa. Tradition places the number of people in the riding party at seventy or seventy-two (both common numbers in Islamic literature). This political act drew the attention of the Umayyads and the Caliph Yazid dispatched an army to intercept Husayn's party before it could reach Kufa. The two groups met at the desert plain of Karbala in the month of Muharram in 680 CE.

The Karbala master narrative is recounted in numerous sources, such as Abu Mikhnaf's eighth century (CE) *Kitab Miqtal al-Husayn* or Husayn Wa'ez Kashefi's highly influential *Rowzat al-Shuhada* (written in 1502 CE), but there is no single canonical account. Tradition reports that Imam Husayn's party included his half-brother 'Abbas, eldest son 'Ali al-Akbar, son 'Ali Zayn al-Abidin (the fourth Imam), sister Zaynab bint 'Ali, infant son 'Ali al-Asghar, and daughter Sukayna, among numerous others. They were encircled by a massive Umayyad army of thousands of soldiers led by Yazid's military commander, Shimr ibn Zuljawshan.

After days of negotiation and skirmishes, the battle began on the tenth of Muharram, known as *Ashura* ("The Tenth"). Vastly outnumbered, Husayn's companions went out to face the Umayyad army and fought heroically (even miraculously) before dying as martyrs under a devastating assault of arrows, spears, and swords. After that, Husayn's family members rode out to fight, beginning with his eldest son, 'Ali al-Akbar, who was also martyred. Overwhelmed by the brutal heat of the desert, Husayn's party, which included women and children, suffered from severe thirst. So he and his half-brother 'Abbas, a major hero of the master narrative, rode toward the Euphrates to retrieve water, but they were blocked by the Umayyad army.

'Abbas, however, rode heroically through a storm of arrows to reach the river and filled a water skin to bring it back to the women and children. He attempted to battle his way back, but the Umayyads severed his hands and then pierced the water skin with an arrow causing all the water to pour out onto the ground. 'Abbas, in tears, reportedly died in Husayn's arms. After the martyrdom of 'Abbas, Husayn carried his infant son, 'Ali al-Asghar, out with him in front of the Umayyad army and implored Yazid's forces to allow his child to have some water. In response, the Umayyad's best archer fired a single arrow that pierced Husayn's arm and killed his infant son, 'Ali, demonstrating the cruelty and barbarism of Husayn's enemies.

With all the male members of Husayn's party killed, except for his son 'Ali Zayn al-Abidin (who was too ill to fight), he rode out to make his heroic last stand in the climatic event of the master narrative. According to the richly detailed and dramatic account of Kashefi, Husayn wore the turban of the Prophet Muhammad, carried the shield of Hamza (see Chapter 4), wielded the famous two-pointed sword of his father 'Ali (Dhul-Fiqar), and rode atop the legendary white horse, Dhul-Janah.[6] The horse Dhul-Janah is commonly depicted in Shi'ite iconography, often bloodied and mourning for Husayn. According to tradition, the horse was originally owned by the Prophet Muhammad, but that would make the horse *at least* forty-nine years old by the time of the Battle of Karbala (horses usually live for around twenty years). Amidst the ensuing battle, Husayn faced the entire army alone and killed hundreds of soldiers in one-by-one combat.

The treacherous Umayyads finally resorted to dishonorable tactics and stormed him from all sides.[7] After sustaining numerous bloody wounds, Husayn was finally decapitated by Shimr, the commander of Yazid's army. Thereafter, Husayn's severed head, along with the surviving women, children, and 'Ali Zayn al-Abidin, were brought back to the Caliph Yazid in Damascus. Husayn's body was entombed at Karbala and a mosque-shrine was later constructed that is one of the most sacred sites in the world for Shi'ite Muslims. One tradition states that Karbala is a piece of heaven on earth where angels once descended and never left. Meanwhile, Husayn's decapitated head was originally enshrined in Damascus, but then relocated to Cairo, Egypt, sometime in the twelfth century (CE). His sister Zaynab was also entombed in Damascus before being relocated to Cairo. The Sayyidna Husayn and Sayyida Zaynab mosques in Cairo are arguably the holiest Muslim sites in Egypt (which is a Sunni Muslim state), although there are several other important sacred sites in Cairo worth noting, such as the tombs of Imam Shafi'i (d. 820 CE) and Sayyida Nafisa.

Shi'ite interpretations of the tragedy at Karbala represent a post-failure rationalization of events, not unlike that of early Christians who sought to explain the failure and humiliating execution of their Messiah through grand cosmic doctrines of redemptive sacrifice and an imminent second coming. For Shi'ite Muslims, the horrific events of Karbala were actually divinely preordained. Apparently, Husayn, the infallible and divinely chosen Imam of all believers, was fully aware of his impending martyrdom. The Imam went to his death willingly, as foretold by prophets and visions throughout history that are related in Shi'ite sources.

According to some traditions, Husayn even turned away the assistance of supernatural beings in order to face the Umayyad army in battle alone. The influential account by Kashefi emphasized the martyrdom of Husayn, "The Prince of Martyrs" (*sayyid al-shuhada*), as the central axis around which all of human history revolves, extending back throughout prophetic history to the time of Adam.[8] Shi'ite tradition teaches that one who grieves for Imam Husayn will have all of his or her sins washed away. Thus, ritual commemorations of Karbala, including elegies, passion plays (*taziyeh*), graphic iconography, and acts of self-mortification, especially on the anniversary of his death on the day of *Ashura*, form the heart of Shi'ite devotional practice.

Husayn and his companions, especially 'Abbas, are the archetypal heroes and martyrs of the narrative. They are portrayed as brave, noble, and willing to sacrifice everything in the struggle against injustice and oppression. On the opposing side is the cruel, treacherous, and barbaric army of the antagonist, the archetypal tyrant Yazid, the Umayyad Caliph. One tradition describes Yazid as "a reprobate, a drinker of wine, and one that kills the innocent soul unlawfully and practices openly all manner of corruption."[9] For Shi'ite Muslims, Yazid is the personification of evil and worldly corruption. The eternal struggle between good and evil, freedom and oppression, justice and injustice, which has played out throughout time, culminated at Karbala with Husayn and Yazid enacting the principal dualistic roles.

Karbala and the Martyrs of Revolutionary Shi'ism

Centuries ago in 1501 (CE), Shah Ismail (d. 1524 CE) established the Safavid Empire of Persia and declared Twelver Shi'ism as the religion of the state. The Safavid Empire was the first sovereign Persian state since the Sasanian Empire fell to Arab Muslims in the seventh century (CE). Before the reign of the Safavids, Persia was predominately Sunni Muslim. For instance, the preeminent Sunni scholar Abu Hamid al-Ghazali (d. 1111 CE) was Persian.

The Safavids, however, made Shi'ite Islam the basis of their new state (with all its political implications for the Shah, who claimed divine authority), and they imposed Twelver Shi'ism on the entire population under their rule. This is still reflected today in modern Iran, where some 95 percent of the population is Twelver Shi'ite. Iraq too, which was once under Safavid control, has a Shi'ite majority population (around 60 percent). The Safavids imported Shi'ite scholars from across the Muslim world, especially from Syria, Arabia, and Iraq, and made Persia (Iran) the world center of Shi'ite Islam (which it still is today). Meanwhile, they persecuted and executed Sunnis who refused to convert to Shi'ism. The Safavids even persecuted Sufi orders due to their rival structures of authority (loyalty to a *pir* or *shaykh*) and many fled to India to live under the more tolerant and ostensibly Sunni Mughal Emperors.

For the Safavids, religious uniformity helped to solidify the empire's territory and ensure the loyalty of the population against the Sunni empires that sat on their borders, namely, the Ottoman Turks and the Uzbeks. During their reign, the Safavids encouraged pilgrimage to tombs and shrines of the Imams, most of which were located in Safavid territory (Iraq and Iran). Pilgrimage to such shrines, especially Imam Husayn's tomb at Karbala, rivaled or even replaced the sacred *hajj* (pilgrimage to Mecca). The holy cities of Mecca and Medina were under Sunni Ottoman control during that time. Many features of Twelver Shi'ite Islam as we know it today, including ritual commemoration of *Ashura*, took definitive shape under the Safavids.

Surprisingly, Safavid political institutions actually ran contrary to normative Twelver Shi'ism. Shah Ismail relied on an eccentric amalgamation of doctrines that proclaimed his infallible divinity and such ideas ran afoul of Shi'ite "orthodoxy." According to "orthodox" Twelver doctrine, only the Holy Imams are legitimate rulers, even though the Imams died centuries ago. There is no legitimate Islamic government until the Twelfth Imam returns from his miraculous occultation (*ghaybat*) at the end of time as the *Mahdi* (see Chapter 8). However, as was the case with Shah Ismail, those details hardly prevented ambitious Shi'ite leaders from devising elaborate justifications for their right to wield political power.

The Guardianship of the Jurist

The chief ideologue of the 1979 Islamic revolution in Iran, the Ayatollah Ruhullah Khomeini (d. 1989), formulated an innovative interpretation of Shi'ite political doctrine designed to circumvent the problem of the absent Imam and Shi'ite eschatology. This doctrine, known as *Velayat-e Faqih* ("Guardianship of the Jurist"), proposed that a leading Shi'ite jurist (e.g., a Grand Ayatollah) could rule a Shi'ite state in the absence of the Imam and act on his behalf. As Khomeini explained: "If we assume that the Prophet and the Imam had been trustees over matters, their task in this respect would not have been very different . . . from the task of any ordinary person designated as a trustee over those same matters. Their guardianship over the entire nation is not different practically from the guardianship of any knowledgeable and just jurisprudent in the time of the absence [of the Imam]."[10]

The Ayatollah, as the chief jurisprudent, could therefore act on behalf of the awaited Imam, and the revolution against Iran's illegitimate monarchy of Shah Mohammad Reza Pahlavi (d. 1980), understood as a manifestation of Yazid, was religiously justified and undertaken in militant fashion. In a sermon given by Khomeini on *Ashura* (the sacred anniversary of Imam Husayn's martyrdom) in 1963, prior to his exile from Iran, he explicitly associated the Shah with Yazid, stating:

> If the Umayyads and Yazid . . . were waging war only with Husayn, why then the savage, inhuman behavior towards the helpless women and the innocent children of Husayn? . . . I think they wanted to destroy the foundation . . . The regime of Yazid [was] against the family of the Prophet . . .They wanted to uproot the sacred [family] tree . . . If the brutal regime of the [Shah] is engaged in a war with the religious scholars, why did it tear apart the Qur'an while attacking the Faisiyeh Seminary? . . .What did it have against the students? . . . It wanted to do away with the foundation . . . It does not want this foundation to exist . . . I advise you Mr. Shah, Shah sir, I advise you to change your ways.[11]

The Shah, perceived as a cruel tyrant and agent of the United States and Israel, had assumed the role of the antagonist Yazid in the political narrative of the Iranian revolution. The Shah, like "the Pharaoh" Anwar Sadat of Egypt, failed to implement God's law and attempted to violently repress the growing Islamic activism among his people.

Khomeini employed the master narrative of Husayn's martyrdom at the hands of Yazid's army to help launch his revolution against the Shah over thirty years ago, but the master narrative is still a prominent force in Iranian politics today. For instance, during the 2009 elections in Iran, incumbent presidential candidate, Mahmoud Ahmedinejad, shockingly compared his opponent, Mir Hossein Mousavi, to the tyrant Yazid. In his campaign speeches, Ahmadinejad attempted to portray himself as the victim of former members of Iran's political establishment, like Mousavi, who were trying to get rid of him in the same way that Yazid had killed Imam Husayn at Karbala.[12] Mousavi, incidentally, was a close associate of Khomeini and served as Prime Minister of Iran for eight years during the disastrous war with Iraq.[13] Ahmedinejad's use of the Yazid archetype was highly unusual since he was the incumbent in power and it did not appear to resonate with the voters. Indeed, aside from Mr. Ahmedinejad's use of the archetype, it remains a normative fixture of Iranian social identity and discourse, often in relation to Western governments and heads of state, such as George W. Bush or Tony Blair. As one contemporary Iranian supporter of Khomeini's ideology put it in 2006: "Bush is Yazid."[14]

In these instances, the role of Husayn is assumed by the Iranian nation as a whole and the hostile foreign powers assume the role of Yazid. The narrative of Husayn and Yazid in this context is rather haunting, given that the story tells us that Husayn entered Karbala fully aware of his impending self-sacrifice. If Iran is faced with a military conflict against Israel or the United States, one could reasonably conclude that self-preservation is not the primary operating principle among Iran's Islamist leadership. That remains to be seen, assuming their religious convictions are sincere and not simply a means of mass mobilization and social control.

After the Iranian revolution, Khomeini intended to export his revolutionary jihad throughout the region and witness the popular overthrow of other "tyrannical" regimes in countries like Bahrain, Lebanon, Iraq, Saudi Arabia, and Egypt. The chief ideologue of the Egyptian *al-Jihad*, 'Abdel-Salam al-Faraj (d. 1982), and his fellow militants were receptive and emboldened by the revolution in Iran, despite the fact that they were Sunni Muslims, and hoped that Sadat's assassination would trigger a full-scale revolution in Egypt, but it never materialized.[15] Rather, Egyptians were horrified by Sadat's death, and public sentiment did not support his assassination. The small and secretive *al-Jihad* group had no popular support whatsoever, unlike the more mainstream Muslim Brotherhood.

In contrast, Khomeini was a cleric of enormous influence with widespread popular support in Iran. His revolution was carefully planned and he negotiated with the entire spectrum of Iran's ideological and economic factions during his rise to power. For his revolutionary success, the Iranian people bestowed the title of Imam on Khomeini, a title traditionally reserved exclusively for the twelve Holy Imams descended from the Prophet Muhammad in Twelver Shi'ite Islam. After his death in 1989, Khomeini's elaborate tomb in southern Tehran became a major pilgrimage site for Iranian Twelver Shi'ites. Meanwhile, the simple tomb of the deposed Shah of Iran lies in exile in a small room in the back of the ar-Rifai mosque in Cairo, Egypt, near the tombs of Egypt's former monarchy.

The Karbala Master Narrative in Extremist Discourse

The militant political mobilization of the Karbala master narrative is not restricted to Iran. In Lebanon, which has a large Twelver Shi'ite minority,

Hezbollah ("The Party of God") utilized the narrative and the teachings of Khomeini in an Arab context, specifically in response to the Arab-Israeli conflict. On November 11, 1982, seventeen-year-old Ahmad Qasir, a Hezbollah *istishhadi* ("self-martyr"),[16] drove a car packed with explosives into an Israeli military base claiming the lives of approximately 150 Israeli soldiers and military personnel.[17] The attack earned him the title of *Amir al-Shuhada* ("Prince of Martyrs") among Hezbollah militants and supporters, a title traditionally reserved for Imam Husayn.[18] Although Hezbollah did not formally declare their existence and the formation of their military wing until 1985, their fighters were active in the early 1980s under an umbrella organization, the Lebanese National Resistance (LNR). They acted under secretive aliases, such as Islamic Jihad (not to be confused with the Palestinian Islamic Jihad or Egyptian *Tanzim al-Jihad*).[19]

Some five months prior to Ahmad Qasir's attack, Israel had invaded southern Lebanon and laid siege to Beirut, attempting to annihilate Yassir Arafat's secular nationalist Palestine Liberation Organization (PLO) based there at the time.[20] The three-month Israeli assault resulted in the death of an estimated fifteen thousand to twenty thousand Palestinians, Lebanese, and Syrians, and some five hundred Israeli soldiers.[21] Qasir's subsequent "martyrdom operation" came to represent the pinnacle of self-sacrifice in Hezbollah's campaign of militant resistance against Israel's occupation and all foreign "imperialist" forces[22] in the Shi'ite regions of Lebanon, particularly in the south. The ideology of the movement was deeply influenced by the teachings of Ayatollah Khomeini, whom Hezbollah recognized as their supreme leader, as well as chief financial supporter. The profound emphasis that Hezbollah's leaders and ideologues placed on martyrdom tapped directly into the Karbala master narrative and followed historical precedents set forth by Iran.

Only two years before the appearance of Hezbollah suicide bombers, or "self-martyrs," in Lebanon, zealous Shi'ites in Iran were sacrificing their lives in the form of the "People's Army," or *Basiji*, against the invasion of Baathist Iraq. "The *Basiji* fought to hold off Iraq's invasion of Khorramshahr in September 1980 and they were known for their 'human wave' assaults in which youths as young as nine years old, as well as middle-aged men, volunteered to use their bodies to clear mines that Iraqi soldiers laid along the border."[23] The most famous of these volunteers was undoubtedly Mohammed Hossein Fahmideh (d. 1980), a twelve-year-old boy from Qum who destroyed an advancing Iraqi tank by throwing himself beneath it with a hand grenade strapped to his body.[24] Khomeini declared him a national hero and icons of Fahmideh are still found throughout Iran. A postage stamp bearing his image was issued in 1986.

The *Basiji*, under the direct orders and guidance of Khomeini, assumed the position of a *Shi'a* vanguard at the forefront of a long chain of heroic martyrs who volunteered to lay down their lives for the preservation of the "true religion" extending all the way back to Imam Husayn. It is this notion of self-martyrdom and sacrifice that came to play such a pivotal role in the development of Hezbollah's ideology sanctioning the use of "martyrdom operations" (i.e., suicide bombings) as a legitimate means of resistance and the greatest form of self-sacrifice that a believer can undertake.

For Hezbollah, engaging in the jihad against Israel and its allies entailed not only a willingness to fight for God's cause, but a willingness to die for the cause, both of which are exemplified in *Shi'a* constructions of Karbala.[25] After all, Husayn had not simply been martyred; from the Shi'ite perspective Husayn had made a voluntary act of self-sacrifice, fully aware of his coming fate as the divinely guided Imam, with all the cosmic significance and eschatological underpinnings that this role entailed. Christian interpretations of the crucifixion of Jesus, as already noted, are not dissimilar in this respect.[26] "Self-martyrdom," in this paradigm, is not an act of suicide (which is prohibited), but a voluntary act in the "cause of God," in this case a defensive struggle against the enemies of Islam.

As of the mid-1980s, Hezbollah has largely abandoned "martyrdom operations" in favor of more conventional methods of warfare.[27] However, the tactic still resurfaces on occasion, such as the 1995 attack by Salah Ghandour, and the rhetoric of martyrdom is still prominently employed by Hezbollah leaders in times of crisis.[28] In a final taped message before his suicide attack, Ghandour is reported to have said: "I, Salah Mohammed Ghandour . . . ask God to grant me success in meeting the master of martyrdom Imam Husayn, this great Imam who taught all the free people how to avenge themselves on their oppressors."[29] Ghandour no doubt saw himself as the latest in a sacred chain of Shi'ite martyrs beginning with those who died on the sacred plain of Karbala.

Analysis of the Karbala Master Narrative

The master narrative of the Battle of Karbala contains the story form that we describe as the noble sacrifice. By appropriating the battle as a dualistic struggle between good and evil with the archetypal martyr accepting his own required noble sacrifice, Shi'ite Islamist extremists provide a religious and historical framework for their actions, including some that may otherwise be interpreted as forbidden under Islam (e.g., suicide). The conflict between good and evil mediated by a hero accepting his destiny as an archetypal martyr for God's cause is therefore only satisfied by standing against an oppressor and accepting death in defiance of tyranny. It is a powerful narrative and one that continues to have appeal among Shi'ite extremist groups today.

Although political quietism has historically figured prominently within Shi'ism, the Karbala master narrative has proven to be a potent framing device for revolution and rebellion, particularly in modern times. The trajectory of the master narrative of Karbala was satisfied by defiant martyrdom (i.e., noble sacrifice) and not by a miraculous victory (at least a *physical* victory). Therefore, the Karbala master narrative encapsulates the iconic words of U.S. General John Stark (d. 1822) of New Hampshire, who famously stated: "Live free or die: Death is not the worst of evils." The existence of a superior military force, which may otherwise discourage rebellion or dissent, carries little power in the face of a master narrative where the hero to be emulated accepts martyrdom in his role as God's chosen leader on earth.

CHAPTER 8

The *Mahdi*

Belief in the appearance of a heroic redeemer or savior at a future time, perhaps the end of time, has been a prominent component of Near Eastern religions since time immemorial. In popular usage, Westerners have often described such notions as "messianic." The root term, "Messiah," is a historically and religiously specific concept that has often been distorted in common parlance. However, its general acceptance within our modern phraseology, as well as its ties to the Judeo-Christian-Islamic lineage, has led us to employ it here in this imprecise yet widely understood manner.

In the Islamic tradition, the best example of an archetypal savior or messianic figure is the *Mahdi* ("the Rightly Guided One"). Surprisingly, the *Mahdi* is never mentioned in the Qur'an or *Sahih Bukhari,* and it may well be a later accretion falsely attributed to Muhammad. Nevertheless, the concept of the *Mahdi* exists in both Shi'ite and Sunni Islam, albeit in very different forms. The concept is most prominent in the beliefs of Twelver Shi'ites, a fact that is still apparent in modern Iran. However, as discussed below, Muslims also believe in the return of the great prophet Jesus (*'Issa*), who is given the honorific title *al-Masih* ("the Messiah") in the Qur'an, and he will reappear before the end of time to help usher in a new era of justice and righteousness across the world. As such, one could argue that the Islamic tradition has no less than two messianic figures. Both of these figures are discussed in this chapter, although the focus remains on the *Mahdi*.

Historically, there are numerous instances of eclectic personalities who have claimed to be the long awaited *Mahdi*, just as various Jews (e.g., Simon bar Kokhba, Sabbatai Zevi) and Christians (e.g., Mother Ann Lee, Arnold Potter, Apollo Quiboloy) have claimed messianic titles for themselves over the centuries. However, the narrative foundation for such claims is rooted in a story about the future and focuses on deliverance or the expectation of justice and redemption in an age yet to come.

Fundamentally, messianic deliverance narratives are about hope, rectifying error, the ultimate goodness of God (despite the appearance of evil in the world), and patience through adversity. Thus, the *Mahdi* master narrative promises Muslims that God will send a righteous guide to lead the *ummah* and bring justice to the world by destroying the unjust power (e.g., armies) of the unbelievers. Since the decline of Islamic civilization in the late Middle Ages and the rise of the European colonial powers (an inversion of the classical world order), this master narrative has carried special resonance among Muslims. In short, the *Mahdi* master narrative promises that the "correct" order of the world will one day be restored with a purified Islam reigning supreme over the entire earth.

The Jewish *Mashiah* as Awaited King

The origin of the term "Messiah" comes to us through Judaism. In the *Tanakh*, Yahweh's people, the Israelites (Hebrews), conquered the land of Canaan (Israel/Palestine) and established their kingdom on the land. After the first Israelite king, Saul, was disgraced, David, the slayer of Goliath, was appointed as the new king. Through David, Yahweh established a covenant that promised David's heirs would unconditionally reign forever. As 2 Samuel, Chapter 7, states:

> [Yahweh said:] When your days are over and you rest with your fathers, I will raise up your offspring to succeed you, who will come from your own body, and I will establish his kingdom. He is the one who will build a house for my Name, and I will establish the throne of his kingdom forever. I will be his father, and he will be my son. When he does wrong, I will punish him with the rod of men, with floggings inflicted by men. But my love will never be taken away from him, as I took it away from Saul, whom I removed from before you. Your house and your kingdom will endure forever before me; your throne will be established forever.'[1]

The Israelite coronation ritual involved anointing the head of the new king with sacred oil. Thus, King David was "the anointed one" of Israel, which in Hebrew translates as *Mashiah* ("Messiah"). As stated in 2 Samuel, Yahweh would be the father of the Messiah, and the Messiah would be Yahweh's son, the "Son of God." In Psalm 2:7, David (allegedly the author of the Psalms) states: "I will proclaim the decree of the Lord: He said to me, 'You are my Son; today I have become your Father.'" David, therefore, was the Son of God.

After his death, all of David's heirs to the throne were called Yahweh's Messiahs.[2] The Davidic monarchy did not last though, contrary to what Yahweh's covenant had promised. It was brought to an end by a Babylonian invasion of Judea in 587 BCE. Nebuchadnezzar, the king of Babylon, besieged Jerusalem and destroyed Yahweh's sacred temple. The end of the Davidic royal line forced a religious rationalization of the disaster (or failure). The deportation of the Jews from Palestine during the Babylonian Exile (ca. 597 BCE–538 BCE) led to the formulation of a belief in a future redeemer who Yahweh would send to restore the lost kingdom and the proper order of the world.

The Jewish exiles came to believe that Yahweh's "anointed one" (Messiah) would one day come to restore the Davidic kingdom of Israel and the worship of Yahweh at a reconstructed temple in Jerusalem. This is evident in the *Tanakh*'s identification of Cyrus, the Emperor of Persia, as the *Mashiah* in Isaiah 45, which states:

> This is what the Lord says to his anointed, to Cyrus, whose right hand I take hold of to subdue nations before him and to strip kings of their armor, to open doors before him so that gates will not be shut . . . I will raise up Cyrus in my righteousness: I will make all his ways straight. He will rebuild my city and set my exiles free, but not for a price or reward, says the Lord Almighty.[3]

Cyrus conquered the Babylonian Empire and tolerated the beliefs of his subjects, including the Jews, allowing them to rebuild their sanctuaries. His designation as the Messiah is highly unusual given that Cyrus was a gentile (a Persian) and a Zoroastrian devoted to Ahura Mazda and other deities (e.g., Marduk). But it does fit contemporary scholars' historical understanding of Judaism's development. Many scholars believe that the Babylonian Exile and subsequent restoration of Jewish religion under Cyrus had profound influence on the development of Jewish beliefs and practices, especially the idea of the resurrection, afterlife, angels, prayer, and the Messiah (influenced by the Zoroastrian *Saoshyant*).

Even after Cyrus' restoration of Jewish religion in Judea and the return of the exiles, which included a new class of scholars known as rabbis, the Jews did not enjoy autonomous sovereignty over the "Promised Land" given to them by Yahweh. They remained a vassal of the Persians, Greeks, and then the Romans. By the dawn of the first century CE, the awaited Messiah was understood as a warrior king from the House of David, born in the city of David's birth (i.e., Bethlehem), who would liberate the Kingdom of Israel from foreign occupation and serve as a beacon of Yahweh's supremacy for the entire world. Liberation from Roman rule was never achieved though, despite the efforts of aspiring Jewish Messiahs, such as Simon Bar Kokhba (d. 135 CE).

In the seventh century (CE), the Romans (Byzantines) were finally defeated by the Caliph of Islam, Umar ibn al-Khattab (d. 644 CE), and the region, including the sacred city of Jerusalem, became part of the early Islamic Empire. In the twelfth century (CE), the preeminent Jewish scholar and physician Moses Maimonides (d. 1204 CE) wrote (in Arabic) his thirteen articles of the Jewish creed in Ayyubid Cairo during the reign of Salah al-Din (Saladin). Among those thirteen core beliefs of Judaism is the important statement: "I believe in perfect faith that the Messiah will come, and we should not consider him as tardy: 'Should he tarry, wait for him.' No date may be fixed for his appearance, nor may the scriptures be interpreted in such a way as to derive from them the time of his coming."[4] Thus, the concept of the coming Messiah remains a core component of Judaism to this day.

The Christian Messiah as Divine Incarnation

After Alexander the Great assumed control of Judea in 331 BCE, the Hellenization of the Eastern Mediterranean region commenced. Greek subsequently became the major language of scholarship, culture, and trade. When Alexander conquered Egypt, he was crowned king and the high priest declared him to be the son of Amun-Ra, the creator deity (already customary among the Pharaohs); many Greeks apparently took the divine designation literally.[5] Cults honoring the divinity of kings and emperors, already common in Persia, continued to endure among the heirs of the Greeks in the region, especially the Romans. Thus, when Christianity was born into the Hellenistic world of the first century (CE), it took root in a religious climate where the deification of revered human beings was the norm and the Jewish messianic appellation of "Son of God" took on a whole new resonance.

During this time, the Hebrew *Tanakh* was translated into Greek, known as the Septuagint, and the term *Mashiah* was translated as *Christos* (Christ). Several decades after the death of the Jewish preacher Jesus of Nazareth (d. ca. 30 CE), oral traditions that conveyed particular Christologies (i.e., theological explanations of Jesus' mission and execution as the *Christos*) were written down in Greek as sequential narratives. Jesus, however, spoke Aramaic, as did his followers.

The earliest of the four Greek narratives canonized by the Church in the fourth century (CE) was the Gospel attributed to Mark (written ca. 70 CE). Mark's author portrayed Jesus as a suffering servant of Yahweh that performed miracles and warned of an impending divine judgment, but who tragically went unrecognized by his people until his martyrdom on the cross. Mark's Christology lies in stark contrast to that attributed to John, written around 100 CE. John reflects elements of Greek Stoicism and even Gnosticism. John's Gospel presents Christ as an earthly incarnation of the eternal and divine *logos*, "the Word made flesh" (John 1:14). His Gospel and high Christology are so distinct that the other three canonical gospels are grouped together by scholars as the "synoptic gospels," differentiated only from John. Later, Church fathers came to interpret Johannine high Christology in support of the doctrines of the Trinity and Incarnation, making the Christ coequal and coeternal with Yahweh ("the Father")—separate persons sharing one divine substance (i.e., Triune monotheism).

The concept of the Incarnation is thoroughly Hellenic in nature, and it ran afoul of Jewish conceptions of monotheism at the time. The Christian Messiah also failed to fulfill the expectations dictated by the *Tanakh* and the Jewish sages, most notably the political failures of the Jesus movement and his execution as a criminal by Roman authorities. The Christian claim that the Messiah came to die as a sacrifice ("the lamb of God"), rather than to establish a new Davidic kingdom on earth was an innovation. As a leading scholar of Jewish Studies, Alan F. Segal, has pointed out: "Nowhere before the beginning of Christianity is there any evidence that the Messiah will suffer, let alone die for humanity's sins."[6] Christianity thus presented the Messiah as the spiritual and not worldly or political savior of humanity. As the Gospel of John (18:36) relates, the Christ declared before Pilate:

> My Kingdom is not of this world. If my Kingdom were of this world, then would my servants fight, that I should not be delivered to the Jews. But now is my Kingdom not from hence.[7]

This concept of a messianic savior may have been foreign to Judaism at the time, but it was well established among the Greco-Roman religions of the Hellenistic world.

The popular Indo-Aryan solar deity, Mithras, was a major rival to Christianity for the first four centuries of its existence. Mithras set the universe in motion through sacrificing the celestial bull (Taurus), and his devotees were purified by participating in ritual meals and baptism with the blood of a sacrificed bull. Mithras was also born on December 25, the ancient winter solstice when the hours of daylight begin to lengthen.[8] The deity's title and principal invocation was also *Deus Sol Invictus Mithras* ("God is the Sun, is unconquered, is Mithras").[9]

The Roman Emperor Constantine, the first Christian Emperor, later associated the resurrected Christ with the unconquered sun (*Sol Invictus*) and the Christian Sabbath was observed on the Day of the Sun (Sunday). In other instances, the great Mother Goddess Isis, originally an Egyptian deity and a precursor to the veneration of Mary, assured her devotees a happy existence in the afterlife through her divine compassion.[10] The god Dionysus, the son of the chief god Zeus and a virgin mortal named Semele, was rejected by his people, killed by the Titans, and returned to life as an immortal deity alongside his father Zeus.[11] The savior narrative expressed in Christian accounts of the Messiah, Jesus Christ, clearly shared many elements found in other existing savior narratives of the Hellenistic world.

Christianity situated the Messiah story in the past, but maintained a normative messianic narrative through articulating the belief in the "second coming" of Jesus in the future, prior to the end of time. According to the *Apocalypse* of John of Patmos ("The Book of Revelation"), Christ will descend to earth dressed in a robe covered in blood, and he will smite the wicked before ruling over the world (Revelation 19:12–16). It states:

> His eyes were as a flame of fire, and on His head were many crowns; and He had a name written that no man knew, but He Himself. And He was clothed with a vesture dipped in blood, and His name is called The Word of God. And the armies which were in Heaven, clothed in fine linen white and clean, followed Him upon white horses. And out of His mouth came a sharp sword with which He shall smite the nations, and He shall rule them with a rod of iron; and He treadeth the wine press of the fierceness and wrath of Almighty God. And He hath on His vesture and on His thigh a name written: King of Kings, and Lord of Lords.[12]

The imagery of the *Apocalypse* expressed in the passage above is vividly reminiscent of the final dualistic battles related by other religious traditions, such as Zoroastrianism (see Chapter 7). The narrative in the Book of Revelation, which was written around 100 CE on the Greek isle of Patmos, would directly shape the eschatological traditions of Islam several centuries later.

The Muslim *Masih* as Human Prophet

The Qur'an refers to Jesus as *al-Masih* ("Messiah"), an Arabic variant of the Hebrew term *Mashiah*, in *surat an-Nisa* (see 4: 171–172). However, the designation is primarily honorific and does not carry the same connotations ascribed to it by Christianity. The Qur'an's use of the term, in reference to Jesus, also distinguishes it from conventional Jewish usage as the restorer of the Davidic kingdom. The Muslim *Masih* thus remains unique from its Jewish and Christian precursors. The Qur'an relates that Jesus (*'Issa*) was miraculously born to a virgin (Mary), and he grew up to perform many miracles, including healing the blind and raising the dead. He was supported by the Holy Spirit (typically identified as the angel Gabriel), and he is referred to as the *kalamullah* ("Word of God"), reminiscent of the opening passage about the *logos* in the Gospel of John. However, the Qur'an explicitly rejects the notion that Jesus is divine or the literal "Son of God." It states:

> Truly the *Masih*, Jesus son of Mary, is a messenger of *Allah* and His Word bestowed onto Mary and a spirit from Him, so believe in *Allah* and His messenger and do not say 'Trinity,' cease; it is better for you. Verily *Allah* is One God, glory be to Him above having a son! To Him belong all things in the heavens and earth. (4:171–172)

The *Masih* of the Qur'an is therefore a human prophet (*nabi*) and messenger (*rasul*) from among the *Bani Isra'il* (Israelites) to whom the *Injeel* (Gospel) was given and whose existence is a miraculous Sign of the One True God. However, as the story goes, Jesus is rejected by his people and a plot is hatched against him to put him to death.

The Qur'an's ambiguous and brief reference to the crucifixion of Jesus has been the subject of much exegetical debate and speculation, as well as inter-religious conflict. The Qur'an states: "And they said: 'Truly we have killed the *Masih*, Jesus son of Mary, the messenger of *Allah*; but they did not kill him and did not crucify him, but so it [only] appeared to them . . . they did not kill him for certain; nay, *Allah* raised him up to Himself'" (4:157). The Qur'an does not tell us anything more than that, leaving plenty of room for later embellished traditions to fill in the gaps in the story. The dominant interpretation of the crucifixion in Islamic thought maintains that Jesus miraculously escaped and ascended into heaven in the body, and he will one day return at the end of time. The Hadith and exegetical commentaries (*tafasir*) provide numerous explanations about how Jesus may have managed to escape his impending execution. Ibn Kathir reports the story of a servant boy who volunteered to take Jesus' place when all of the twelve disciples (*ansar*) were too afraid to do it when told of the coming events at the last supper. "*Allah* made him [i.e., the boy] look exactly like Jesus," writes Ibn Kathir.[13] Another Muslim tradition suggests that Judas Iscariot was made to look like Jesus and he was crucified in his place as punishment for his betrayal. Other traditions suggest that it was Simon of Cyrene, or even an angel in his place on the cross.

But not all Muslims accept these imaginative interpretations. Some contend that Jesus did physically die, even though his spirit lives in heaven. As the Qur'an states: "Do not think of those that are slain in the path of God as dead; nay, they are alive with their Lord receiving sustenance" (3:169). In materials attributed to Umayyad supporters of the seventh century (CE), the assassination of the third Caliph Uthman ibn Affan (d. 656 CE) was compared to the martyrdom of Jesus. The Umayyad governor of Iraq, al-Hajjaj ibn Yusuf al-Thaqafi (d. 715 CE), is reported to have said: "Jesus the son of Mary in the eyes of *Allah* is like Uthman."[14]

Another possible explanation of the Qur'an's account of the crucifixion is the possibility of Gnostic influences in Arabia. The reader will recall from Chapter 7 that Christian Gnostics believed that Jesus was an emissary of the spirit realm and the crucifixion was only an illusion because he did not have a real physical form. Regardless, whichever explanation Muslims choose to believe, they are essentially unanimous in their belief in his return to earth near the end of time.

The "second coming" of Jesus is equally as vague as the crucifixion in the Qur'an, but the idea certainly captured the imagination of subsequent Muslim exegetes and took shape as a grand eschatological narrative on its own. The Qur'an states: "And there is none from the People of the Book that will not believe in him [i.e., Jesus] before his death, and on the Day of Judgment he will be a witness against them" (4:159). The Hadith and exegetical commentaries state that Jesus will return prior to the Day of Judgment and kill the *Dajjal*, the one-eyed Anti-Christ. The Qur'an makes no mention of the *Dajjal*, however it does make one vague reference to the *dabba* ("beast") that may be a reference to the seven-headed beast (with the number 666) described in the eschatological imagery of the Book of Revelation (see Rev. 13:11–18). The Qur'an also explicitly mentions Gog (*Yajuj*) and Magog (*Majuj*) from the Book of Revelation (see 20:7–8), stating: "Until Gog and Magog breach the opening and they spring forth from every side, and the True Promise draws near" (21:96). The Hadith also adds that Jesus will descend from the heavens over the minaret of the grand mosque in Damascus, lead the Muslims in prayer, "break the cross, kill the pigs, and abolish the *jizya*" (poll tax), and call all people to embrace Islam.[15] He will then live for forty years, die, and, according to some traditions, be buried beside Muhammad's tomb in Medina.

As noted above, Jesus is not the primary figure in Muslim messianic narratives, despite his Qur'anic designation as the *Masih*. The case might be made that the *Mahdi* is simply a historical Islamized variation of the Biblical second coming of Christ narrative. One Muslim tradition even identifies the *Mahdi* as the returned Jesus, although this is not the dominant view among Muslim scholars.[16] Rather, Islamic tradition refers to the coming of a second figure, called *al-Mahdi* ("the Rightly Guided One"), who will appear at the end of time amidst great turmoil, assist in the establishment of a new era, and even interact with the returned Jesus. This *Mahdi*, as we will see, exists in different forms within both Shi'ite and Sunni Islam.

The Hidden Imam as *al-Mahdi* in Twelver Shi'ism

Adherents of Twelver Shi'ism, the largest sect of the Shi'ites, believe that the Imamate continued on through nine successive male descendents of Imam Husayn (d. 680 CE) after the tragic events at Karbala (see Chapter 7). Over the years, all of these Imams were persecuted and martyred by political usurpers, heretics, and infidels. Due to this oppressive environment, the second-to-last Imam apparently hid the existence of his son from public knowledge. Shi'ite tradition relates that the Twelfth Imam, Muhammad ibn Hasan al-Askari (b. ca. 869 CE), was just a young boy when he miraculously vanished in the cellar of his father's house and escaped the Abbasids intent on capturing and killing him. His father, the Eleventh Imam, Hasan al-Askari (d. 874 CE), was allegedly poisoned in Samarra, Iraq, by the Abbasid Caliph. His mother, according to tradition, was a Byzantine princess descended from St. Peter (the disciple of Christ).[17] Muhammad was born when Hasan al-Askari was still imprisoned. Historically, almost nothing is known about the life of the Twelfth Imam, and some scholars have questioned whether he ever existed at all.[18] Twelver Shi'ites believe that he was between five and eight years old (traditions vary) when he began his Minor Occultation (*ghaybat al-sughra*) around 874 CE following his father's death in Samarra. He was reportedly fully grown at the time of his Occultation despite his young age.

During the period of the Minor Occultation, the Imam communicated with his followers through four successive intermediaries or deputies, known as *wikala* or *sufara*, a method that his father also used during his imprisonment. The deputies would provide guidance from the Hidden Imam, sometimes even written instructions or letters, for the *Shi'a* community and collect taxes (i.e., *khums* and *zakat*) on his behalf. This continued until the death of the last of the four deputies, Abu'l-Husayn 'Ali ibn Muhammad as-Samarri, in 941 CE. From then on, the Imam entered the Great Occultation (*ghaybat al-kubra*) and this period will continue until he returns at the end of time as the *Mahdi* to restore order, piety, and justice to the entire world.

The Hidden Imam, *al-Mahdi,* is known by many names, including *al-Qa'im* (the Rising One), *Wali al-Asr* (Master of the Age), *Hujjat Allah* (Proof of God), *al-Muntazar* (the Awaited One), and *Sahib al-Zaman* (Lord of the Age), among others. He continues to live by *Allah*'s decree without aging and walks the earth invisibly among the people. According to *Shi'a* tradition, the world will one day devolve into chaos, immorality, and ignorance. Wickedness and evil will reign throughout the earth. The religion of Islam will be abandoned, infidelity will dominate, and the Qur'an will be little more than a dusty and forgotten relic of the past. Some *Shi'a* traditions report that a descendant of Abu Sufyan of the Umayyads (grandfather of Yazid), called Sufyani, will emerge at this point and mislead the people with false piety and rise to power in the Middle East.[19]

At that time of total darkness, the *Mahdi* will reappear (*zuhur*) from his Occultation in the holy city of Mecca on the day of *Ashura*, the anniversary of Imam Husayn's martyrdom, carrying Dhu'l-Fiqar (the sword of 'Ali) and he will avenge the *Ahl al-Bayt* (the Prophet's family) by destroying the wicked and ushering in a new era of justice, equity, and peace.[20] According to the *Bihar al-Anwar* ("Oceans of Lights") compiled by Muhammad Baqir (d. 1698 CE): "When our Qa'im emerges with the command, *Allah*, the Exalted, will make him place his hand over the heads of the people so that their consciences and their intellects will be perfected."[21] The Imam *al-Mahdi* will reign over the world for a period of seventy years, then die, and, according to some traditions, rise from the dead after forty days.[22]

The *Mahdi* in Sunni Islam

As noted above, the *Mahdi* does not appear in the text of the Qur'an (at least explicitly) or the authoritative traditions of *Sahih Bukhari.* Nevertheless, it does come out in the traditions of other Sunni collections of Hadith compiled in the ninth and tenth centuries (CE). We should note that the division between Sunni and Shi'ite was still rather tenuous at the time of their compilation, and the presence of Shi'ite-oriented ideas in Sunni traditions attributed to Muhammad is not unusual. The same can be said regarding distinctly Christian and Jewish ideas that are not found in the Qur'an, but are clearly present in the much later (post expansion) Hadith traditions.

Even though the Sunni variation of the *Mahdi* shares the same core archetypal story form, the Sunni *Mahdi* differs substantially from its Shi'ite counterpart. The most obvious difference is that the Sunni concept of the *Mahdi* is not associated with Muhammad ibn Hasan al-Askari, and it has no connection to the *Shi'a* Imamate or a "Hidden Imam" in occultation. The *Mahdi* of Sunni Islam is not an infallible vessel for the "Light of Muhammad" either. Rather, he is a more earthly albeit righteous and pious descendent of the Prophet from the Quraysh and his name will also be Muhammad ibn ʻAbdullah. As a saying of the Prophet relates: "The world will not pass away before the Arabs are ruled by a man of my family whose name will be the same as mine."[23] Another tradition related in *Sunan Abu Dawud* further states:

> Narrated Abu Said al-Khudri: The Prophet (peace be upon him) said: The *Mahdi* will be of my family, and will have a broad forehead, a prominent nose. He will fill the earth with equity and justice as it was filled with oppression and tyranny, and he will rule for seven years.[24]

The fact that the Sunni *Mahdi* is far less mystical and fantastic than the Shiʻite Hidden Imam means that it can arguably be more readily appropriated by Muslims inclined toward making messianic claims, although the concept still remains more important to Shiʻism.

Perhaps the most famous example of a Sunni Muslim invocation of the *Mahdi* master narrative is the rebellion of Muhammad Ahmad (d. 1885) in Sudan. During the nineteenth century, Ottoman Egypt occupied Sudan and established a regional base in Khartoum. In 1882, the British assumed official control of Egypt from the Ottomans and began a colonial occupation that lasted until the mid-twentieth century. The peoples of Sudan came to resent the foreign rule of the "Turks" and the British, their exploitation of Sudan's resources, and harsh taxation.[25]

In 1881, a charismatic Sudanese Sufi ascetic and preacher, Muhammad Ahmad ibn ʻAbdullah, declared himself to be the awaited *Mahdi* who will purify Islam and rallied Sudanese Muslims to expel the Turko-Egyptian and British occupation forces from the country and establish a sovereign Islamic state in Sudan.[26] In less than four years, he and his lightly armed *Ansar* ("helpers") swept their way to shocking military victories, including a massacre of some 8,000 Anglo-Egyptian troops, and accumulated significant booty, including great wealth and European weaponry.

His efforts began to capture the imagination of Sunni Muslims from Nigeria to Arabia. In January of 1885, the *Mahdi* and his forces captured the capital of Khartoum and the British General, Charles Gordon, was decapitated. The *Mahdi* then established his capital in the village of Omdurman along the Nile. The *Mahdi*'s rise to power would not last however, thus negating his extraordinary claims. He died of an illness in June 1885 at the age of forty-one, and he was succeeded by his "Caliph" ʻAbdallah, who was killed by the British in 1899. An elaborate tomb-shrine of the *Mahdi* still stands in Omdurman, Sudan, today.

The *Mahdi* Master Narrative in Extremist Discourse

The deliverance stories of a righteous figure that will come to restore Islam throughout the world and destroy the wicked nations following a period of great turmoil has obvious relevance to the aspirations of Islamist extremists. The Twelver Shi'ite variant of the *Mahdi*, in particular, has remained a potent force in shaping ideological readings of world events and assumed institutionalized form in the Islamic Republic of Iran. The Constitution of Iran, promulgated after the 1979 Revolution, states that: "During the Occultation of the *Wali al-'Asr* (may God hasten his reappearance), the *wilayah* and leadership of the *ummah* devolve upon the just and pious *faqih* (jurist), who is fully aware of the circumstances of his age." This statement reflects Khomeini's aforementioned doctrine of *velayat-e faqih* (see Chapter 7), arguing that the chief jurist, the Grand Ayatollah, can assume political leadership on behalf of the Hidden Imam until his return as *al-Mahdi*. This notion is further evident in numerous statements by Iran's senior political and religious leadership who regularly infuse their positions with the divine authority of the Hidden Imam to insulate them from criticism or refutation.

President Mahmoud Ahmadinejad has promoted the idea that he has a personal mystical connection to the Imam, and made such statements as: "We have a mission to turn Iran into the country of the Hidden Imam."[27] In a speech delivered by Ahmadinejad before the United Nations General Assembly, he further stated:

> Let us, hand in hand, expand the thought of resistance against evil . . . The Promised One who will come accompanied by Jesus Christ, and accordingly design and implement the just and humanistic mechanisms for regulating the constructive relationships between nations and governments. Oh great Almighty, deliver the savior of nations and put an end to the sufferings of mankind and bring forth justice, beauty, and love.[28]

Meanwhile, in the wake of antigovernment protests in Iran, Ayatollah Mesbah Yazdi, a spiritual guide of the Iranian president, declared that it is the duty of all Shi'ites to obey Grand Ayatollah 'Ali Khamenei (the successor of Khomeini) because he is the shadow of the Hidden Imam on earth.[29] Both Ahmadinejad and Yazdi have been rumored to be part of a messianic group in Iran called the Hojjatieh Society, who, according to some claims, work to hasten the *Mahdi*'s return through apocalyptic conflict.[30] This accusation is controversial and disputed, however, because the late Ayatollah Khomeini outlawed the traditionally quietist group in 1983.[31] Nevertheless, the implicit worldview underpinning such messianic notions is one that sees

Iran as the last bastion of God's religion in a world dominated by evil and tyranny. As such, Iranian actions perceived by the West as aggressive and militaristic, may be seen within Iran as defensive and righteous in nature as acts in service of the grand plan of the Lord of the Age, Imam *al-Mahdi*.

Beyond Iran, in neighboring Iraq, the radical dissident and Shi'ite cleric, Muqtada al-Sadr, is the ideological and spiritual leader of a notorious Twelver Shi'ite militia made up of impoverished Shi'ites, known as the Mahdi Army. Al-Sadr has encouraged fierce anti-American sentiment among his followers by preaching that the United States invaded Iraq because the government knew about the imminent return of the *Mahdi* in Iraq, and the Americans wanted to capture and decapitate him to prevent the new just world order.[32] His messianic Shi'ite militia has also been responsible for the deaths of Iraqi Sunnis, non-Muslims, Iraqi government officials and employees, as well as rival Shi'ite clerics and their supporters in Iraq. Elsewhere in the Arab world, the deputy secretary general of Lebanon's Hezbollah organization, Shaykh Na'im Qassem, penned a book in 2007 entitled *The Savior Mahdi* in which he noted an increase in messianic fervor in the world. Popular pamphlets sold in Hezbollah-controlled territories have also described the 2006 war between Israel and Hezbollah as a "divine victory" in which *al-Mahdi* took part, wielding the sacred sword Dhu'l-Fiqar.[33]

Analysis of the *Mahdi* Master Narrative

The *Mahdi* master narrative is a continuation of a deliverance story form that has been passed on throughout the Near East for untold centuries and among a multitude of religious traditions. The *Mahdi*, like the *Mashiah* or *Masih*, is clearly a savior archetype, which also shares some elements of the champion archetype. The distinction lies in the fact that a savior archetype is projected into the future as the harbinger of an ideal age of restoration that remedies all the suffering, tyranny, and turmoil currently being endured in the world. The champion, by contrast, is an archetype tied to events in the past. The functions of this story form are far-reaching and may be utilized in many ways. For Islamist extremists, the *Mahdi* master narrative is a force for mobilization, and its eschatology infuses immediate sociopolitical conditions with a religious significance that can be interpreted through the authoritative pronouncements and guidance of the *ulama* or ayatollahs. It also reinforces a binary worldview of inevitable conflict where the United States, Israel, or even rival Muslim factions, can be cast as antagonistic members of a worldly party destined for ultimate destruction at the hands of the *Mahdi* or his pious deputies in the coming age.

Savior archetypes and deliverance story forms are most important to people enduring struggles, conflicts, and suffering. This is very much apparent among the Shi'ites, who historically have been a persecuted minority dominated by the Sunnis (although Shi'ite exceptions, like the Safavids, have indeed existed). Thus, the Shi'ite master narrative of the Battle of Karbala has been a powerful force for enduring these conditions and, when needed, facing persecution and death without wavering in one's convictions.

CHAPTER 9

The Infidel Invaders

Invasion stories figure very prominently in extremist rhetoric. They offer an essential framework for the depiction of violent acts as part of a defensive struggle for the liberation of a people or land from an aggressive occupier. These tales are so significant that the invasion story form is featured prominently in two master narratives, namely, the Crusader master narrative and the Tatar master narrative.

These two master narratives differ in their historical settings, events, and archetypal characters. However, the narrative trajectory of the invasion and desire-to-satisfaction story form remain essentially the same. Both master narratives contain an invasion by a foreign power that desecrates and destroys Muslim lands and cities, killing many in the process, followed by the emergence of a Muslim champion that defeats the invader and initiates a reversal of fortunes that preserves Islam (i.e., the correct order of things). That said, the enemies in these two master narratives have different archetypal roles and their aims and motivations differ as well. Contemporary analogical invocations of these master narratives thus take on a degree of special application in their usage, as we will see at the end of this chapter.

The invasion story form is obviously not unique to Islam. One example of an invasion story of traditions from pre-Islamic times can be found in the Biblical story of King Nebuchadnezzar's (d. 562 BCE) conquest of Judea and destruction of Solomon's temple in Jerusalem. We have already discussed the Babylonian Exile in some detail in Chapter 8, but a few points are worth reviewing here.

The invasion story, related in the Book of Jeremiah, begins with the Babylonian invasion of the Kingdom of Judah (Judea) and the destruction of Jerusalem and its holy places, including the Temple of Solomon. Devastated by this invasion and the destruction of its land and culture, the Judeans awaited the emergence of a champion or savior to deliver them from their brutal occupiers and captors. The savior that emerges in the story is Cyrus the Great of Persia, described as the Messiah (see Chapter 8), who defeats the Babylonians and returns the Judeans back to their land to restore the worship of Yahweh. We will see this basic story form repeated in the master narratives analyzed below.

The Crusader Master Narrative

On November 27, 1095 CE, in Clermont, France, Pope Urban II (d. 1099 CE) called for a Christian military campaign to capture the holy land of Palestine from the Muslims ("the Saracens"), who he described as a "despised and base race, which worships demons" and establish Christian sovereignty over the holy city of Jerusalem.[1] The Christian volunteers who answered his call to war with cries of "God wills it!" came to be known in Latin as *crusignatus*, or those who take the cross (i.e., crusaders). The volunteers received a cloth cross to be worn or sown into their clothing, took special vows and enjoyed privileges of protection at home and remission of sins through service and martyrdom for Christ abroad.[2]

Some seven months earlier, the Byzantine Emperor in Constantinople had asked for military support from Rome against the encroaching Seljuk Turks who were migrating into Anatolia from the East. But the timing of the Emperor's request facilitated the expansion of the campaign's goals and aims. Christian campaigns against Muslim kingdoms in Spain (the *Reconquista*) and Sicily were already underway; pilgrimage to the Holy Land had been disrupted by the Turkish migration; and efforts to unify feuding Europeans were ongoing and an external infidel foe was important as an outlet for endemic internal violence. The Muslim Middle East, meanwhile, was fragmented into many feuding states and kingdoms incapable of mustering a unified force to resist the unexpected influx of European armies from the West.

The First Crusade (1096–1099 CE) reached Jerusalem on June 7, 1099 CE, when the city was under the control of the Fatimid Caliphate of Egypt. The Fatimids, who were Ismaili Shi'ites, had just recently recovered Palestine from the Sunni Seljuk Turks. The city was home to some 20,000 inhabitants at the time (equal to the population of Paris), including Muslims, Jews, and Christians, and protected by a system of defensive walls, ramparts, and a moat.[3]

Enthralled by a state of exaltation and accompanied by the relics of Christian saints, the Crusaders filled the moat and breached the walls of the city on July 15 under the leadership of Godfrey of Bouillon (d. 1100 CE).[4] The ensuing slaughter of men, women, and children in Jerusalem in the name of Christ has since become legendary for its infamy. The famous chronicler and archbishop William of Tyre (d. 1186 CE) described the aftermath of the Crusader siege of Jerusalem as follows:

> It was impossible to look on the vast numbers of the slain without horror; everywhere lay fragments of human bodies, and the very ground was covered with the blood of the slain. Still more dreadful was it to gaze upon the victors [i.e., Crusaders] themselves, dripping with blood from head to foot.[5]

The Crusaders established Jerusalem as a Christian city and either converted or simply desecrated the Muslim and Jewish holy sites in the area. The reader will find a detailed discussion of the transformation of Muslim holy sites in Chapter 12 of this book in the context of the *Nakba* master narrative.

Of the 60,000 people who initially set out on the First Crusade in 1096 CE, most (among those who survived the ordeal) returned to Europe as heroes, leaving a smaller garrison of Crusader knights (e.g., the Hospitallers) behind to safeguard the newly established Kingdom of Jerusalem and the small Latin Crusader states along the Mediterranean coast.[6] Some immediate efforts to reclaim the city by the Muslims (e.g., the Fatimids) failed, and attention remained focused on inter-Muslim conflicts in the East. As one Muslim poet lamented in the wake of the Crusader victory:

> How many a mosque have they made into a church! The cross has been set up in the *mihrab*; the blood of the pig is suitable for it; Qur'ans have been burned under the guise of incense; do you not owe an obligation to God and Islam, defending thereby young men and old? Respond to God: woe on you! Respond![7]

The Crusader Latin states of Edessa, Antioch, Jerusalem, and Tripoli were established in the years following the success of the First Crusade. However, the Frankish overlords and settlers had to acknowledge the realities on the ground and pragmatically accepted the existence of non-Christian inhabitants in their lands. Border skirmishes and battles never ceased, save for the occasional treaty or alliance, so formidable stone castles (e.g., Krak des Chevaliers) were constructed and served as their principal strongholds in the region.

Meanwhile, beyond the castle walls, the Near Eastern world remained dominated by Islam. For instance, when a second wave of Crusaders eagerly set out in 1101 CE, they endured heavy losses against the Turks in Anatolia, although the survivors did manage to reach Jerusalem and provide much needed reinforcements for the fledgling Latin states.[8] The peoples under their reign included a variety of ethnic and religious groups, including Franks, Gauls, Greeks, Armenians, Arabs, and even a small number of Jews, among others. Muslim farmers and villagers were permitted to remain in some cases because, as King Baldwin I (d. 1118 CE) put it, "of their usefulness in cultivating the land."[9] The Muslims paid a poll tax and up to half of their crop yield to their Frankish overlords, which was akin to taxes paid under prior Muslim rulers.[10] However, in legal matters the Muslims were third-class subjects at the bottom of the social hierarchy.

By the middle of the twelfth century, an important Muslim ruler rose to power in Aleppo, Syria, known as Nur al-Din (d. 1174 CE). He unified the Muslim city-states of Syria and led an army against the Crusaders in the Latin state of Antioch. Nur al-Din defeated the Crusaders at the Battle of Inab in 1149 CE, where the Prince of Antioch, Raymond of Poitiers, was slain by Nur al-Din's Kurdish general, Asad al-Din Shirkuh. Raymond's head was sent to the Abbasid Caliph in Baghdad as a statement of Nur al-Din's status as a champion of Sunni Islam.[11]

After taking Damascus, Nur al-Din raced against the Crusaders to conquer Egypt from the Shi'ite Fatimids, who were growing increasingly weak after two centuries of rule. In 1169, Nur al-Din's Kurdish generals, Asad al-Din Shirkuh and his nephew Salah al-Din al-Ayyubi, succeeded in wrestling Egypt from the Fatimids and restored Sunni Muslim rule. Thereafter, Egypt and Syria were united under the banner of Sunni Islam and a Muslim Sultanate surrounded the Latin states by land. But Nur al-Din, much to the delight of the Crusaders, died in May of 1174. A new champion would have to emerge to preserve the fragile Muslim unity and continue the struggle (jihad) against the Crusaders in the holy land. The Muslims found that champion in Salah al-Din al-Ayyubi, more commonly known in the Western world as Saladin.

Saladin (d. 1193 CE) emerged as Nur al-Din's successor as Sultan over Syria and Egypt and established the Ayyubid dynasty (1171–1250 CE). He was a devout Sunni, an adherent and patron of the Shafi'i school of law and Ash'arite school of theology, and was famous for his chivalry. On July 4 of 1187 CE, he led an army against the Crusaders at the Battle of Hattin near the Sea of Galilee. The Franks were led by the King of Jerusalem, Guy of Lusignan (d. 1194 CE), and Reynald of Chatillon (d. 1187 CE), but Saladin proved to be the superior strategist and commander on that day. The Crusaders were soundly defeated at Hattin, and Guy and Reynald were taken as prisoners to Saladin. He demonstrated respect and gallantry toward King Guy, but Saladin detested Reynald and beheaded him. Reynald was a notorious figure who had attempted to besiege Mecca and Medina, violated numerous truces, and reportedly plundered the pilgrimage caravan of Saladin's own sister in 1186.[12] After his important victory at Hattin, Saladin advanced onto the holy city of Jerusalem.

The Muslim siege of Jerusalem began in September of 1187 (CE). On the night of Friday, September 25, Saladin assembled mangonels (siege engines) to attack the substantial fortifications and towers that defended the city. His cavalry, infantry, and archers, meanwhile, engaged Latin forces near the walls. When the walls surrounding the city were breached shortly thereafter, a council of Latin overlords gathered to discuss the availability of reinforcements and potential terms for surrender. Saladin's siege apparently had the support of Jerusalem's Syrian and eastern Christians in the city, who were marginalized and viewed as barely above the "Saracens" (Muslims) by the Latin Christians.[13] Saladin also had an alliance with the Orthodox Christians of Byzantium under Emperor Isaac II Angelus (d. 1204 CE) against their mutual enemies, the Latin Crusaders and Seljuk Turks.[14] As Saladin's army besieged Jerusalem, Isaac's navy was attacking Latin Cyprus, but unlike Saladin he failed to achieve victory.

On October 2 (Rajab 27), the anniversary of the Prophet Muhammad's Night Journey to Jerusalem, the Latin Crusaders surrendered the city to Saladin. Greek and other Eastern Orthodox Christians (e.g., Armenians) were permitted to remain in the city on the condition that they pay the poll tax (*jizya*), and the remaining goods and property of the expelled Latins were purchased by or given over to them and the Muslims. The Latin churches in the city, except for those that had previously been mosques (e.g., *al-Aqsa*), were converted to the Greek rite and placed under the control of the Byzantine Patriarch.

Meanwhile, the Latins paid ransoms of ten dinars per man, five dinars per woman, and two dinars per child to leave with what property they could carry.[15] Those Latins unable to pay were enslaved, but thousands were manumitted by Saladin per different requests. Saladin's magnanimous conduct following his victory was in striking contrast to the savagery that the Crusaders inflicted upon the Muslims and Jews in Jerusalem in 1099 CE. The Muslim chronicler Ibn al-Athir (d. 1233 CE) wrote of Saladin: "This noble deed of liberating Jerusalem was achieved by none after Umar ibn al-Khattab except for Salah al-Din, and this deed suffices for his glory and honor."[16]

Only weeks after the surrender of Jerusalem to Saladin, Pope Gregory VIII launched the Third Crusade to retake Jerusalem from the Muslims. Led by King Richard of England, "the Lionheart" (d. 1199 CE), the largest Crusader force since the First Crusade invaded the Middle East and succeeded in securing the existence of the small Latin states on the coast. However, Richard failed to conquer Jerusalem and returned home after a truce with Saladin in 1192 CE.

The reputation of Saladin as the great champion of Islam was diminished by stalemates and even defeats in battle with Richard, but when

Saladin died of an illness in 1193, he was the reigning sovereign of Jerusalem and the Sultan of an empire that continued among his dynasty (the Ayyubids) for some sixty years (before passing it on to their Mamluks). The Crusades against the Muslim Middle East continued until the late thirteenth century when the last Latin state of Acre was defeated by the Mamluks in 1291 CE (see Chapter 12). However, additional Crusades, primarily against the Ottoman Turks in Eastern Europe and Cyprus, were waged for centuries thereafter.

The onset of European colonialism in the Middle East in 1798, the year of Napoleon's arrival in Egypt, quickly reminded the Muslims of the Crusades. This perception persisted and grew as the great Western powers of the age, particularly the British and the French, conquered and colonized some 90 percent of the Muslim world, including Palestine and the holy city of Jerusalem.

For Sayyid Qutb (d. 1966), who was born in British-ruled Egypt, the Crusades were an expression of unbridled hatred, motivated not by penance, pilgrimage, or the promise of earthly or otherworldly rewards, but by an insatiable hatred of Islam and a thirst for its destruction among the Europeans. The rise of Islam in the seventh century had, in his view, posed the most serious threat to Europe's ruling elite in history, who, in turn, responded by constructing all manner of lies and distortions in an attempt to demonize Islam and its adherents in the minds of the European populace and to justify their malevolent and militant aspirations against it. He wrote:

> The enmity that the Crusaders stirred up was not confined to the clamor of arms, but was, before all else and above all else, cultural enmity. The European mind was poisoned by the slurs which the Crusader's leaders cast on Islam as they spoke of it to their ignorant Western compatriots. It was in that age that there grew up in Europe the ridiculous idea that Islam was a religion of unbridled passion and violent sensuality, that it consisted merely of formal observances, and that it had no teaching of purity or of regeneration of the heart. And this idea has remained as it started . . . Thus was the seed of hatred sown.[17]

For Qutb, the Crusades were no less than a genocidal force[18] that produced unspeakable atrocities, exemplified by the fall of Jerusalem in 1099 CE during the time of the First Crusade.[19] The Crusaders were the very embodiment of ruthlessness and treachery. In a brief but telling account of the events at Jerusalem, Qutb wrote:

> The Muslims sought refuge and sanctuary in the *Aqsa* mosque, but the Crusaders followed them inside and dispatched them with their swords so

> that blood flowed through the sacred precincts in a flood. In this act, the Crusaders violated a solemn treaty that their leaders had made with some of the Arabs. This was only one example of the barbarity of the Crusaders, which included the raping of women, mutilation of the living, and the torture of old women and children.[20]

Qutb then followed his unflattering depiction of the Crusaders with a depiction of the Muslims as the very embodiment of nobility and compassion, writing: "The Muslims [were] imbued with the Islamic spirit, which was strong enough to check the desire for vengeance in Muslim hearts and to keep them within the bounds of humanity and religion."[21] This nobility, he further noted, was not limited to the figure of Saladin, as has often been the case in Western accounts of the Crusades, but was, in his view (despite clear evidence to the contrary), true of the entirety of the Muslim forces involved. "The conduct of the Muslims during the Crusades," he wrote, "showed the full inspiration of the strong spirit of Islam as it arose superior to lowliness, treachery, and ruthlessness."[22]

Although Christianity has been irrevocably tied to the events of the Crusades, Qutb believed that the Crusaders' hatred of Islam was born not out of Christianity or the Church itself, but out of what he described as "the crusading spirit." He argued that Europe was never at any time in its history truly Christian.[23] But, rather, that the true culture of Europe was essentially irreligious and based on the ancient Roman view of life as a matter of material and economic advantage, and thus independent of absolute values.[24] "European imperial interests," he writes, "can never forget that the spirit of Islam is like a rock blocking the spread of imperialism [and must thus] either be destroyed or pushed aside."[25]

For Qutb, himself an Islamist, Islam was not simply a collection of beliefs and rituals, but a dynamic sociopolitical and economic system, and thus, prior to the birth of Communism, the only considerable obstacle standing in the way of the destructive ambitions of the West for centuries. The Christian conquest of Muslim Spain, which Qutb did not identify as a Crusade, was nevertheless an expression of this same "crusading spirit," and a poignant example of its senseless, irrational, and violent nature. "The cries of joy," he wrote, "which all over Europe greeted [the expulsion of the Muslims from Spain] were uttered in full knowledge of the consequences that would arise; for the result was that science and learning were blotted out, and in their place came the ignorance and the barbarity of the Middle Ages."[26]

The "crusading spirit," he further argued, has since remained latent within the European mind, in the thinking of every European man and woman throughout history, even during the sectarian wars of the Reformation or the overall decline of the Church's power and influence in Europe. Referring to the British conquest of Palestine during World War I, Qutb noted the words of General Allenby, who, upon entering the city of Jerusalem, is reported to have said: "Only now have the Crusades come to an end."[27]

The Crusades of the Middle Ages were thus deeply woven into Qutb's interpretation of modern events, bolstering his fears and sense of paranoia of a large-scale movement (perhaps even conspiracy) against the Muslim world that admittedly seemed to be materializing before his very eyes. As he wrote:

> In the present age, when Europe conquered the world, and when the dark shadow of colonization spread over the whole Islamic world, East and West alike . . . Europe mustered all its forces to extinguish the spirit of Islam, it revived the inheritance of the Crusaders' hatred, and it employed all the materialistic and cultural powers at its disposal.[28]

In response to questions about the extent to which European colonialism was in fact a modern expression of the Crusades, given the decline of Christianity and the political role of the Church in the nineteenth and twentieth century, Qutb contended that even though human beings may disregard the religious beliefs of their past, they nevertheless psychologically retain certain "superstitions" or worldviews that centered on those discarded beliefs.[29] Qutb's observation may thus explain, at least on some level, the often unwavering support that the modern state of Israel has received from the Western world to the great dismay of its Arab neighbors. He states:

> Despite the fact that the religious convictions that gave rise to European hostility to Islam have now lost their power . . . the ancient antipathy itself still remains as a vital element within the European mind. So far as the strength of this antipathy is concerned, it undoubtedly varies from one individual to another, but that it exists is indisputable. The spirit of the Crusades, though perhaps in a milder form, still hangs over Europe; and that civilization in its dealing with the Islamic world.[30]

As such, Qutb dismissed other theories circulating at the time that attempted to explain the West's apparent antipathy toward Islam, such as the alleged financial influence of American Jews, notions of English ambition and Anglo-Saxon guile, or the politics of the Cold War.[31] For Qutb, the real reason was nothing more than the crusading spirit, a single destructive force that linked even communist Russia and capitalist America together.[32]

Qutb's modern interpretation of the narrative indicates several important points for our analysis of story forms and archetypes. The crusader archetype is not inherently Christian, but rather Western or European. The crusader may only seek material ends with no religious implications for his actions, because the West is only nominally, even hypocritically, Christian. However, the idea of a Christian soldier immediately resonates with the historical figure of the Crusader as well. In addition, the crusader seeks the occupation and colonization of Muslim lands, particularly Palestine, thus we may consider the crusader archetype synonymous with the "colonizer." In Chapter 12 of this book (the *Nakba* master narrative), we will examine how the idea of the "Zionist" also becomes conflated with the crusader, despite the fact that the historical Crusaders massacred Jews.

Continuing along the trajectory of this story form, the narrative then introduces a champion archetype in the person of Salah al-Din (Saladin), who unites and leads the Muslims in a great victory over the Crusaders and liberates the holy city of Jerusalem for Islam. His victories manage to initiate a broader reversal of fortunes in the Muslim struggle against the Crusaders and the final Latin states are eliminated by the fierce Mamluks of Egypt under the Sultans Qalawun and al-Ashraf Khalil by the end of the thirteenth century. Europeans would not conquer Palestine again until the twentieth century during World War I.

The Tatar Master Narrative

At the beginning of the thirteenth century, Genghis Khan (d. 1227 CE) united the warring tribes of the Mongolian steppe and initiated an aggressive campaign of territorial conquest that established one of the largest empires in history. In the Muslim sources, they are known as the Tatars (or Tartars), derived from a Turkic word for horsemen.

The Mongols were a tribal confederacy of nomadic horsemen who practiced an indigenous animism or shamanism, although there were also significant Buddhists and Nestorian Christians among them. They fashioned a formidable military force, infamous for their brutality and merciless offensives, and even employed psychological warfare against their often numerically superior adversaries. For instance, during the bloody sacking of the once great Muslim city of Nishapur in 1221 CE, the Mongols made pyramids out of the severed heads of the city's inhabitants, including men, women, and children.[33] By the middle of the thirteenth century, the Muslims of the Near East were still battling the Crusaders, while further east, Hulagu Khan (d. 1265 CE), the grandson of Genghis Khan and brother of Kublai Khan, led the Mongol hordes on a sweeping conquest of Persia into the land of the two rivers, Iraq.

The Mongols reached Baghdad, the glorious capital of the waning Abbasid Caliphate, in January of 1258. They reportedly had the support of some Shi'ites interested in the downfall of the Sunni Caliphate. Hulagu sent his emissaries to the city demanding the Caliph's surrender and submission to his commands, reportedly threatening: "When I lead my troops in wrath against Baghdad even if you hide in the sky or in the earth . . . I shall bring you down . . . I shall not leave one person alive in your realm, and I shall put your city and country to the torch."[34] The Caliph, al-Mustasim (d. 1258 CE), dismissed Hulagu's warnings (despite the Caliph's inferior army) and arrogantly told him to return to Central Asia. Enraged, the Mongols began their siege on February 1 and attacked the walls, ramparts, and towers defending the city. On February 10, the city's defenses were in peril and the Caliph marched out to negotiate terms of surrender with Hulagu, accompanied by three thousand of Baghdad's dignitaries (most of them were taken away and killed).[35]

Hulagu instructed the Caliph: "Tell the people of the city to throw down their weapons and come out so that we may make a count."[36] The Caliph had no options and agreed; the soldiers disarmed and came out of the city. The Mongols slaughtered them and then entered the city to carry out Hulagu's plans for Baghdad.

Over the following days, the entire city was plundered and burned to the ground, except for the homes and possessions of Baghdad's Christians, because Hulagu's senior wife, Doquz Khatun (d. 1265 CE), was a Christian.[37] The accumulated treasures, sacred relics, manuscripts, vast libraries, and architectural monuments of nearly six centuries of Abbasid rule were destroyed. Finally, on February 20, 1258, the Caliph, his eldest son (his heir), and attendants were executed, ending the Abbasid Caliphate (r. 750–1258 CE).[38] As the early twentieth century Orientalist Joseph de Somogyi wrote in 1933: "Hardly ever has Islam survived a more disastrous and more mournful event than the destruction of Baghdad by the Mongols of Hulagu Khan."[39]

Following the destruction of Baghdad, including the deaths of anywhere between 100,000 to 1 million people (estimates vary), the Mongols advanced through Syria and besieged city after city, including Damascus, save for those that immediately bowed in submission to Mongol rule. By 1260, the Mongols had reached the sacred land of Palestine and stood within marching distance of Jerusalem.

The Ayyubid dynasty of Saladin had passed the Sultanate to its former Mamluk generals only a few years prior, and the Mamluk Sultan Sayf al-Din Qutuz (d. 1260 CE) and Mamluk general Baybars (d. 1277 CE) rode out to face the seemingly invincible Mongol hordes. Hulagu Khan, meanwhile, departed with some of his troops to China for the selection of a new Great Khan following the sudden death of his brother Mongke. The remaining Mongol force was left to the control of a Nestorian Christian, Kitbuga (d. 1260 CE).

The Mamluks and Mongols faced each other in heavy combat at 'Ayn Jalut ("Spring of Goliath") on September 3, 1260 CE. The Mamluks, many of whom were Turks, were very similar to the Mongols in their military skills, strategy, and arms, prompting one Syrian chronicler to remark that the Mongols battled "pests of their own kind" in Palestine.[40] The resulting Mamluk victory was the first major Muslim triumph over the Mongols and it brought an end to the Mongol westward expansion, saving the three holy cities, as well as Egypt and North Africa, from the onslaught. Kitbuga, the leader of the Mongol forces, was killed in the battle. Meanwhile, Hulagu Khan died in 1265 CE, and, although he might have been a Buddhist, he was buried according to Mongolian ancestral tradition and ritual, which included human sacrifices.[41]

The defeat of the Mongol army at 'Ayn Jalut did not mark the end of the Mongols' power in the region. The Mamluks had stopped their expansion, but the Mongol empire remained in the lands they had conquered, including Iraq and Persia where the Ilkhan dynasty reigned. Conflict on the borders persisted for many years to come.

Meanwhile, in keeping with the past destruction wrought by the conquerors, the Mongols initially persecuted Muslims and suppressed Islam in their domains, favoring Buddhists and Christians. But in time the tide turned and the conquerors converted to the religion of the conquered (Islam) beginning as early as the 1260s. Ghazan Khan (d. 1304 CE), who had earlier ties to Christianity and Buddhism, converted to Sunni Islam (largely for political reasons it seems) and adopted the name Mahmud in 1295 CE.[42] The conversion of Ghazan Khan initiated a larger trend in the Ilkhanate, Islam was patronized, and the advances of Buddhism and Christianity in the empire were reversed. However, the conversions of Mongol rulers like Ghazan Khan were treated with skepticism by some, including the great Syrian Hanbalite scholar, Ahmed ibn Taymiyyah (d. 1328 CE).

Ibn Taymiyyah, whose writings would later inspire (in part) the Wahhabi and Salafi movements in Sunni Islam, represented a revival of the heretical Kharijite doctrine of *takfir* (i.e., declaring professing Muslims to be unbelievers). This was due in large part to Ghazan Khan's rulings and judgments according to the *Yasa* of Genghis Khan. In 1206, Genghis Khan promulgated a code of laws based on the ancestral traditions, customs, laws, and ideas of the Mongols, which were to be binding on his people and their descendants, and copies were kept in the treasuries of Mongol rulers for consultation as need arose.[43] Therefore, despite his identification with Sunni

Islam, Ghazan Khan did not judge according to the Qur'an and Sunnah of the Prophet Muhammad (i.e., the *shari'ah*). The Mongols also revered Genghis Khan as an exemplary ruler and leader far more than the Prophet Muhammad.

This fact prompted Ibn Taymiyyah to write that his conversion was a farce and that he is an unbeliever that should be fought (or rebelled) against in jihad by the believers. Ibn Taymiyyah's views were apparently even shared by Ghazan's brother and successor, Oljeitu (d. 1316 CE), who said (perhaps for political ends) of his brother in a letter to the Mamluk Sultan: "He was a Muslim on the outside, but an infidel on the inside."[44] The idea of declaring a Muslim ruler to be an infidel based on his failure to implement Islamic law (*shari'ah*), as expressed by Ibn Taymiyyah's rejection of Ghazan Khan, would later resurface in the writings of extremists such as 'Abdel-Salam al-Faraj, the ideologue of the extremist group responsible for the assassination of Egyptian President Anwar Sadat in 1981.

The Tatar master narrative contains multiple story forms and archetypes. The invasion story form of the Mongol conquest of the eastern Islamic world and the horrific destruction of Baghdad, including the execution of the Abbasid Caliph, conveys the catastrophic desecration and occupation of Muslim lands by archetypal barbarians. It then introduces a Muslim champion to reverse the course of events in favor of Islam. The barbarian archetype, as opposed to the crusader archetype, lacks the same devious plots and designs to colonize Muslim lands. Instead, the barbarian is savage, often pagan, and seeks destruction and plunder for the simple sake of destruction, like inhuman monsters with little interest in wealth or cities to make their own.

The champion archetype in the Tatar master narrative is the Mamluk, specifically the Sultans Qutuz and Baybars, who defeated the Mongol army of Hulagu Khan at 'Ayn Jalut in 1260 CE. This important Mamluk victory ended the Mongol expansion westward and initiated a reversal of fortunes for the Muslims. The Mongols were not expelled and sent back to the steppes of Central Asia, but remained and converted to Islam thereby transforming them into civilized figures. Islam was preserved and grew again from the ashes of destruction into new imperial powers under Mongol patronage (e.g., Timurids, Safavids, Mughals).

Another story form that exists in the Tatar master narrative is a ruse story, as indicated by Ghazan Khan's politically motivated conversion to Sunni Islam and Ibn Taymiyyah's accusations of infidelity against him. Ghazan Khan and other converted Mongol leaders assume the role of the archetypal imposter, who pretends to be something that he is not for the sake of personal gain or political ends. Ghazan's actions, specifically his adherence to the *Yasa* of Genghis Khan rather than the *shari'ah* of Islam, expose his true infidel or pagan nature and the archetypal sage or scholar, in this case Ahmed Ibn Taymiyyah, sees through his lies and exposes him as a pagan that should be fought in a jihad for Islam. This particular story form would later prove to be very popular among Islamist extremists interested in denouncing regimes they see as insufficiently "Islamic."

The Infidel Invaders Master Narratives in Extremist Discourse

The Crusader and Tatar master narratives have numerous analogical functions in Islamist extremist rhetoric, particularly with regard to U.S. military activities in the Middle East. Although the two master narratives differ and utilize different archetypes, they have both been deployed to characterize American leaders, policies, and actions in alarmingly hostile terms.

For example, the Syrian al-Qaeda ideologue, Abu Mus'ab al-Suri, in his manifesto, "The Call for Global Islamic Resistance," described the plight of the world's Muslims by stating: "We are today faced with this [U.S.] assault, with no Salah al-Din to confront the Crusaders, and no Qutuz to confront the Tatars, and no al-Iz [al-Din] ibn 'Abdel-Salam or Ibn Taymiyyah mobilizing the Muslims and running ahead of them."[45] Al-Suri's treatise is filled with such material. Indeed, references to the Crusader and Tatar master narratives exist in great abundance in a myriad of extremist Islamist sources.

In his influential 1965 radical treatise, *Ma'alim fi'l-Tariq* ("Milestones"), Sayyid Qutb discussed the attempts of European leaders, whom he referred to as "enemies of Islam," to hide what he considered the true Crusader nature of colonialism in the twentieth century, including Zionism. He wrote:

> We see an example of this today in the attempts of Christendom to try and deceive us by distorting history and saying that the Crusades were a form of imperialism. The truth of the matter is that the latter-day imperialism is but a mask for the crusading spirit, since it is not possible for it to appear in its true form, as it was possible in the Middle Ages.[46]

Qutb concluded his remarks by calling for Islamic unity and religious revival as the only true path to victory against European colonial occupation, perhaps echoing the ideas of an Islamist predecessor in Egypt, Hasan al-Banna (d. 1949). In it, Qutb recounted the victories of Saladin and the Mamluks, stating:

> The unveiled crusading spirit was smashed against the rock of the faith of Muslim leadership which came from various elements, including [Saladin]

> the Kurd and Turan Shah [*sic*] the Mamluk, who forgot the differences of nationalities and remembered their belief, and were victorious under the banner of Islam.[47]

Qutb is thus in agreement with scholars who have noted the impact that internal divisions among the Muslims (e.g., between the Seljuks, Abbasids, and Fatimids) had on the success of the First Crusade, most notably on the loss of Jerusalem. However, Qutb not only likened this trend to the modern divisions of the transnational Muslim community (*ummah*) as a precursor to the onset of colonialism, but to the rise of nationalist ideologies in the Middle East, a trend that he despised and harshly denounced. "Those who deviate from [the Islamic system] and want some other system," he wrote, "whether it be based on nationalism, color and race, class struggle, or similar corrupt theories, are truly enemies of mankind!"[48]

For a more contemporary invocation of these narratives, al-Suri's aforementioned text is particularly informative, but for the remainder of this chapter we will survey a selection of more recent extremist materials.

Following the Fort Hood shootings in the United States on November 5, 2009, and the failed Nigerian Christmas Day "underwear bombing" operation thereafter, the American-Yemeni radical, Anwar Awlaki, emerged as a prominent extremist ideologue. In a telling lecture, widely disseminated over the internet through downloadable audio and text files, Awlaki delivered a lengthy commentary on a treatise penned by an al-Qaeda in the Arabian Peninsula (AQAP) extremist, Yusuf al-'Uyari, who was killed by Saudi Arabian security forces in 2003. In his English translation and discussion of al-'Uyari's Arabic text, entitled "Constants on the Path of Jihad," Awlaki states:

> When the Tatars entered Iraq . . . they killed over 1 million people . . . [they] defeated the Muslims in every single battle. So the Muslims . . . fell into despair; they felt that the Tatar was undefeatable . . . [But] *Allah* purified the Muslims through those trials and they became sincere . . . in their Jihad; they then defeated the Tatar in the battle of 'Ayn Jalut. . . . When the Muslims won, they didn't win because of strength . . . Muslims don't win based on their numbers or resources. They win based on *Allah*'s will. Victory is a gift from *Allah*.[49]

The implications of such statements are that individual Muslims need to act in order to reverse the fortunes of the seemingly invisible Tatars of today, namely, the Americans in Iraq. Muslims should fight these "Tatars" in jihad even if they lack the numbers and resources to do so, because victory belongs to *Allah* and martyrdom awaits those who die in the path of *Allah*. Either way, the faithful believers are assured victory. It would seem that the individual militants involved in the Fort Hood and Christmas Day attacks took his message to heart.

In his 1999 treatise "Allah's Governance on Earth," the notorious exiled Egyptian extremist, Abu Hamza al-Masri, wrote a chapter entitled "Examples of the Old Tatars and the New Tatars." In it, the armless veteran of the wars in Afghanistan and Bosnia states:

> The Tatars of today have raised their heads and have swooped down on the unsuspecting Muslims again. The lands of the Muslims have again fallen into foreign hands, with our women being raped and abused beyond belief. The *kufr* is so great, its actual size and ramifications are known entirely only to *Allah*. This is how great it has become. Listen to the words of one of our martyred brothers, Muhammad 'Abdus-Salam al-Faraj who paid with his life for speaking about the Tatars of today.[50]

The "martyred brother" to whom Abu Hamza refers in this passage, Muhammad 'Abdel-Salam al-Faraj (d. 1982 CE), invoked numerous master narratives in his own earlier manifesto, *al-Faridah al-Ghaybah* ("The Neglected Duty"), which we have examined elsewhere in this book. One example of al-Faraj's use of the Tatar master narrative reads as follows:

> The laws that rule the Muslims today have been infidel laws . . . since the disappearance of the Caliphate in 1924, the eradication of all the laws of Islam and their replacement by laws imposed by the infidels . . . What was true during the time of the Tatars is true today.[51]

But such references are not limited to texts or publications. For instance, Francis J. "Bing" West of the Council on Foreign Relations noted in his 2005 book, *No True Glory*, that radical Sunni imams and *khatibs* in Iraq proclaimed U.S. President George W. Bush as the second coming of Hulagu Khan in their mosque sermons during the American invasion. References to the Shi'ite allies of Hulagu Khan during his conquest of Baghdad in 1258 CE were also made by these preachers to inflame sectarian tensions. As West reports:

> Just before the Americans drove into Fallujah in April 2003, the mufti Jamal, the senior Sunni cleric in the city, warned the residents that the American invaders would turn Iraq over to the Shiites. The radical clerics were calling President Bush 'Hulagu II,' a reference to the conquest of ancient Baghdad by the Mongol leader Hulagu, assisted by a Shiite leader who betrayed the ruling caliph. The Americans, the mufti told the citizens, were modern-day Mongols, infidel invaders and occupiers.[52]

Such instances reveal in vivid terms the manner in which extremists have employed the master narrative to frame contemporary events and conflicts, including the U.S. invasion of Iraq, despite obvious cultural disparities between the Americans and the Mongols.

Analysis of the Infidel Invaders Master Narratives

All of these references to the Tatar and Crusader master narratives are used to frame contemporary conflicts and events, whether it is British colonialism in Egypt, Zionism in Palestine for Sayyid Qutb, or the United States and Operation Iraqi Freedom for Anwar Awlaki. These master narratives remind Muslims to look into the past to understand the present, just as they look to the example of the Prophet Muhammad (the Sunnah) in the seventh century (CE) to inform their daily conduct and lives in the twenty-first century. In both instances, the narrative trajectory directs audiences to defeat the modern-day "Crusaders" or "Tatars" and liberate the lands of Islam. These master narratives furthermore establish a historical precedent whereby non-Muslim powers, by their very nature, seek to conquer and destroy the Muslim world and its holy places.

The historical period encapsulated by each master narrative is quite large and therefore they each provide a wide array of events and characters that can be invoked for ideological ends. The Tatar master narrative alone contains no less than three story forms with accompanying archetypes in its various components; however, the principal story form is invasion. This sort of internal complexity and variety makes these master narratives particularly useful for framing a range of events and circumstances and helps to ensure their cultural longevity and persistence among extremists seeking to persuade Muslim audiences. This is an important quality for these master narratives to possess since neither have roots in the Qur'an or the lifetime of the Prophet.

CHAPTER 10

Shaytan's Handiwork

The problem of evil in the world has long perplexed believers in the Abrahamic religions. Monotheism is a difficult concept to reconcile with the innocent suffering, death, disease, and devastating catastrophes that plague our world. Innocent suffering seriously challenges the comforting notion of a just and loving God that deserves our devotion.

Long before the historical emergence of Abrahamic monotheism, polytheistic and henotheistic traditions, such as those in ancient Egypt or Canaan, attributed innocent suffering to rival deities and cosmic forces in conflict. Ascribing evil to a particular deity or supernatural being proved to be a popular explanation for the problem of evil (i.e., theodicy) and a fixture of the religious imagination. The idea persevered in modified forms in the theodicies of all three of the Abrahamic religions (to varying degrees) despite the problems that the idea of the "Evil One" poses for monotheistic belief systems.

In common parlance, the Abrahamic descendent of deities like Set or Ahriman (see Chapter 7) is known as the Devil (from the Greek *diabolos*) or Satan. In the Qur'an, he is known by the Arabic name Iblis or the title *al-Shaytan*. The Muslim *Shaytan* is identifiable with the Jewish and Christian figures of Satan, but remains unique in its Islamic appropriation or manifestation. The story of the origins of Iblis and his role in the world, including his hatred for human beings, is an important one. It still informs the lives of devout Muslims around the world and shows up even in the daily routine of the five obligatory prayers (*salat*).

As we will see, there are actions, ideas, and objects attributable to *al-Shaytan*'s machinations in the world, such as the consumption of alcohol or gambling, that can motivate violence or militant action by Islamist extremists. In this chapter, we will examine the role of the *Shaytan* in Islam and how common Western elements of daily life, namely, alcoholic beverages such as wine, are understood as the snares and handiwork of the *Shaytan* that lead humans astray from *Allah*'s path and form a flashpoint for cultural tensions in the modern Muslim world.

Origins of the *Shaytan*

In ancient Egypt, many centuries before the Hebrew Bible was written down, people feared and revered the god Set (or Seth). Traditionally depicted as red in color and having the head of a beast, Set was the god of chaos in a world where the preservation of order (*maat*) was sacrosanct. Storms, violence, earthquakes, the desert, foreign lands (especially western Asia), as well as pigs, dogs, hippopotamuses, crocodiles, snakes, donkeys, and scorpions were all associated with Set.

One of the most prominent stories associated with Set was his epic battle with Horus, god of kingship, law, and light. Horus was the divine defender of Egypt against the destructive forces of chaos. His father Osiris, who became the god of the dead and the underworld, was murdered and dismembered by Set, so Horus went out to battle Set to avenge his father and inherit his father's earthly throne. Horus and Set engaged in many battles and contests that personified the struggle between good and evil (or between *maat* and chaos) and Horus ultimately emerged as the victor. A popular icon of ancient Egypt depicts Horus with a spear in his hand defeating Set in the form of a crocodile. The Greeks identified Set with Typhon, the monstrous winged serpentine storm deity who battled Zeus in an epic struggle. Belief and worship of Set persisted in Egypt until the fourth century CE when imperial Christianity wiped out the public observance of the old religions.

When the Hebrew Bible began to assume written form around the fourth or fifth century BCE, a minor figure gradually emerged in the literature known as the Satan ("adversary"), presumably from the Hebrew word for "obstacle."[1] Some scholars have also suggested the word may have evolved from the aforementioned name Set. Contrary to popular belief, the Satan was not the tempting serpent who lured Eve into sin while in the Garden of Eden. That conflation occurred much later in subsequent Jewish and Christian thought. Indeed, in the earliest books of the Bible, Yahweh is the source of both good and evil, creation and destruction. It was not until the books of Job and Zechariah that those attributes began to be disassociated with Yahweh and ascribed to the malevolent being known as the Satan.

The Book of Job relates that Yahweh presides over a court of heavenly hosts, called "sons of God." Among those hosts is a mysterious "adversary" that challenges Yahweh to test the faith and devotion of his righteous servant Job on earth by allowing him to inflict horrible calamities and death upon his family (see, e.g., Job 1:13–20). It is important to note that the Satan, at this point in his development, is only a servant of Yahweh and an adversary of human beings. He is not the cosmic evil adversary of God envisioned by later apocalyptic writings and sects, such as Christianity. That notion of Satan did not emerge until after the Babylonian Exile and the restoration of Jewish religion under Cyrus the Great of Persia.

As discussed previously in Chapter 8, the Babylonian Exile resulted in the "mixing" of certain Zoroastrian elements with Rabbinic Judaism. The dualism of Zoroastrian theology, which centers on the cosmic struggle between Ahura Mazda (god of light) and Ahriman (god of darkness), clearly informed Jewish thinking on the problem of evil and human suffering. The result was a monotheistic variation of dualism and the formation of a Jewish hierarchy of personified angelic and demonic beings at war with one another over human souls in the service of Yahweh and His archenemy, the Satan. Ultimately, by the time of the Christian New Testament, Persian, Greek, Syrian, and other foreign notions of "the Evil One" and his diabolical minions had been thoroughly Hebraized and subordinated to the religion of Yahweh.[2]

The New Testament took shape at a time of serious sociopolitical upheaval and religious creativity and diversity in Roman-occupied Palestine. According to the Jewish historian Josephus (d. 100 CE), one of the major Jewish sects of the time, the Essenes, saw themselves as the "sons of light" destined to defeat the Satanic "sons of darkness" in an imminent final battle at the end of time.[3] The Christian Gospels, likewise, depicted Satan as a seductive being trying to lure Jesus over to his side with promises of great kingdoms and luxuries on earth. The synoptic Gospels of Mark, Matthew, and Luke, all situate this encounter in the desert, the domain of Set. Matthew's Gospel relates:

> Then the Devil took [Jesus] up to a very high mountain, and showed him all the kingdoms of the world in their magnificence, and he said to him: "All these I shall give to you, if you will prostrate yourself and worship me." At this, Jesus said to him, "Get away, Satan!" . . . Then the Devil left him and behold angels came and ministered to him.[4]

The Gospels further depict Jesus traveling through the countryside to cities and towns exorcising demons or evil spirits that had inhabited the bodies of human beings. As the Gospel of Mark relates: "He cured many who were sick with various diseases and he drove out many demons, not permitting them to speak because they knew him" (Mark 1:34). The Satan and the evil spirits that serve him are clearly not agents serving Yahweh in such stories but enemies to be defeated by the Messiah.

Surprisingly, the section of the New Testament where Satan is most prominent was also the last to be written and nearly excluded from the Biblical canon in the fourth century CE. The Book of Revelation was written by John of Patmos around 100 CE, long after the time of Jesus and his disciples. However, the vivid account of the end times and the final battle between the forces of good and evil contained in the document profoundly influenced the concept of Satan as the archetypal "Evil One" in Western religious thought.

The Book of Revelation is distinctly dualistic and depicts Jesus as a cosmic destroyer who will vanquish all evil and corruption from the world. Opposing Jesus in this cosmic battle is Satan in the form of a red, seven-headed dragon, now identified with the serpent in the Garden of Eden. It states: "Then war broke out in heaven . . . The huge dragon, the ancient serpent, who is called the Devil and Satan, who deceived the whole world, was thrown down to earth, and its angels were thrown down with it" (Rev. 12:7–9). As the prophetic narrative continues, Satan's primary agent, "the Beast" or Anti-Christ, emerges and deceives the masses before being defeated by Jesus and his angels. Many scholars believe that the "beast" of Revelation actually refers to the Roman Emperor Nero (d. 68 CE), the first emperor to actively persecute the early church.

By the end of the sixth century CE, Christianity was firmly established as the official religion of the Roman Empire and encompassed the Mediterranean world. Egypt developed its own sect of Christianity, the Coptic Church, which espoused a doctrine of monophysitism that was considered to be a heresy by the dominant Roman Church. Furthermore, it was in Egypt, during the fourth century, that St. Anthony (d. 356 CE) pioneered Christian monasticism by retreating from the world to enter a life of asceticism in the desert to engage in a spiritual battle against demonic forces.

The first account of St. Anthony's battle with demonic forces was penned by Athanasius of Alexandria (d. 373 CE). As he writes: "For the Lord was working with Anthony, the Lord who for our sake took flesh and gave the body victory over the Devil, so that all who truly fight can say, 'not I but the grace of God which was with me.'"[5] Athanasius' narrative relates that St. Anthony was physically assaulted by demons that nearly beat him to death. Remaining steadfast in his faith, St. Anthony was later visited by demons in the form of ferocious beasts, including lions, serpents, scorpions, bulls, and wolves. The Devil then went on to try to tempt St. Anthony with apparitions of gold and silver, but again Anthony could not be fooled by the snares of the Evil One. As Athanasius writes:

> "This is some wile of the devil. O thou Evil One, not with this shalt thou hinder my purpose; let it go with thee to destruction." And when Anthony had said this it vanished like smoke from the face of fire.[6]

The aggressive dualistic struggle between good and evil, evident in the story of St. Anthony in Egypt from the fourth century CE, builds on the ideas expressed in the canonical Gospels and the Book of Revelation dating back to the late first century.

In neighboring Arabia, the Coptic, Chalcedonian, Nestorian, and other eastern sects of Christianity remained restricted to the north of the Peninsula and Yemen on the southern coast, except for isolated pockets, particularly monks living in ascetic devotion in the deserts. As discussed in Chapter 6, far more prominent in the Hijaz region of Arabia where Islam developed were tribes of Jews, although the majority of tribal peoples (including the Quraysh) were animists adhering to Arab ancestral customs. By the time of Muhammad's religious mission in the early seventh century CE, the religious climate in the Hijaz region of Arabia likely included the presence of Jewish notions of the adversarial Satan, and to a lesser extent the eastern Christian dualistic "Evil One" leading his army of demons against the righteous servants of God.

The Story of Iblis in the Qur'an

The Qur'an emphasizes absolute monotheism (*tawhid*) as the core doctrine of Islam. *Allah*, therefore, is described as the source of everything in creation, whether good or evil. *Allah* has no rival or partner in anything and all of creation exists solely by His Will. As the Qur'an states: "For to *Allah* belong the forces of Heaven and Earth and *Allah* is Great and Wise" (48:7). Given this emphasis on *Allah*'s unrivaled oneness and supremacy over creation, it should be no surprise that the *Shaytan* of the Qur'an is a minor figure akin to the figure found in the Biblical Book of Job.

The Qur'an relates that when Adam was created by *Allah* at the pinnacle of creation, all the hosts of heaven were commanded to bow down before him. Adam, the Qur'an tells us, was created from water and dust mixed into clay and infused with the breath of life to serve as *Allah*'s vicegerent on Earth. The angels, who were created from light, obeyed *Allah* and bowed down before Adam, despite the fact that they believed they were better suited to act as *Allah*'s vicegerent.

However, among the hosts of heaven at this event was a *jinni* named Iblis. The *jinn* are a race of beings created after the angels on the timeline of creation, but before Adam, and the *jinn* were made of smokeless fire. They are incorporeal like the angels, but possess the power to choose their actions like human beings. Thus, the *jinn* can be good or evil. Iblis believed that he was superior to this new being made of clay and refused to bow down before Adam. As the Qur'an relates:

> Iblis was not among those that bowed down. [*Allah*] said: "What prevented you from bowing down as I commanded you?" He said: "I am better than him. You created me from fire and created him from clay." [*Allah*] said: "Get you down from here; it is not for you to be arrogant here, so get out, for you are among the debased!" [Iblis] said: "Grant me respite until the Day of Resurrection!" (7:11–14)

Allah granted Iblis his request, despite his act of hubris and arrogant disobedience. His punishment was thus delayed until the Day of Judgment when all of humanity will be held accountable for their deeds and enter either heaven or hellfire. Iblis declares that he will prove his superiority over Adam to *Allah* by tempting and luring as many of his descendents into sin and ultimately into hellfire as possible, even if it means entering Hell himself. As the Qur'an states:

> [Iblis] said: "Because you have cast me out, I will lie in wait for them along the Straight Path. Then I will besiege them from the front and the back, from their right and their left, and you will find that most of them are not grateful." [*Allah*] said: "Get out from here, disgraced and driven out. For whoever follows you from among humanity I will fill Hell with all of you." (7:16–18)

Determined in his malevolent mission to prove the inferiority and unworthiness of humanity to *Allah*, Iblis assumes the role of *al-Shaytan* ("the Satan") and goes to the Garden (Eden) to guide Adam and his wife astray and persuade them to eat from the forbidden tree. In the Garden, "*al-Shaytan* then whispered to them," the Qur'an relates, explicitly placing Iblis in the role played by the serpent in the Hebrew Bible and conflated with the Devil in the Christian Book of Revelation. But the Qur'anic *Shaytan* is most fundamentally akin to the early Jewish "adversary" of humanity found in the Book of Job who serves as an otherwise powerless agent of Yahweh. Iblis is "the whisperer" (Qur'an 114:4) who tempts the hearts of men to go astray from the Straight Path that *Allah* has revealed to them through His prophets. He is the enemy of humanity, but not the dualistic adversary of *Allah*.

Although he is ultimately a minor figure in Islamic cosmology with no power independent of *Allah*, perhaps more of a *trickster archetype* than a devil archetype, the insidious whisperer Iblis remains a serious threat to the salvation of individual Muslims. His sole existence is devoted to leading human beings astray from *Allah*'s guidance into self-destruction. As such, invocations of *Allah*'s protection against the machinations of *al-Shaytan* are commonplace in Muslim devotional life. For example, it is common knowledge that observant Muslims perform *salat*, or formal prayer, five times daily. But what non-Muslims may not know is that each prayer begins with the Arabic invocation "*audhu billahi min ash-shaytan ar-rajeem*," meaning "I seek refuge in *Allah* from the Satan, the Accursed One." The same invocation is always spoken before devoutly reciting from the Qur'an. We should also note that the last two *surah*s of the Qur'an, *al-Falaq* (113) and *an-Nas* (114), both serve as special prayers to protect human beings against evil, including "he that whispers in the hearts of men" (114:5).

The Prohibition of Alcohol

The traditional Islamic prohibition against the consumption of alcohol and intoxicants, as well as gambling and divination, is well known. But these prohibitions, like other elements of Muslim belief and practice, occurred through a series of certain historical events that are more obscure. Most importantly for our interests, the Qur'an situates these practices in terms of the *Shaytan*'s plots to deceive the human race and lead them astray. As with many legal injunctions in Islamic thought, these prohibitions are based on events that occurred in Medina after the *hijra*.

According to post-Qur'anic traditions (e.g., Hadith) and exegetical commentaries, it was commonplace in the days of *jahiliyyah* for the Arabs to drink wine and play gambling games. We further read in the books of Hadith that wine at that time was made from five things: wheat, barley, dates, grapes, and honey. These pastimes persisted into the early years of Islam, until impious behavior associated with these activities began to create problems for the community. The first Qur'anic reference to the consumption of alcohol is in the Medinan *surah*, *al-Baqarah*. It states:

> They ask you concerning wine (*al-khamr*) and gambling. Say [to them]: "In them is a great sin, and some benefit to people; but the sin is greater than the benefit" (2:219).

Later on, an incident reportedly occurred where one of the Muslims performed *salat* while drunk and garbled his words and recitation of the

Qur'an. This incident prompted a new revelation to come down to the Prophet that prohibited the believers from performing prayers under the influence of alcohol. The verse states: "Oh you who believe! Do not approach *salat* [i.e., prayer] in a drunken state until you know what you are saying" (4:3). Finally, as inappropriate behavior persisted among some of the Muslims in Medina that drank alcohol, particularly among the Hypocrites (see Chapter 5), the Qur'anic prohibition came down in a verse explicitly associating it with the *Shaytan*'s handiwork. It states:

> Oh you who believe! Truly wine and gambling, idols, and divination arrows are an abomination among *Shaytan*'s handiwork; avoid them so that perhaps you may prosper. *Shaytan* wants to foster enmity and hatred between you with wine and gambling, and divert you from the remembrance (*dhikr*) of *Allah* and prayer (*salat*); so will you abstain? (5:90–91).

After these verses were revealed, the news was spread throughout Medina, so the Muslims brought out their jugs and skins of wine and poured them out onto the ground. The seemingly innocuous prohibition in the Qur'an is amplified in the later Hadith collections, where corporal punishment for drinking is stipulated. As *Sahih Bukhari* states, the punishment for drunkenness is lashing, typically forty (although the Caliph Umar stipulated eighty lashes):

> Narrated Abu Huraira: A drunk was brought to the Prophet and he ordered him to be beaten (lashed). Some of us beat him with our hands, and some with their shoes and some with their garments (twisted in the form of a lash). When that drunk had left, a man said, "What is wrong with him? May *Allah* disgrace him!" *Allah*'s Apostle said, "Do not help Satan against your (Muslim) brother."[7]

The sale and trade of alcohol was also forbidden, as a tradition relates that the Prophet said: "Verily He Who has forbidden its drinking has forbidden its sale also."[8] Another tradition, related in *Sahih Muslim*, states that one ceases to be a believer when drinking alcohol until stopping. It states: "No one who drinks wine is a believer as long as he drinks it, and repentance may be accepted after that."[9] It is also reported in *Sahih Muslim* that one of the signs of the Last Hour will be the widespread consumption of alcohol.

The seminal treatise on *usul al-fiqh* (Islamic jurisprudence) by the famous Sunni jurist Muhammad ibn Idris al-Shafi'i (d. 820 CE), called *ar-Risala*, elaborates on Muslim legal formulations relating to these injunctions. The legal principle of *qiyas*, or analogy, is often used in reference to the verses and traditions regarding wine cited earlier. Al-Shafi'i writes that "if there is no indication as to the right answer, it should be sought by *ijtihad*, and *ijtihad* is *qiyas*."[10]

On the basis of analogy, the Qur'anic prohibition against wine has been extended to all forms of alcohol and even to all forms of intoxicants. Despite its enormous popularity in much of the Muslim world, Muslim jurists have even debated the permissibility of drinking coffee because of its properties as a stimulant. However, the dominant view applies the prohibition only to substances that "cloud the mind" and inhibit proper judgment.

The *Shaytan*'s Handiwork Master Narrative in Extremist Discourse

The infamous characterization of the United States as the "Great Satan" by the Ayatollah Khomeini (d. 1989) of Iran has been a fixture of Western popular imagination that has yet to fade from our collective consciousness. But this ominous designation distracts us from the normative associations that more commonly frequent extremist discourses regarding the *Shaytan*'s machinations in everyday Muslim life. A splendid example comes to us from the small island nation of Bahrain that will elucidate the ruse story form contained in this master narrative further.

The kingdom of Bahrain has long been one of the most liberal societies in the Gulf, where alcohol, nightclubs, movie theaters, rock concerts, and art galleries attract huge numbers of tourists, mostly from neighboring ultraconservative Saudi Arabia. But in 2002, greater democratic reforms under King Hamad allowed Sunni and Shi'ite Islamists to achieve sweeping victories in parliamentary elections. It was the first such election in Bahrain in thirty years.

As Islamism has increasingly asserted itself in Bahrain, the lucrative tourism industry has become a frequent target of political attacks, despite the serious economic implications. Violent extremist attacks have also emerged, particularly among Muslim youths in the country. For example, in March of 2004, one hundred Shi'ite Islamist extremists, mostly youths, stormed a French restaurant in the capital city of Manama with knives and set fire to cars owned by its patrons. One of the Islamists was stabbed by a patron in the ensuing chaos. That same month, five men were arrested for attacking homes belonging to foreigners and a store selling alcohol. On the political end, all of the ills of Bahraini society have been conflated with alcohol by the Islamist parties. For them, these ills clearly suggest the satanic nature afforded to alcohol by Islam, particularly the master narrative of *Shaytan*'s handiwork.

In recent years, antialcohol measures have gained significant ground in Bahrain's parliament. Sunni and Shi'ite Islamists, as well as some liberals, have been united in these efforts. In 2008, the parliament passed a resolution calling for a ban on alcohol throughout the country and the closing of all nightclubs. More modest measures have already succeeded in banning alcohol sales in the Bahrain international airport and on the national airline, Gulf Air. Another measure banned the sale and serving of alcohol in one and two star hotels, leading some hotels to turn their ballrooms into five-star restaurants to take advantage of liquor permits and the lucrative business alcohol creates.[11] Sheikh Ibrahim al-Hadi, a Sunni Islamist MP, subsequently accused such hotels of "cheating" and threatened to launch a campaign against "those who want to corrupt the country."[12]

The discourse surrounding the antialcohol measures paints an image that suggests that Bahrain is teetering on the verge of imminent destruction due to alcohol's presence in the country. Such discourses clearly diverge from rational and empirical inquiries on the subject. As one Salafi-Sunni Islamist MP, Ibrahim Busandal, put it: "Whether they are producers, drinkers, distributors, sellers, or those who eat from its money, [they] are all damned by God; alcohol is the biggest sin, the mother of all sins."[13]

The Islamist campaigns to ban alcohol in Bahrain might seem insignificant (even humorous) to outsiders, but what cannot be overlooked is the fact that the antialcohol campaigns are frequently linked to xenophobic sentiment, both against Westerners and Arabs from elsewhere in the region (e.g., Saudi Arabia). Foreigners are viewed by Bahraini Islamists (as well as others) as the primary consumers for the alcohol industry in Bahrain.

This is a significant link for those in the United States, because Bahrain is the home of the U.S. Fifth Fleet, stationed on a strategically vital U.S. naval base originally established in 1949. The base is especially important given Bahrain's geographic proximity to Iran and the Strait of Hormuz. The Fifth Fleet is also responsible for battling the proliferation of piracy emanating from Somalia. Thus, among the approximately three thousand U.S. servicemen and women on the naval base, those looking for a beer on a Saturday night in Manama are unwittingly acting as agents in the "satanic corruption" of Bahraini society and (in the Islamist view) opening the door to a whole range of vices and crimes, including prostitution, rape, and homosexuality, that threaten to destroy their country.

The Islamists of Bahrain, whether they are violent extremist mobs or refined members of parliament, have woven all of these elements and social ills together around the seemingly insignificant consumption and sale of alcohol. This is no accident. It is rooted in the master narrative of the *Shaytan*'s handiwork. The desire-to-satisfaction trajectory of the narrative is the defeat of the malevolent archetypal trickster, the *Shaytan*, in order to stay on the straight path to salvation. Human beings, such as tourists or foreign workers, who drink, sell, or trade in alcohol, are analogous to satanic agents, because they are either caught in the *Shaytan*'s snares or working to lead the Muslims astray. Therefore, someone selling beer and wine in a store to feed his family suddenly becomes a satanic agent or a corrupter of Muslim society that could be attacked for the sake of the community and its salvation.

Analysis of the *Shaytan's* Handiwork Master Narrative

The *Shaytan*'s handiwork master narrative encodes the seemingly harmless and mundane as something far more nefarious than outside observers may otherwise recognize. There are many elements of the traditional Muslim concept of the *Shaytan* and his activities in the world to guide people astray. However, in this chapter, we have focused on the way everyday elements of societies in the modern world can be associated with this master narrative and become targets for violent extremist acts. For instance, as already discussed, an ordinary restaurant where families dine can be framed as part of a satanic plot against Islam due to the fact that it serves wine to its patrons. Or a hotel resort with a casino catering to tourists can serve as a basis for foreigners to be cast as agents of the *Shaytan* and corrupters of a Muslim society. Even a children's game can be condemned as a satanic plot when properly framed. For example, this was the case when the children's game *Pog* was denounced in Egypt around 2001 as a form of gambling that corrupted young Muslims.

The ruse story form and trickster archetype of the *Shaytan*'s handiwork master narrative are particularly interesting because of their ability to frame the seemingly innocuous as sinister and dangerous. The obvious targets are those forbidden by *shari'ah*, especially alcohol and gambling given that they are explicitly forbidden and associated with *Shaytan* in the Qur'an. However, through analogy and other means, there is little reason to believe that the master narrative cannot serve as a framing device by Islamist extremists to justify or motivate violent action against a wide array of social or cultural elements for their own ideological interests.

CHAPTER 11

1924

After the death of the Prophet Muhammad in 632 CE, the Muslim community (*ummah*) established a religio-political office that assumed Muhammad's temporal leadership responsibilities (but not his prophethood), called *al-Khilafah* ("viceroy") or the Caliphate. This office was largely political, sometimes only ceremonial, and existed in one form or another for thirteen centuries until it finally came to an end in its Ottoman manifestation in 1924.

There is no Caliphate, at least on any significant level, in the Muslim world today. Therefore, Sunni Islam (Shi'ites have the rival Imamate) has continued to exist for over eighty years in the absence of this major institution of the religion, once thought to be indispensible. Surprisingly (not really), efforts to restore the Caliphate have seldom moved beyond romantic rhetoric, nostalgia, and conferences. The prospects for its revival remain extremely bleak.

Nevertheless, the story of the Caliphate's demise in 1924 has become a major master narrative of extremist discourse and it has adopted a variety of imaginative elements that defy the mundane accounts found in the average Western history book. In fact, according to the Islamist extremist version of events, the abolition of the Ottoman Caliphate in 1924 by Mustafa Kemal Atatürk (d. 1938) was all part of a grand ruse and sinister conspiracy against Islam. Among the many strange elements in the alleged conspiracy, we find that Atatürk was a secret Jew (apparently a member of the Dönme sect) working on behalf of global Zionism to eliminate Islam.

There is a striking contemporary parallel to the 1924 master narrative found in the United States surrounding the election of Barack Obama as U.S. president in 2008. Various far-right elements in the United States maintain that Obama is really a secret Muslim and part of a grand conspiracy to destroy the United States of America. Some variants of the narrative claim that Obama has ties to Egypt's Muslim Brotherhood or that he took his oath of office on the Qur'an instead of the Bible. David Gaubatz, an anti-Islam activist with ties to numerous U.S. Congressmen, wrote at the time of the election that "a vote for Hussein [*sic*] Obama is a vote for Shari'ah law."[1]

Other stories, espoused by those known as "Birthers," maintain that Obama is not a U.S. citizen and that his Hawaii birth certificate was forged by sinister conspiratorial elements in the federal government, perhaps Islamist infiltrators. Claims of Obama's secret Muslim identity and other nefarious plots have been circulated by numerous sources in the United States, including several spurious e-mail messages. One such e-mail stated the following:

> Lolo Soetoro, the second husband of Obama's mother, Ann Dunham, introduced his stepson to Islam. Obama was enrolled in a Wahabi [*sic*] school in Jakarta. Wahabism [*sic*] is the RADICAL teaching that is followed by the Muslim terrorists who are now waging Jihad against the western world . . . The Muslims have said they plan on destroying the U.S. from the inside out, what better way to start than at the highest level through the President of the United States, one of their own!!!![2]

This bizarre, fictitious conspiracy narrative is strikingly similar to Islamist extremist accounts of Atatürk and his establishment of the secular Republic of Turkey in the aftermath of World War I. In some ways, the two stories are a direct inversion of each other. However, the 1924 master narrative has endured for decades and it is still referenced in attempts to frame or explain contemporary events in the Muslim world.

The circumstances surrounding the history of the Caliphate and its eventual abolition in Turkey are complex and require some explanation. A historical overview is therefore important for our interests, given that so much of the 1924 master narrative is at odds with the facts of history. Indeed, the entire concept of the Caliphate as it exists in modern Muslim discourse is too often at odds with the historical record. This is the subject that we begin with now as we examine the 1924 master narrative.

The Caliphate—Ideal versus Reality

Traditional Muslim accounts portray the office of the Caliphate, the temporal successor of the Prophet Muhammad, as a noble line of universal Muslim rulers of the *ummah* that embody Islamic power and prestige at the glorious height of Islamic civilization, going back in an unbroken chain to the time of the Prophet in Medina (i.e., the Medinan Paradigm). The reality, however, is quite different.

The Caliphate was a very troubled institution from the start. Not only did the "Rightly Guided" Caliphs, namely, Abu Bakr, Umar, Uthman, and 'Ali, face serious internal opposition (three of the four were assassinated), but the Caliphate very quickly devolved into a worldly kingship surrounded by bloody political intrigue. The Caliphs of the ensuing dynasties proved to be no different than any ambitious king or emperor in Europe's many feuding and scandalous Christian kingdoms. For many generations, multiple Caliphates even existed simultaneously. The most notable case of multiple Caliphates occurred when the Abbasid Caliphate existed in Baghdad, the Fatimid Caliphate in Cairo, and the Umayyad Caliphate in Cordoba, during the tenth and eleventh centuries (CE).

Countless Muslim empires, emirates, and kingdoms also existed beyond the Caliph's influence or direct rule, such as the domain of the Sunni Ghaznavids in South Asia or the many Muslim empires of West Africa (e.g., Mali, Songhay). At still other times, the Caliphate existed as little more than a minor ceremonial office devoid of any real political power. This was the case among the Abbasid Caliphs when the Twelver Shi'ite Buyids conquered Baghdad and ruled Iraq in the tenth and eleventh centuries, or when an Abbasid Caliphate was installed in Mamluk Cairo after the Mongol destruction of Baghdad in 1258 CE (see Chapter 9).

In fact, it was the decline and chaos around the office of the Abbasid Caliphate that drove Abu al-Hasan al-Mawardi (d. 1058 CE) to write his seminal treatise on caliphal authority, *al-Ahkam al-Sultaniyya wal-Wilayat al-Diniyya* ("The Ordinances of Government"), in the eleventh century. The Ottoman adoption of the office, after their conquest of Egypt's Mamluk Empire in 1517, hardly lived up to the idealized Islamic ruler presented in Muslim mythology either. It was even common practice for Ottoman Sultans to murder potential political rivals within their own families, including their own sons and brothers, upon assuming power. The 1924 master narrative fails to recognize any of these unsavory details or any other negative elements of the Caliphate.

Given the prominence afforded to it in most Muslim literature and religious scholarship, it may surprise our readers to know that the concept of the Caliphate is not found in the Qur'an. The concept is entirely post-Qur'anic and thus lacks any explicit divine sanction in the eternal Speech of *Allah*. Rather, its initial development seems to have emerged out of political necessity more so than anything else. As the historian Marshall Hodgson put it: "Though the Qur'an enforced the idea of a community, in which pious action was completed by joint action in the cause of God, it provided directly for no government other than that of the Prophet himself."[3]

Muhammad's death threatened to dismantle the innovative tribal confederacy that he had established in Arabia, and its continued existence required the creation of a unifying office of leadership, assumed by Abu Bakr (the first Caliph). Historian Jonathan Berkey has argued that the initial Caliphate was something akin to a "king of the Arabs" rather than a universal Islamic leader. He states: "A caliph such as Umar [the second Caliph, r. 634–644 CE] seems to have regarded himself, first and foremost as the leader of the Arabs, and their monotheistic creed as the religious component of their new political identity."[4] Thus, the Caliphate, having no basis in the Qur'an, was very clearly a product of the empires that followed Muhammad's modest Arabian city-state, even if it has been ascribed to the Prophet in subsequent Muslim traditions, literature, history, and scholarship. These facts are important as we examine the way the Caliphate is described in the 1924 master narrative.

Atatürk and the End of the Caliphate

By the beginning of the twentieth century, Islamic civilization had fallen deeply into decline and far behind the progress of Western Europe. The last great symbol of Muslim power, the rapidly crumbling Ottoman Empire, was popularly dubbed the "sick man of Europe." Just a fraction of its former size, the Ottoman Empire faced serious internal disarray by the end of the nineteenth century.

The Ottoman Sultan and Caliph 'Abdul-Hamid II (d. 1918) brutally crushed internal dissent against his autocratic rule and emphasized his role as Caliph to try to appeal to pan-Islamic sentiment among his ethnically diverse Muslim subjects, including Turks, Kurds, Arabs, Slavs, Circassians, and others. But in 1908, a revolution by Turkish nationalist-constitutionalists known as the "Young Turks," or the Committee of Union and Progress (CUP), forced 'Abdul-Hamid II to capitulate the throne. Thereafter, 'Abdul-Hamid II lived out the rest of his years in exile in Salonika (Thessaloniki, Greece) until war forced his relocation to Istanbul where he died in captivity.

Inspired by modern European progress, the Young Turks were a secretive league of Turkish army officers and intellectuals intent on restoring the Ottoman constitution of 1876, which was suspended by 'Abdul-Hamid II. After the Caliph was deposed in 1908, his half-brother Mehmed V (d. 1918) was installed as a ceremonial Caliph with no real power by the revolutionaries. Autocracy quickly resurfaced in the Empire among the CUP thereafter.

Real political power over the Ottoman Empire resided with the "Three Pashas" of the CUP, who asserted their control after a coup in 1913 that ousted the non-CUP Ottoman grand vizier (i.e., prime minister). Led by the "Three Pashas," the Young Turks allied the Empire with Germany and entered World War I against the Triple Entente of Russia, Britain, and France (including their colonial territories). Of particular significance, for our interests, is the Arab revolt against Ottoman rule during the war.

The Arabs sided with the Christian British Empire against the Muslim Ottomans in hopes of securing independent Arab states (e.g., Jordan). Ethno-nationalism, not Pan-Islamism, was the dominant ideological current of the age. The British were the Ottomans' greatest adversaries in the war, and the British navy, as well as its control of formerly Ottoman Egypt, formed the greatest threat to the Turks.[5] The "Three Pashas," meanwhile, demonstrated their incompetence at leading the crumbling Ottoman Empire with failed policies and military defeats in the war. The British and their Arab allies eagerly struck away at Ottoman holdings in the Middle East, including Palestine (opening the door for Zionist colonization).

By the end of the war in 1918, the Ottomans were on the verge of total annihilation. However, a Turkish military officer and war hero, Mustafa Kemal (d. 1938), rallied the remaining Ottoman troops and maintained an army to salvage the future of Turkish nationhood.[6] The "Three Pashas," meanwhile, fled to Germany in disgrace. Soon, the new Ottoman Caliph, under British pressure, was condemning Kemal and mobilizing against him and his loyal forces. The Greeks and other ethno-nationalist minorities from former Ottoman territories mobilized as well, hoping to establish valuable holdings for their own nation-states. Kemal and his army succeeded in defending what is now the state of Turkey in Anatolia, defeating the Greeks and others, to emerge as a national hero. For these efforts and his later political achievements, he received the honorary surname Atatürk in 1934, meaning "Father of the Turks." Elsewhere, two of the "Three Pashas" were assassinated by Armenian militants in Europe, and the third was killed in Tajikistan fighting the Soviet Red Army.

In the years that followed, Atatürk set about establishing the Turkish nation-state as a secular republic with an overtly Western orientation. In his view, modern civilization was synonymous with European secularism; therefore, the creation of a viable, modern, Turkish nation-state required Turkish conformity to European sociopolitical norms. In October of 1923, Ankara (not the Ottoman capital of Istanbul) was designated as the capital of the Turkish republic and Atatürk was appointed as the first president of Turkey. In 1924, he abolished the Caliphate and all religious schools (*madrasas*), and then in the following year he outlawed the wearing of the turban and fez and implemented the Gregorian calendar.[7] In 1928, Atatürk replaced the Arabic script with a new Latin script and removed the constitutional clause that established Islam as the state religion.[8] He also abolished the use of *shari'ah* (Islamic law), implemented legal codes based on European law, and outlawed the influential Sufi orders. In 1933, the Turkish government even required that the Qur'an be read in Turkish (not Arabic), as well as the call to prayer (*adhan*) to be in Turkish. In short, Atatürk systematically purged Islam from public life in Turkey in an alarmingly rapid fashion, and a national personality cult surrounding Atatürk developed in its place. Turkish secularism, therefore, differs substantially from American secularism. The Turkish state, even as many of Atatürk's reforms have since waned, remains very active in regulating and controlling the practice of religion in its borders.

Atatürk's policies were praised in the United States and the West, but proved to be deeply unsettling for much of the Muslim world. Efforts were mobilized almost immediately to restore the Caliphate in different regions, but the prominence of ethno-nationalism among Islam's global community (*ummah*) never allowed such efforts to gain substantial momentum. One of the most notable of these movements was the failed Khilafat Movement, associated with the 'Ali brothers, in British India, which began in 1919 immediately after the war. The Hashemite Sharif of Mecca, Husayn ibn 'Ali (d. 1931), also proclaimed himself Caliph in 1924, but his proclamation went largely unrecognized and his kingdom in the Hijaz (including Mecca) was conquered that year by the Saudi Wahhabites, paving the way for the creation of Saudi Arabia. At the time, Husayn's son 'Abdallah (future King of Jordan), stated to a British newspaper:

> [The Turks] have rendered the greatest possible service to the Arabs. I feel like sending a telegram thanking Mustafa Kemal. The Caliphate is an Arab institution. The Prophet was an Arab, the Qur'an is in Arabic, the Holy Places are in Arabia, and the Caliph should be an Arab of the tribe of Quraysh… Now the Caliphate has come back to Arabia.[9]

A Caliphate Conference also convened at Jerusalem in the British Mandate of Palestine in 1931 to try and advance the cause of the Caliphate's restoration. The Grand Mufti of Jerusalem was quoted as stating at the time: "The question of restoration of the Caliphate will not be decided at our All-Muslim Congress in Jerusalem next December, but, while no Caliph will be elected by the Congress, we will deal with the question abstractly."[10] Meanwhile, the Turkish government actively lobbied the British Empire to prevent the Caliphate conference from taking place and ensure that the restoration of the Caliphate will not be permitted in the British Empire (e.g., Egypt, India, Palestine).

The reformist scholar Rashid Rida (d. 1935), one of two figures credited with the founding of the Salafi movement in Sunni Islam, lived in colonial Egypt (British rule) and Syria (French rule) during the turbulent events surrounding the end of the Caliphate. His ideas would prove influential in the historical development of Islamism in Egypt. At the time of the war, Rida's thought reflected an eclectic mixture of Arab nationalism, modernism, and classical Sunni orthodoxy. Convinced of the imminent fall of the Ottomans, he saw the Arab alliance with the British as an opportunity to establish an independent Arab Caliphate, and British officials in Egypt and Sudan apparently supported the idea.[11] But an official proclamation drafted by Rida and presented to the British government in London was soundly rejected.[12] Britain would only accept an Arab Caliphate devoid of temporal power and subservient to British rule. As A. H. Grant, Britain's secretary to the Foreign Department, related in 1914: "What we want is not a united Arabia, but a weak and disunited Arabia, split up into little principalities so far as possible under our suzerainty, but incapable of coordinated action against us, forming a buffer against the Powers of the West."[13]

In 1922, Rida penned a treatise on the Caliphate, entitled "The Caliphate or the Supreme Imamate." In it, he argued in favor of the necessity of having a Caliph, even citing a hadith that equates dying in the absence of a Caliph with dying in the days of *jahiliyyah*.[14] The powers of the restored Arab Caliphate would be "limited by the prescriptions of the Qur'an and the Sunnah, by the general example of the *Rashidun* [i.e., Rightly Guided] caliphs and by consultation."[15] But Rida's modernist views also led to innovations that departed from classical thought on the Caliphate. He advocated the idea that the Caliph should be democratically elected by a council of representatives from Muslim societies consisting of not only the *ulama*, but political officials, intellectuals, prominent merchants, physicians, lawyers, and others.[16] This council would also have legislative powers within the parameters of the Qur'an and Sunnah. Returning to the original textual sources, or *ijtihad*, after all, was a core component of the Salafi movement. The renaissance of the Muslims, Rida argued, was "dependent on *ijtihad*."[17]

Thus, the underlying significance of the Caliphate for Rida was in terms of Muslim political independence from the dominant colonial European powers of the time, and as a unifying institution that reflected centuries of Muslim prestige. Nevertheless, as history attests, the efforts of Rida and other Caliphate activists never yielded any results and Sunni Islam has continued to exist without a Caliph to this day.

The 1924 Master Narrative in Extremist Discourse

At the start of this chapter, we noted the parallels between the ruse story form in the 1924 master narrative and the right-wing conspiracy theories that developed in the United States surrounding the 2008 election of President Barack Obama. In the May 2009 issue of the online extremist magazine, *Jihad Recollections*, the cover image actually depicts Obama and Atatürk with the title "Obamaturk" overhead and overlaid with chains and the repeated number "1924." The featured article in the magazine condemns Obama's 2009 speech in Turkey and states: "[Obama] started off by praising Kemal Atatürk [in his speech], who single-handedly dismantled the greatest nation *Allah* ever let exist on the face of the earth."[18] This is an interesting claim by the extremist authors for many reasons.

First, this is obviously a radical overstatement of the facts, placing the blame for the Ottoman Caliphate's end solely on an *archetypal imposter*, Atatürk. As we discussed above, the historical circumstances surrounding the demise of the Caliphate are complex and numerous, including several internal Muslim revolts against the Ottomans. As previously mentioned, the Arabs (including the Sharif of Mecca) fought on the side of the Christian British Empire against the Turks.

Second, the statement seems to claim that the Ottoman Empire was the "greatest nation *Allah* ever let exist." The Ottomans were certainly one of the greatest empires in world history, but they hardly matched either the scriptural piety or territorial domain of the classical Caliphates (e.g., Harun al-Rashid). This statement suggests an exaggerated focus on military prowess as the utmost determinate of greatness, probably because Ottoman conquest was directly largely at Europe, and reflects a romantic narrative profoundly detached from historical realities.

The exclusive blame placed on Atatürk for the end of the Caliphate is extraordinary in the 1924 master narrative, but it should not surprise us given that the Kemalist personality cult in Turkey credits Atatürk with the same accomplishments. When we consider the fact that a leading variant of the 1924 master narrative contends that Atatürk was secretly Jewish, the exclusivity of the master narrative begins to resemble the "cosmic" destructive capabilities often attributed to Jews in European anti-Semitic literature, especially in the "Protocols of the Elders of Zion" that originated in Tzarist Russia. But, just as we observed in the Obama "secret Muslim" conspiracies, there is a small grain of truth to the Atatürk tale.

Obama's grandfather was indeed a Muslim, although Obama himself is a Protestant Christian. Likewise, several leading figures among the Young Turks, such as Mehmet Javid Bey, were adherents of the Jewish Dönme ("convert") sect, although Atatürk was a nominal Sunni Muslim. The Dönme are the descendents of a seventeenth century messianic Jewish movement that recognized Sabbatai Zevi (d. ca. 1676) as the long awaited Jewish Messiah. Arrested as a treasonous rebel by the Ottoman Caliph Mehmet IV (d. 1693), Zevi ultimately converted to Islam rather than accept martyrdom at the hands of the Sultan's executioner. While many Jews felt betrayed by his conversion, Zevi's most ardent devotees followed his example and outwardly converted to Islam while still continuing to practice Judaism in secret. The Dönme community continued to live in the Ottoman Empire, especially in the prosperous city of Salonika, also the city of Atatürk's birth, before their expulsion by the Greeks after World War I.

One of the most eccentric examples of a claim that Atatürk was secretly Jewish is a web site called "AtaJew.com." Although it now contains only articles and links, the web site used to depict Atatürk as a "Jewish Dictator" with several crudely modified images of Atatürk adorned with a Star of David on his hat or clothing. The web site also claims that Atatürk was a British agent, a Freemason (a common element in Western conspiracy theories) and a homosexual. For instance, the AtaJew.com web site states:

> To this date, there is extreme confusion among Muslims and non-Muslims alike around the world regarding who was Freemason Mustafa Kemal, the Gay dictator of Turkey. Recently, yet other evidences have surfaced that Gay Mustafa Kemal, the cruel dictator of Turkey, was not only a non-Muslim doenmeh [*sic*], but also a secret Jewish descendant of 17th-century Jewish false messiah Sabbatai Tzwi (Zevi)![19]

The internet, of course, is rife with dubious information, and individuals can post such content anonymously. The anonymity may be important in this case because insulting Atatürk is a crime in the Republic of Turkey. For example, a prominent secular Turkish filmmaker, Can Dündar, is currently on trial in Turkey for "insulting Atatürk" with his documentary film *Mustafa* and faces up to seven years in prison. We should also note that the "Atajew.com" web site contains a link to download a digital copy of the aforementioned spurious anti-Semitic treatise, "The Protocols of the Elders of Zion," along with many other works.

The idea of a vast global conspiracy led by Jews, particularly Zionists, presented in "The Protocols" took root in the Middle East during World War II when Nazi Germany actively courted the Arabs to join them in their fight against the British. Although he rejected all Western ideologies, the Egyptian Islamist ideologue Sayyid Qutb (d. 1966 CE) also wrote a treatise in the early 1950s entitled *Our Struggle with the Jews* that conveyed ideas that seem to reflect those commonly expressed in Western anti-Semitic literature. Qutb wrote:

> And a Jew was behind the incitement of various kinds of tribal arrogance in the last Caliphate; the (fomenting) of revolutions which began with the removal of the *shari'ah* from the legislation and substituting for it 'The Constitution' during the period of the Sultan, Abdul-Hamid II; and the 'hero' Ataturk's ending of the Caliphate. Then behind the subsequent war declared against the first signs of Islamic revival, from every place on the face of the earth . . . stood the Jews.[20]

This notion of a Jewish conspiracy against Islam situates the downfall of the Ottoman Empire and the Caliphate at the center of modern historical events and seeks to explain, in grand terms, the current predicament of so many in Muslim societies. But it would be a mistake to reduce the 1924 master narrative to an anti-Semitic story about Jewish machinations against Islam. Rather, the most important element of the master narrative is still the abolition of the Caliphate and the implications of that event for the future of Islam.

In a statement posted online on April 5, 2009, by the North African extremist group, al-Qaeda in the Land of the Islamic Maghreb (AQLIM), that was addressed to the people of Algeria prior to presidential elections on April 9, 2009, the 1924 master narrative emerged yet again. This time, even though framed as a Jewish and Christian plot, the end of the Caliphate is described in the thematically broader context of an infidel Western plot to besiege all Muslims in order to destroy Islam. The intent of the AQLIM statement is clearly to rally the audience against further "Westernizing" social trends, such as voting secular parties into power. It contends that Atatürk's reforms did not improve the conditions of Muslims, but only made things worse. It claims that secularism is designed to keep Muslims weak, divided, and subject to Western power for the sake of exploitation and greed. This is a curious claim given that Turkey enjoys a far better standard of living, as well as military strength, than many other Muslim nations. Furthermore, Turkey has not had the benefit of lucrative oil wells either. Nevertheless, the AQLIM message states:

> The worst catastrophe that befell the ummah was the collapse of the Caliphate that was defending the religion of Muslims and managing their life according to the moderate Shariah. Then, the ummah was controlled by a group of agent rulers who implemented the plots of the Jews and the Christians against the ummah of Islam in order to disturb it from within and

> destroy it from without: to destroy its creed, ideas, culture, and manners. They are destroying every seed that can be planted in the righteous soil of the ummah. They are fighting its righteous sons who want God's Word to be superior and religion to be only from God. That is to say, they tightened their control over Muslims' countries, imposed secularism upon the weak people, and excluded religion from everything relating to power. By using those treacherous rulers who do not belong to us and are our bitter enemies, the infidels plundered and ransacked our rights by their cunning and deception. Rulership, or what is known in the jurisprudence books as an imamate or caliphate, is of great importance in Islam since it is the guard of this religion and the extended hand that spreads it and protects it from the greedy and from fools.[21]

A similar invocation of the 1924 master narrative was made by the ideologue of al-Qaeda, Ayman al-Zawahiri, on the anniversary of the September 11 attacks in 2006. A jihadist web site attributed to the Islamic Renewal Organization posted several links to an interview with al-Zawahiri by Al-Sahab Media Production, wherein he stated: "After the fall of Ottoman Caliphate [in 1924] a wave of psychological defeatism and ideological collapse spread."[22] Al-Zawahiri's use of the 1924 master narrative is surprisingly more rational than the other examples cited above, nevertheless the message is the same: the abolition of the Caliphate in 1924 devastated the *ummah* and caused many of the problems that Muslims are facing today. In the extremists' view, restoring the political power of Islam, whether through the Caliphate or an Islamic state, is the only way to rectify these matters.

Analysis of the 1924 Master Narrative

The 1924 master narrative works out of a known conflict between Muslims, Jews, and the West. At the heart of its ruse story form is the antagonist and archetypal imposter, Atatürk, who is only posing as a Muslim, when, in fact, he is secretly a Jew (as well as a Freemason). Under his leadership, the Caliphate is dissolved and various negative Western influences are introduced (successfully) into formerly Ottoman Turkey. Clearly, this archetypal imposter is trying to destroy Islam. In order to satisfy the conflict in a way acceptable to Islamists, there must be a concerted effort by all to expose these lies, reverse the innovations introduced, and stop the decline of Islam by restoring the Caliphate.

The 1924 master narrative is a perfect example of how stories are used to try and explain the world around us. In doing so, stories can be crafted to communicate an ideology that shapes how people perceive the world, its history, and the nature of human conflicts. As time passes and past historical facts become more and more obscured, these stories can even assume the appearance of fact, especially when repeated through multiple channels that saturate audiences. For Islamist extremists, the 1924 master narrative is not simply an analogy that parallels other events or conflicts (e.g., "Obamaturk"), but an undeniable fact of history that has shaped the contemporary world and the Muslim societies that exist within it.

CHAPTER 12

The *Nakba*

The loss of a sacred land, and the quest to reclaim it, is a story that echoes throughout the annals of history and mythology around the world. In the United States, the Lakota Sioux lament the loss of *Pahá Sápa*, or the Black Hills of South Dakota, to the federal government. In 1980, the U.S. Supreme Court ruled that the Black Hills was taken illegally by the government and awarded over one hundred million dollars in damages to the Sioux. However, they refused to accept the money awarded and continue to demand the return of their sacred land.

Elsewhere, Orthodox Serbs continue to claim the independent Muslim-majority Republic of Kosovo as a sacred part of Serbia and an integral component of their ethno-religious identity. Vajrayana Buddhists in South Asia reject China's claims over the land of Tibet and protest the destruction of its traditional Buddhist culture, while the U'wa tribal people of Colombia struggle against an American oil company and the Colombian government's designs for their sacred ancestral lands in the rainforests.

In each of these cases, the land is connected to a specific people through a historical bond and a foundational myth(s) that carries important religious significance. In most cases, the stories and myths feature archetypal protagonists and antagonists as key agents in the sequence of events that lead to the loss of the land or its anticipated recovery.

For Palestinian Arabs, the shocking loss of their homes and lands to the new state of Israel in 1948 is known simply as *al-Nakba*, meaning "the Catastrophe." But in the case of Palestine, this loss of land had ramifications far beyond any particular ethno-national group. Muslims around the world consider the land of Palestine, known in Arabic as *Filistin* and *al-Ard al-Muqadassa al-Mubaraka* ("The Holy and Blessed Land"), as a sacred trust (*waqf*) that belongs to the entire Muslim *ummah* for all time.

At the heart of Palestine sits the holy city of Jerusalem (*Medinat al-Quds*), which has profound religious significance for all Muslims, whether

Sunni or Shi'ite. Elsewhere, sacred tombs, shrines, and houses of worship dot the landscape and bring the stories of the Bible and Qur'an to life. The loss of this small stretch of land was a disturbing event for Muslims around the world, and for many it remains absolutely unacceptable. In the case of Islamist extremists, the *Nakba*, or the disastrous loss of sacred Palestine, must be avenged through violence and the land taken back through jihad for the establishment of Islamic rule.

The Night Journey to Jerusalem

The ancient city of Jerusalem or *Medinat al-Quds* ("The Holy City") is the third of the three holy cities of Islam, along with Mecca and Medina in western Saudi Arabia. The religious significance of Jerusalem for Muslims is based on three primary points. The first is the role of Jerusalem as the city of the prophets, where figures that are immortalized in the Qur'an, such as Jesus, David, or Solomon, once worshipped and conveyed the Word of *Allah* to their people. This point extends to the whole of Palestine, especially to sacred sites like the Tomb of the Patriarchs (or *al-Haram al-Ibrahimi*) in Hebron.

The second point is that Jerusalem was the original *qibla* for the Muslims during the lifetime of the Prophet Muhammad. The *qibla* is the direction that Muslims face during their five daily prayers. The Jews also faced Jerusalem during their daily prayers at that time (as many still do today). Among the Muslims, this practice continued until after the *hijra* in 622 CE, when a Medinan revelation from *Allah* abrogated it and ordered the Muslims to distinguish themselves from the Jews by turning toward Mecca instead. As the Qur'an states: "So We shall turn you toward a *qibla* that pleases you; turn your faces in the direction of the sacred mosque (*al-masjid al-haram*) [in Mecca]."[1]

The third point of significance is the story of Muhammad's miraculous night journey from Mecca to Jerusalem and his ascension through the seven heavens toward the abode of the divine presence. The *Isra* and *Mi'raj*, or the Night Journey and Ascension, is only a passing reference in the Qur'an, but it is related in vivid detail in the Hadith and other traditions (e.g., *Seerah*), as well as Islamic art. The Qur'an states: "Glory be to Him that transported His servant [i.e., Muhammad] by night from the *Masjid al-Haram* [in Mecca] to the *Masjid al-Aqsa* [in Jerusalem], that area which We blessed in order to make clear Our Signs."[2] The Qur'an makes no further reference to this miraculous event, although many exegetes consider a passage from *surat an-Najm* (53:13–18) to be a reference to Muhammad's journey through the heavens.

The Hadith, specifically *Sahih Muslim*, and the early hagiography of Ibn Hisham explain that Muhammad was sleeping one night beside the Ka'aba in 619 CE (or 620 CE), when the angel Gabriel (*Jibreel*) woke him from his slumber. Gabriel presented Muhammad with a tall, white, mystical steed called al-Buraq, which later Muslim artisans would commonly depict as an angelic winged beast with the head of a man (or woman) akin to the ancient Persian *lamassu*. Together, Gabriel and Muhammad (riding on al-Buraq) traveled at the speed of light from Mecca to Jerusalem. There, in the precincts of the Noble Sanctuary (*al-Haram al-Sharif*), also known as the Temple Mount, Muhammad fastened al-Buraq to the "tie-ring of the prophets" and offered two units (*rakat*) of prayer to *Allah*. When he completed his prayers, Gabriel brought three (some versions say two) bowls before him and asked the Prophet to choose one. The three bowls contained wine, milk, and water, or wine and milk according to the version with only two bowls. Muhammad chose the milk, which was the correct choice, the middle path.

Gabriel and Muhammad then began the miraculous ascent through the seven heavens and ultimately to the abode of the divine presence. Muslims regard the point of departure for this holy ascent as the rock sitting under the stunning golden Dome of the Rock (*Qubbat as-Sakhrah*). This monumental and iconic Muslim shrine was originally constructed by the Caliph 'Abd al-Malik ibn Marwan from 685 to 691 CE.

From this location, Muhammad and Gabriel ascended to the first heaven where they were met at the heavenly gate by Adam, who invoked peace and blessings upon Muhammad. They then traveled to the second heaven, where they were received at the gate by Jesus and John the Baptist with greetings and blessings. At the third heaven, they were met by the prophet Joseph, famous for his beauty, who again invoked peace and blessings upon Muhammad. At the fourth heaven, Muhammad and Gabriel were met at the gate by the prophet Enoch (Idris), who ascended into the heavens in the body according to the Bible and Qur'an. He too invoked peace and blessings upon Muhammad. Then at the fifth heaven, they were met at the gate by the prophet Aaron, who invoked peace and blessings upon Muhammad. At the sixth heaven, they were met at the gate by Moses, on whom *Allah* revealed the Torah, and he invoked peace and blessings on Muhammad. At the seventh heaven, they were met at the gate by Abraham, father of the prophets, and he invoked peace and blessings on Muhammad. There he found the Lote Tree marking the boundary beyond which none may pass because it is the abode of the mysterious divine presence.

At this point in the story, Qur'anic exegetes have connected the aforementioned verses from *surat an-Najm* to the ascension of Muhammad. The

Qur'an states: "Truly He saw him on his heavenly arrival, near the Lote Tree, near it is a Garden of the Abode; then the Lote Tree enveloped what it enveloped, the eyes never turned away, nor did it exceed proper bounds; truly he saw the greatest of the Signs of his Lord!"[3]

The transcendent experience of Muhammad is ambiguous at this point in the texts, almost silent, but the sources agree that he received knowledge and commands directly from *Allah*. Some traditions say that *Allah* commanded Muhammad to have his *ummah* pray fifty times a day (yes, fifty), but when he descended down through the heavens he met with Moses who inquired about his encounter. Moses insisted that fifty prayers a day was too many and impossible for human beings to fulfill. So Muhammad returned to the Abode to ask *Allah* to lessen the burden, which He did by removing five prayers. This course of events was ultimately repeated again and again until Muhammad was too embarrassed to ask *Allah* to go any lower than five prayers a day. Thus, the tradition says, the number of obligatory daily prayers became fixed at five for the Muslims. Thereafter the Prophet descended and returned to Mecca, miraculously completing in only a single extraordinary night the journey that ordinarily takes an Arab caravan a month.

While the story of *Isra* and *Mi'raj* is sacred to all devout Muslims, it carries special significance for Muslim mystics (i.e., Sufis) as the paradigm of the mystical journey. Muslims generally disagree over whether the Night Journey of Muhammad occurred in the physical body or as a purely spiritual, mystical experience akin to a shamanic flight. Regardless, Muhammad's journey to *Masjid al-Aqsa* in Jerusalem was a real event for Muslims whether his visitation was spiritual or physical. Today, the *al-Aqsa* Mosque and Dome of the Rock that stand within the same sacred complex remain as monuments to the significance of this story in Muslim devotional life. Islamic tradition relates that one prayer at *al-Aqsa* is equivalent to five hundred prayers elsewhere.

A Short Historical Narrative of Muslim Palestine

The land of Palestine, sitting at the crossroads between the three continents of the ancient world, has been inhabited and conquered by countless peoples since time immemorial. Once known as Canaan, tribal peoples lived and worshipped deities, such as El and Baal, at several settlement centers there, including the village of Shalem (i.e., Jerusalem). In the twelfth century BCE, the Israelites settled in Canaan, presumably coming from Egypt. The Book of Joshua recounts the bloody conquest that the Israelites unleashed on Canaan, but the archeological record casts serious doubt on the Biblical version of events. The city of Jerusalem, which remained a Canaanite city after the invasion, reportedly fell to King David around 1000 BCE, and thereafter it was designated as the new capital of the Israelite monarchy and the center of Yahweh worship (equated with El).

In 930 BCE, civil war divided the Kingdom of Israel into two states with Israel in the north, and Judah located in the south. In 722 BCE, the Assyrians invaded and destroyed the northern kingdom of Israel, leaving only Judah remaining. In 586 BCE, the Babylonians invaded and conquered the Kingdom of Judah, ending Jewish rule in the region. Then in 539 BCE, the Persians conquered the Babylonians and assumed control of the land, until the Greeks under Alexander the Great (d. 323 BCE) conquered the entirety of the Persian Empire.

After his death, Alexander's massive empire fragmented and the Greek Ptolemaic dynasty of Egypt ruled over Palestine. In 198 BCE, the Seleucid Empire of Syria conquered the land from the Ptolemies, outlawed Judaism, and sparked the Maccabean revolt that initiated the Hasmonean period from 166 to 63 BCE. The Roman Empire thereafter conquered Palestine in 63 BCE, where it ruled until 638 CE when the Caliph Umar ibn al-Khattab (d. 644 CE), second successor of the Prophet Muhammad, conquered Palestine and the holy city of Jerusalem to usher in the age of Muslim rule.

The Muslims defeated the Romans (Byzantines) at the Battle of Yarmuk in 636 and the whole of Palestine capitulated to the Muslims by 638 CE. The eastern Christian sects and Jews in the region reportedly preferred the rule of the Muslims over that of Heraclius and Byzantium.[4] It is reported that when the Muslims took Jerusalem, the Christian Patriarch of the city, Sophronius (d. 638 CE), insisted on surrendering only to the Caliph Umar. Upon hearing this, Umar came to the city and toured it with the Patriarch, and then oversaw the *'Uhda al-Umariyya* ("Covenant of Umar") that granted certain rights and freedoms (as well as limitations) to the Christians and their holy places in return for the payment of a tributary tax (*jizya*).

In many cases, houses of worship (i.e., churches) in Palestine were initially shared by Christians and Muslims. Tradition says that the Patriarch toured the Church of the Holy Sepulcher with Umar and invited him to offer his prayers there, but Umar declined for fear that the Muslims would convert the sacred church into a mosque. Instead, he prayed outside the church on the site where the Mosque of Umar (*Masjid Umar ibn al-Khattab*) now stands, although the current structure dates from the twelfth century CE. During his tour of the city, Umar also visited the Noble Sanctuary (or Temple Mount) and ordered the construction of a mosque (*Masjid al-Aqsa*) on the dilapidated site.

To the southeast of Jerusalem, the ancient city of Hebron was another major religious center as the site of the cave-tomb of the great prophet Abraham (*Ibrahim*), as well as the prophets Isaac (*Ishaq*) and Jacob (*Yacub*). Abraham is revered in Islam as the *khalil* ("friend") of *Allah*, the forefather of Moses, Jesus, and Muhammad, and the builder of the *Ka'aba* in Mecca along with his firstborn son, the prophet Ishmael (*Ismail*). Thus, Hebron is known as *al-Khalil* among the Muslims and the gate from Jerusalem that leads to Hebron is called *Bab al-Khalil* ("the Gate of the Friend").[5] For several centuries after the Muslim conquest, the majority of the population of Muslim-ruled Palestine remained Christian, and a large Palestinian Christian community remained until the middle of the twentieth century when many fled the Arab-Israeli wars to settle elsewhere, especially in the West where churches helped to facilitate resettlement.

Muawiyyah ibn Abu Sufyan (d. 680 CE), the first Umayyad Caliph, was crowned as Caliph in Jerusalem after the murder of the "Rightly Guided" Caliph, 'Ali ibn Abu Talib (d. 661 CE). The dynasty he began, the Umayyad Caliphs, developed the Noble Sanctuary (*al-Haram al-Sharif*) into the elaborate complex that we see today, although numerous renovations and reconstructions have occurred over the centuries. The existence of the early *al-Aqsa* mosque of Umar is verified by the account of a French Christian pilgrim, Arculf, dating from 670 CE.[6] But the Umayyad Caliphs 'Abd al-Malik ibn Marwan (d. 705 CE) and al-Walid I (d. 715 CE) expanded the complex to include the aforementioned Dome of the Rock, completed in 691 CE, and *Masjid al-Aqsa*, completed in 705 CE, which replaced the earlier wooden mosque of the Caliph Umar on the site. Scholars have speculated about the different intentions at play in the early Muslim focus on the Noble Sanctuary. One explanation, based on anti-Umayyad treatises penned under the Abbasid Caliphs, posits that the Umayyads intended to make the Noble Sanctuary a rival to Mecca as a site of Muslim pilgrimage, because Mecca was under the control of Ibn al-Zubayr (d. 692 CE), a rival of the Umayyads.[7] However, this explanation appears to be incorrect.[8]

After the Abbasids overthrew the Umayyads in 750 CE, several restorations of Muslim holy sites in Palestine occurred under the Caliphs al-Mansur (d. 775 CE) and al-Mahdi (d. 785 CE), including the restoration of *Masjid al-Aqsa* following a devastating earthquake. Under the Fatimid Caliph al-Aziz (d. 996 CE), the Ismaili (Sevener Shi'ite) Fatimid Caliphate of Cairo (*al-Qahirah*), a rival to the Abbasids, captured Palestine and the holy cities. The Fatimids were Ismaili Shi'ites and generally tolerant of Jews and Christians, who were plentiful in Cairo. However, the sixth Fatimid Caliph (as well as Imam), al-Hakim (d. 1021 CE), was notoriously cruel, and religious minorities suffered during his reign. Inexplicably, in 1009 CE he ordered the destruction of the Church of the Holy Sepulcher in Jerusalem. Aside from the fact that he was likely insane, scholars do not know why he destroyed the sacred church, and his Fatimid successors, the Caliphs 'Ali al-Zahir and al-Mustansir, rebuilt it.

During the late eleventh century, the Sunni Seljuk Turks moved into Palestine from the east and wrestled control from the Shi'ite Fatimids in the Holy Land. Around the year 1095 CE, the famous Sunni theologian, jurist, and mystic Abu Hamid al-Ghazali (d. 1111 CE) traveled west from his native Persia to Jerusalem. During his lengthy sojourn at a *madrasa* overlooking the precincts of the Noble Sanctuary, he wrote portions of his seminal Sunni treatise, *Ihya 'Ulum ud-Din* ("Revival of the Religious Sciences"), including the Ash'arite theological treatise *ar-Risalah al-Qudsiyyah* ("The Jerusalem Epistle").

In 1099 CE, only a year after the Fatimids regained control of Palestine from the Turks, the Crusaders captured Jerusalem and great slaughter and desecration of Muslim, Jewish, and eastern Christian ("heretic") holy sites ensued (see Chapter 9). At the time, the Muslim world was fragmented and rife with internal conflict, preventing the formation of any serious campaign to regain Palestine and the holy city until the Kurdish general Salah al-Din (Saladin) al-Ayyubi (d. 1193 CE) emerged and mobilized a Muslim force in the twelfth century.

In all, Jerusalem remained under the control of the Crusaders for eighty-eight years, during which time the Dome of the Rock and *al-Aqsa* Mosque were used by Christian military orders, especially the Knights Templar, as a church, palace, and even storage facility. The Christians introduced paintings, altars, a cross above the dome, an iron grill around the rock, and a covering slab over the rock when they converted the Dome of the Rock into a church dedicated to the Virgin Mary.[9] The Crusaders also seem to have strangely mistaken the *al-Aqsa* Mosque for the Temple of Solomon (destroyed by the Babylonians in 586 BCE), calling it *Palatium Salomonus.* Serious restoration and rebuilding efforts were undertaken by Salah al-Din and his Ayyubid successors to rectify the Crusaders' alterations and desecrations of Muslim holy sites after the city was regained.

After Jerusalem was retaken by the Muslims in 1187 CE, Palestine passed from the Ayyubids into the control of the Mamluk Sultans of Egypt and the last pockets of Crusaders along the coast were defeated by the late thirteenth century. The Mamluks showed great interest in architecture and constructed dozens of *madrasas*, tombs, mosques, and *zawiyas* (also known as *khanqahs* or *ribats*) in Jerusalem near the Noble Sanctuary and other sites.[10] In Hebron (*al-Khalil*), the Mamluks restored the *Ibrahimi* Mosque at the cave-tomb of the Patriarchs and constructed a wall at the entrance to the cave restricting access to the holy graves.

By the 1240s, the Mongol hordes (Tatars) had rampaged through Muslim Persia and Mesopotamia and reached northern Palestine. In 1260, under threat, a Mamluk army under Sultan Sayf ud-Din Qutuz (d. 1260 CE) and Baybars (d. 1277 CE) faced the Mongols in the famous battle of *'Ayn Jalut* in northern Palestine, just south of the town of Nazareth. The decisive victory of the Mamluks over the Mongols brought an end to the unchecked campaigns of the Mongol hordes eastward and spared Palestine, Arabia, Egypt, and North Africa from destruction. As the great Muslim scholar Ibn Khaldun (d. 1406 CE) would later write, the Mamluks "saved Islam."[11] Years later, fearing further Crusades from Europe, the Mamluks had all of the important ports on the Mediterranean coast of Palestine destroyed. This seriously damaged trade and commerce in the region for years and led to a decline in the population and cultural life of Palestine.

In 1517 CE, the Ottoman Turks expanded their powerful empire by defeating the Mamluks and incorporating Syria, Palestine, the Hijaz, and Egypt into their domain. The Ottoman Sultan, Selim the Grim (d. 1520 CE), feared that the Mamluks may form an alliance with their archrivals, the Shi'ite Safavids of Iran, and launched a preemptive strike that benefited from Mamluk treachery and desertions.[12] The Ottomans thereafter ruled over the holy cities until their defeat in World War I (see Chapter 11).

Incorporated into the complex Ottoman bureaucracy, Palestine experienced renewed life and development as a home to Muslims, Christians, and Jews. The seventeenth century travel account of Salim 'Abdallah al-Ayyashi (d. 1679 CE) relates his journey as a pilgrim from Mecca to Palestine beginning with his arrival in Gaza. Ayyashi described Gaza as a spacious city filled with groves, orchards, trees, houses, palaces, and a great Mamluk mosque in its center (*al-Masjid al-Kabir*), where prices were cheap and fruit was plentiful.[13] Ayyashi also described the existence of a tomb attributed to the Prophet Muhammad's grandfather, Qasim ibn 'Abdul-Muttalib, on the Gaza coast, and a shrine devoted to Imam Shafi'i, who was born in Gaza, but died in Cairo, Egypt.

Ayyashi then travelled to Asqalan (Ashkelon), where he prayed and read from the Qur'an at the mosque-tomb of Salman al-Farsi, and then visited al-Ramla where he listened to a religious lecture by a Shafi'ite jurist, toured a number of Sufi sites with a revered shaykh, including the White Mosque, and the tomb of one of the Prophet's companions, al-Fadl ibn Abbas.[14] From al-Ramla, Ayyashi traveled to Jerusalem where he toured the Noble Sanctuary. While there, he noted the large number of fellow Moroccan Muslims, Sufi ascetics or *faqirs*, the architectural glories of the Dome of the Rock, the wonderful olive and fig trees in its vicinity, and even visited a number of Christian shrines, especially those associated with Jesus and

Mary.[15] After a week in Jerusalem, Ayyashi traveled through Bethlehem to Hebron where he stayed for several days near the tomb of the prophets Abraham (*Ibrahim*), Isaac (*Ishaq*), Jacob (*Yacub*), and Joseph (*Yusuf*), and participated in *dhikrs* with Muslim mystics (i.e., Sufis).[16] From the seventeenth century onwards, Palestine remained a center of Muslim piety, pilgrimage, and devotion up to the modern period, when dramatic political developments pushed the region into turmoil and disrupted Palestinian Muslim, as well as Christian, life.

In the late nineteenth century, Theodore Herzl (d. 1904), an Austrian Jew and journalist, observed the Dreyfus Affair in Paris, France, and concluded that Jews would never enjoy freedom and security until they had a state of their own. The political ideology that Herzl articulated called for the creation of a Jewish nation-state as a homeland for all Jews (as one nation) and came to be known as Zionism. Although several different locations were proposed for the creation of this new Jewish nation-state, including Argentina and Uganda, the land that was ultimately chosen by the Zionists was Ottoman Palestine, the Biblical "Promised Land." In 1880, nearly 75 percent of the global Jewish population was living in Eastern and Southern Europe, but a resurgence of European anti-Semitism (e.g., the Russian pogroms from 1881–1882) shook the optimistic attitude that many Jews had for the new secular modern age.

The first wave (*aliyah*) of Jewish migration to Palestine consisted mostly of "cultural Zionists" who were secular-leftist Russian and Polish Jews intent on living in cooperation with the indigenous Palestinian Arabs.[17] But the political Zionists, like Herzl and the First Zionist Congress, had far greater aspirations. Europe, at the time, saw the Middle East, Africa, and Asia as lands to be conquered and "civilized," and political Zionism reflected those imperial attitudes.[18]

The second and third waves of immigrants (1904–1923) were explicitly interested in establishing a distinctly Jewish state in Palestine rather than living among the existing Arab communities, and many of Israel's first leaders (e.g., David Ben Gurion) emerged from this group.[19] The outbreak of World War I in 1914 resulted in the loss of Ottoman Palestine to the British Empire, which established it as a British Mandate.

Between 1924 and 1939, Jewish immigration, mainly from Central Europe, increased to an average of 16,000 people per year, peaking between 1931 and 1935 as Nazism grew in Germany, and the influx triggered violent Arab riots in Palestine from 1936 to 1939.[20] In 1931, the Jewish population of Palestine was 17 percent of the overall population, but by 1939 it had risen dramatically to 31 percent.[21] The majority of the Jewish immigrants settled in Jerusalem, Jaffa, Haifa, and al-Ramla, where they established separate Jewish social and cultural institutions with financial support from overseas.[22]

Relations between the new Jewish settlers and the British authorities were also strained, despite explicit British support for the creation of a Jewish state in Palestine. In November of 1917, the Balfour Declaration had declared Britain's support for the "establishment in Palestine of a national home for the Jewish people," despite the fact that 90 percent of the population of Palestine at the time was Arab (Muslim and Christian).[23] For the Arabs, political Zionism and its substantial European and American support amounted to little more than colonial occupation.

The *Nakba* Master Narrative and the Loss of Palestine

In the Arab world, May 15, 1948, is commemorated and lamented as *Yawm al-Nakba,* the "Day of the Catastrophe." For Israeli Jews, however, the day prior is a time of celebration, known as Independence Day. In the 1940s, European plans to partition the British Mandate of Palestine were proposed as a possible solution to rival Jewish and Arab aspirations for national self-determination. Some Palestinians, including the Mufti of Jerusalem, pledged their support for Nazi Germany during World War II in hopes that a German victory would result in an Arab state free of British overlords and Jewish settlers. Still others pursued international channels and political deals to find a solution, but yielded little success. Tensions accelerated as Britain was weakened by the war and withdrew from most of its colonial holdings (e.g., India). War between Zionist and Arab forces in Palestine simmered on the horizon.

World War II resulted in the creation of the United Nations (UN) in place of the failed League of Nations. The UN was backed by, and based within, the United States, which was a leading political and financial supporter of political Zionism. As the atrocities of the Nazi genocide against the Jews of Europe came to light, world sympathy fell to the Jews. The momentum of world opinion favored Zionist aspirations in Palestine when the UN Partition plan was approved by a vote of 33 to 13 (ten abstentions) in November 1947. The approved plan gave the Jewish state 75 percent of Palestine, including the fertile coastal region, but at the time Jews represented only about 33 percent of the population and owned 7 percent of the land.[24] The Palestinian Arabs rejected the partition plan.

When violent clashes broke out between Jews and Arabs after the British ended the Mandate, the Zionist forces, namely, the Haganah (including the Palmach), Irgun, and the Stern Gang (Lehi), benefited from European weaponry and resources, mostly obtained illicitly.[25] The Zionists began to implement a campaign known as Plan D (*Dalet*) to deal with the presence of hundreds of thousands of Palestinian Arabs inhabiting the land that the Jewish nationalists sought for their nation-state (i.e., the state of Israel).[26] Orders consisted of large-scale intimidation of Arabs, laying siege to and bombarding villages and population centers (e.g., Deir Yassin); setting fire to homes, properties, and goods; expelling residents; demolishing homes; and planting mines in the rubble to prevent expelled Arab inhabitants from returning.[27]

The UN Partition of Palestine (Resolution 181) was universally rejected by the Arab states in the region, and the Zionist declaration of statehood on May 14, 1948, sparked all-out war. The neighboring states, specifically Egypt and the young nation-states of Iraq, Jordan, Syria, Saudi Arabia, and Lebanon declared war on Israel. The initial expectation was that the combined Arab states would crush the nascent Jewish state. But the entrenched, well organized and well equipped Zionist forces proved to be far more resilient and capable than the combined, yet inferior and disorganized, Arab forces. In the case of Jordan, King 'Abdullah (d. 1951) even negotiated a tacit agreement with the Zionist leadership to divide Palestine between them.[28]

By the end of combat in 1949, the war resulted in the deaths of approximately 6,000 Israelis and approximately 15,000 Arabs. In the process, the victorious Israelis succeeded in annexing even more territory than the UN partition had originally granted them. Israeli control of the land expanded to 77 percent of Palestine, which became the state of Israel. The Palestinian Arabs were left with the remaining 23 percent. This territory consisted of the West Bank (governed by Jordan) and Gaza Strip (governed by Egypt).

By the end of the Arab-Israeli War (1948–1949), 750,000 Palestinian Arabs, or half of Palestine's indigenous Arab population, were refugees, 531 villages were destroyed, and 11 urban Arab neighborhoods had been purged of their residents.[29] "The most outstanding incident, which shocked the world and accelerated the panicked flight of the Arab inhabitants, was the massacre of over 250 [Arab] men, women, and children in the village of Deir Yassin [on the road to Jerusalem] on April 9, 1948."[30] Israeli Prime Minister Menachim Begin (d. 1992), the leader of the Irgun attack on Deir Yassin, later stated: "The massacre was not only justified, but there would not have been a state of Israel without the victory at Deir Yassin."[31]

The loss of Palestinian homes and villages is powerfully reflected in the keys to the homes and shops that Arab refugees carried with them into exile. When the Palestinians fled or left their villages, the houses, buildings (including mosques and churches), property, and agricultural lands (e.g., orchards, olive groves) they left behind were claimed by Zionist forces and newly arrived Jewish immigrants. Thus, the rusty keys that Palestinian families, especially elders, still carry with them and display to others are reminders of the unjust loss of their homes and lands, as well as their historic claims to them. In fact, the symbol of the key has grown to be a part of Palestinian national identity, so much so that decorative keys now exist made of plastic or wood, sometimes reading "*al-Nakba* May 15, 1948" in Arabic along the side. The key has even evolved into the form of a giant float parading down the streets of the West Bank on the anniversary of the *Nakba*.

The Setback of the Six-Day War

Although the term *"al-Nakba"* refers specifically to the events of 1948, the story of Palestine's loss is incomplete without the subsequent story of the debacle of the Six-Day War of 1967. As mentioned previously, the Arab-Israeli War concluded in 1949 with the West Bank (including East Jerusalem) and Gaza Strip under the control of Jordan and Egypt, respectively. But the "setback," or *al-naksa*, of the Six-Day War ended with Israel expanding its territory even further to occupy both the West Bank and Gaza Strip, as well as other territories (e.g., Sinai), thus completing Israeli control over the entirety of Palestine. Under international law, it is illegal to annex territory occupied in war, so these lands came to be known as the "Occupied Territories," being neither a Palestinian state nor an official part of Israel (despite settlement activity).

Most notably from an Islamic perspective, the loss of the West Bank to Israel meant the loss of East Jerusalem, which includes the "Old City" housing the Noble Sanctuary. For many Muslims, the idea of Islam's third holiest site falling under the control of non-Muslims (i.e., Jews) was unthinkable. This situation has only further been exacerbated by extremist Jewish (and Christian) groups (e.g., Gush Emunim) that hope to see the destruction of the Islamic holy site so that a new Jewish temple to Yahweh can be constructed in its place.

The Six-Day War represented the climactic battle between Arab nationalism and Jewish nationalism (i.e., Zionism) in the Middle East. When Arab nationalism was crushed in a humiliating fashion by Israel, Islamism stepped in to fill the void left behind. The hero (perhaps demigod) of Arab nationalism was Egypt's Gamal Abdel-Nasser (d. 1970). No one else in the Arab world inspired and commanded the devotion of the Arab peoples like the charismatic military officer Nasser. He was a revolutionary and espoused a Pan-Arab brand of socialism that railed against imperial exploitation of the developing world at the hands of the great world powers of the day. Nasser even met with the American Muslim leader and black nationalist, Malcolm X (d. 1965), who named one of his daughters after Nasser, during

Malcolm's travels to Cairo in the 1960s. According to Nasser's 1959 tract, *The Philosophy of the Revolution,* he stood for the liberation of all Arabs and Afro-Asian states colonized or dominated by the Western powers, with Egypt playing a key role as the nexus between the Arab, African, and Islamic world.[32] Nasser's ideology had definite Marxist influences, but it denied the class struggle, retained private ownership of property and land (under strict limits), and rejected atheism by maintaining Islam as the religion of the state.[33] However, he also imposed state control over Egypt's *ulama* (religious scholars) and mosques, most notably the great mosque-*madrasa* of al-Azhar, in order to reinforce the powers of the state and silence potentially powerful voices of dissent.[34]

In the days leading up to the war, Nasser received Syrian and Soviet intelligence reports that Israel was planning a major attack against Syria.[35] Egypt and Syria had united as a single country, the United Arab Republic, under Nasser from 1958 to 1961, but Syria seceded. By 1967, Nasser's position as the leader of the Arab world was being challenged by Saudi Arabia's King Faisal, who aggressively opposed Nasser's socialist ideology, and an Israeli attack on Syria would have been disastrous for him. Nasser ordered UN forces out of the Sinai and mobilized Egyptian troops along the border (much of Egypt's army was fighting in Yemen), restricted Israeli ship movement in the Gulf of Aqaba, and amplified his public rhetoric against Israel.[36] Yet, as Yitzhak Rabin, Menachim Begin, and Lyndon Johnson went on to admit, Nasser had no intention of launching an attack on Israel and drawing Egypt into another war.[37] Nevertheless, Egypt's upsurge of activity and particularly its closure of the Strait of Tiran were seized upon by Israel's leadership as a justification for military action and further territorial state expansion.

In June 5, 1967, Israel launched a "preemptive" strike against Egypt, and engaged Syria and Jordan. By June 6, Egypt's entire air force had been destroyed by Israeli air raids before any of its planes could leave the ground. Four days later on June 10, the war was over. Israel had soundly defeated the Arab states, killing between 25,000 and 30,000 Arabs and inflicting massive damage on their military facilities and property that set back economic development for years.[38] Israel's territory now included the entire Sinai peninsula and Gaza Strip from Egypt, the West Bank (including East Jerusalem) from Jordan, and the Golan Heights from Syria. We should note that 34 American seamen were also killed and 164 wounded in the Six-Day War when the U.S. intelligence ship the *USS Liberty* was attacked by Israeli aircraft and gunboats in international waters.[39] The incident was officially declared a mistake, but remains steeped in controversy.

The humiliating defeat of the Arab states in the Six-Day War was so devastating that Nasser offered to resign from office. The promises of secular Arab nationalism were dashed and the loss of Arab life and lands to the small Jewish state proved traumatic. During the war, the Arab media had disseminated propaganda reporting Arab victories and the march toward Jerusalem. This made the defeat, just days in the making, all the more shocking to the Arab street.

The Islamists stepped forward at this moment offering a powerful explanation. They contended that the 1967 defeat was *Allah*'s punishment for the Arabs because they had abandoned Islam in favor of infidel ethnonationalist ideologies, like Nasserism. As Ayman al-Zawahiri would later state: "The direct influence of the 1967 defeat was that a large number of people, especially youths, returned to their original identity: that of members of an Islamic civilization."[40]

The *Nakba* Master Narrative in Extremist Discourse

The centrality of the conflict over Palestine in Islamist discourse cannot be overstated. In his militant treatise, *The Defense of Muslim Lands*, 'Abdullah Azzam (d. 1989) expressed this point by writing: "Palestine is the foremost Islamic problem. It is the heart of the Islamic world, and it is a blessed land."[41]

The *Nakba* master narrative is invoked as a default grievance by Islamist extremists when another context or relevant master narrative is not immediately apparent. This was the case when Usama Bin Laden framed the failed 2009 Christmas day "martyrdom-operation" of the Nigerian "underwear bomber," Umar Farouk 'Abdulmutallab, as an act of retaliation for the loss of Palestine. Bin Laden stated: "The United States will not dream of enjoying safety until we live it in reality in Palestine . . . God willing our attacks will continue as long as you support the Israelis."[42] Likewise, Ayman al-Zawahiri has consistently justified attacks on the United States by invoking the *Nakba* master narrative. In his treatise, *The Exoneration*, al-Zawahiri wrote:

> The United States also dispersed the Palestinians and settled the brothers of apes and pigs in their place in Palestine. It has supported the criminal Jewish state with money, weapons, and expertise. How could America perpetrate these actions and not be viewed as the Islamic nations' enemy that fights against them?[43]

But for other extremist groups, such as Hamas or Hezbollah, the master narrative has a far more direct connection. Indeed, the *Nakba* master narrative is a part of their origin stories. Historically, these groups exist as part of a reactionary Islamist "resistance" movement to Israel in the wake of the military and diplomatic failures of Arab governments and other international agencies (e.g., UN) to find a just resolution to the conflict. The same can be said of nationalist guerrilla groups, such as the Palestinian Liberation Organization (PLO).

The "Islamic Resistance Movement" (*Harakat al-Muqawama al-Islamiyyah*), better known as Hamas, published its ideological charter "The Islamic Covenant" from its headquarters in Gaza in August of 1988.[44] The covenant challenged Israel and Yasser Arafat's PLO and declared Hamas to be the sole legitimate representative of the Palestinian people.[45] Originating out of a local Gaza branch of the Egyptian Muslim Brotherhood, Hamas Islamists seek the creation of an Islamic state in Palestine and the removal of the "Zionist entity" (i.e., Israel) that occupies it. The 1988 charter states:

> The Islamic Resistance Movement [Hamas] believes that the land of Palestine has been an Islamic *waqf* throughout the generations and until the Day of Resurrection, no one can renounce it or part of it, or abandon it or part of it. No Arab country nor the aggregate of all Arab countries, and no Arab King or President nor all of them in the aggregate, have that right, nor has that right any organization or the aggregate of all organizations, be they Palestinian or Arab, because Palestine is an Islamic *waqf* throughout all generations and to the Day of Resurrection.[46]

The cofounder and spiritual leader of Hamas was Shaykh Ahmed Isma'il Yassin, a quadriplegic who was assassinated by an Israeli helicopter gunship in 2004. In 1991, the military wing of Hamas, called the Izzedine al-Qassam Brigades, was established and quickly began a campaign to kidnap and execute suspected Palestinian collaborators with Israel.[47] By 1993, Yassin's group initiated a campaign of "martyrdom operations," sending Muslim fighters to blow themselves up as suicide-bombers against Israeli military and civilian targets. Suicide is forbidden in Islam, but Yassin and other Hamas leaders defended the tactic by characterizing the conflict with Israel as a defensive struggle against a powerful aggressor that has wrongfully occupied Muslim sacred land and persecuted its people. Despite Hamas' identity as a distinctly "Islamic" organization, its leaders and defenders repeatedly invoked the plight of the Palestinian people in terms of the *Nakba* master narrative, rather than exclusively relying on Islam's sacred texts to convey and qualify a defense of the controversial military tactic.

Analysis of the *Nakba* Master Narrative

The *Nakba* master narrative features a deliverance story form wherein a people of the land, the Palestinians, struggle to escape the clutches of an archetypal colonizer, in this case "the Zionists." The European origins of many Israelis and their migration to Palestine during the time of the hated British Mandate certainly facilitated the conflation of the Zionist with the archetypal crusader in Islamist accounts of the Arab-Israeli conflict. Indeed, the hyphenated term "Zionist-Crusader" is common in Islamist extremist rhetoric. Framed in this way, the events of 1948 are understood as a catastrophe (*nakba*) through which the correct order of the world was inverted in favor of a seemingly weak and foreign people, the Jews, who were so few in number compared to the Arab and Muslim nations. The corrupt, even defiled, world left in the wake of the Zionist occupation and ongoing colonization must be overturned. As such, the desire of the master narrative can only be satisfied through a militant struggle (jihad) that leads to the restoration of Palestine in its prior condition as a Muslim land of imagined tranquility and piety for all time.

The deliverance story form of the *Nakba* master narrative took on renewed significance when the Arab nations led by Egypt's Gamal Abdel-Nasser were soundly defeated in 1967, failing to satisfy the desire of the narrative. The *naksa* or "setback" of the Six-Day War discredited the nationalists in their efforts to resolve the conflict. In the aftermath of the 1967 defeat, the Islamists took renewed ownership over the *Nakba* master narrative, arguing that only an army of Muslim believers could achieve victory against the "Zionist occupiers." Thus, the *Nakba* master narrative not only reminds audiences of the loss of Palestine, but the ongoing failure of Arab and Muslim nationalist governments to reclaim it.

CHAPTER 13

Seventy-Two Virgins

The emergence of Muslim suicide-bombers in the final decades of the twentieth century transformed otherwise obscure Islamic traditions (*ahadith*) into a topic of sensational public interest, as well as ridicule. According to these traditions, Muslim men that die waging jihad against the enemies of Islam will be rewarded by *Allah* in heaven (*jannah*) as martyrs (*shuhada*) and receive seventy-two virgins to enjoy in blissful ecstasy. This notion seems to be particularly attractive to young males who live in otherwise sexually repressive societies (e.g., Saudi Arabia, Afghanistan), perhaps due to stifling economic limitations, and are yet to marry.

But perpetrators of "martyrdom operations" have hardly come exclusively from this segment of Muslim societies. Indeed, even women have acted as suicide-bombers, such as the revenge-driven "Black Widows" of Chechnya. The connection, therefore, between the seventy-two virgins traditions and the complex phenomenon of suicide-bombings in the Muslim world is limited and hardly causal in nature.

At its core, the seventy-two virgins master narrative expresses a desire to escape a world of suffering for one of blissful joy, personified by the dark-eyed maidens of Islamic tradition. However, reaching this blissful world in heaven and escaping the earthly world of struggle and suffering is not an easy journey. It requires remarkable steadfastness and devotion. Islam, after all, requires attention to the meticulous details of ritual and law. Simply believing is not enough (according to most scholars). But, according to the seventy-two virgins master narrative and other traditions expressing similar redemptive notions, martyrdom in the cause of Islam can give a person instant access to that blissful world and wash away all of one's inequities and sins. Thus, the journey can be a very easy one if the believer dies on the path of *Allah* (*fi sabil Allah*). The notion of instant salvation through martyrdom is not unique to Islam either. Indeed, the idea was likely appropriated from existing Jewish and Christian sacred texts and martyrologies, as well as other regional traditions, during the advent and expansion of the nascent Islamic community.

The concept of the afterlife reveals much about the function of religion. One need not focus on martyrdom to see the many peculiar promises made to those who live and die in devotion and obedience to their religious traditions. Theorists of religion have long examined this curious component of religion, particularly among the Abrahamic religions. Karl Marx (d. 1883), as most in the Western world know, saw religion as "the sigh of the oppressed" and the "opium" of the masses. Heaven, in his view, was an illusory promise of an imaginary future designed to control the masses through ruling institutions and encourage them to accept their difficult lot in life. But such explanations do not adequately address "religions of revolution" that motivate the masses to overturn the status quo and fight against dominant sociopolitical institutions.[1]

The famous psychologist Sigmund Freud (d. 1939) conceived of religious ideas as "illusions, fulfillments of the oldest, strongest and most urgent wishes of mankind" and stated that "the prolongation of earthly existence in a future life provides the local and temporal framework in which these wish-fulfillments shall take place."[2] Wish fulfillment may well be a piece of the puzzle, but, as with Marx, it is hardly the whole picture. Indeed, some religions do not even seek entrance into a blissful afterlife at all. Regardless, Marx and Freud both alluded to an important underlying function of religious ideas about the afterlife, which is that these afterlife concepts and narratives valorize human suffering and self-sacrifice.

Historical Origins of Heaven

The ancient Egyptians envisioned an elaborate afterlife that closely resembled life on earth. The afterlife was generally understood in physical terms and required the preservation of the body (through embalming and mummification), as well as attention to all its needs, such as food and drink. This is still evident in the elaborate tombs uncovered in Egypt in modern times, most notably those of Pharaohs such as Tutankhamen (d. 1323 BCE).

The rulers of Egypt had monumental burial structures built with numerous storerooms to accommodate furnishings and supplies, including huge quantities of food in ceramic jars, luxurious stoneware dishes, tools, household furniture, and game boards.[3] After death, Egyptians believed that the dead faced judgment before a tribunal led by Osiris, god of the underworld, and their hearts were weighed on a scale to determine whether they would enjoy eternal life among the gods or the "second death" of the damned. The hearts of the wicked, we are told, would be thrown into the mouth of a demonic monster known as *Amemet* ("Swallower") or *Am-mut* ("Swallower of the Damned") and devoured.[4] The righteous, however, will follow the heavenly trek of Re, the sun god, through the Field of Offerings each day, and then reunite with their mummified bodies each night as Re enters the underworld to be reborn the next day (at sunrise). As the *Book of the Dead* reports, the righteous will enter the lush green lands and waterways of the Field of Offerings (or Field of Rushes), "being a blessed one there, plowing and harvesting there, eating and drinking there, making love there, and doing everything that one was used to do on earth."[5]

Prior to the Hellenic period, Judaism did not articulate a belief in heaven or hell. The Jewish concept of an afterlife was limited to *sheol*, a dark abyss-like underworld, where everyone (sinner and saint) dwelled in misery after death. This idea, which was so different from that espoused by the Egyptians, may well have originated in Mesopotamian religion.[6] Any rewards for devotion and obedience to Yahweh's commandments were to be enjoyed in this life (e.g., fertile crops, offspring, victory in war). Actions or beliefs had no impact on existence after death in *sheol*. The Hebrew Bible even states that Yahweh is completely absent from *sheol*. For instance, Psalm 88 asks:

> My couch is among the dead with the slain who lie in the grave. You remember them no more; they are cut off from your care. . . . Is your love proclaimed in the grave, your fidelity in the tomb? Are your marvels declared in the darkness, your righteous deeds in the land of oblivion?[7]

The absence of Yahweh made death all the more tragic and lamentable. However, by the second century BCE, Antiochus Epiphanes (d. 164 BCE), the Greek emperor of the Seleucid Empire, ruled over the Jews and new religious ideas soon followed.

As recorded in the Hebrew Bible, 1 Maccabees, Antiochus besieged Palestine and the city of Jerusalem, slaughtered thousands, and outlawed the traditions and rites of the Jews in favor of the worship of Zeus, the Greek supreme god. Greek persecution of Judaism ultimately prompted the Maccabean revolt (167–160 BCE) and the formulation of new concepts of the afterlife that provided persecuted Jews solace for the suffering and death of the time.

The miseries of *sheol* hardly motivated martyrdom for the religion of Yahweh, but resurrection in a future life of blissful happiness certainly did. As a Jewish mother, witnessing the persecution of her sons, proclaims in 2 Maccabees (7:23): "Therefore, since it is the Creator of the universe who shapes each man's beginning, as He brings about the origin of everything, He, in His mercy, will give you back both breath and life, because you now disregard yourselves for the sake of the law [i.e., Torah]." Thus, out of persecution and martyrdom at the hands of the Greeks emerged the belief in the resurrection of the dead, eternal life in heaven, and the punishment of the wicked in hell, among the Jews. As the Book of Daniel, written during the persecution of the second century BCE, relates: "Many of those who sleep in the dust of the earth shall awake; some shall live forever, others shall be an everlasting horror and disgrace."[8]

By the time of Roman rule, Palestine was home to numerous Jewish sects, including the Pharisees and the Sadducees. The experience of the Jews during the Babylonian Exile profoundly shaped the Pharisees. Historically, they were the precursors to Rabbinic Judaism and their devotional life revolved around the synagogue, the rabbis, and the study of Torah. The Pharisees also professed an elaborate belief in the resurrection of the body and its continued existence in heaven or hell. The Sadducees, on the other hand, maintained the old Jewish temple rites revolving around animal sacrifice and denied the resurrection of the body. Scholars have argued that the Pharisees incorporated beliefs and ideas into Judaism during the Exile, specifically from Zoroastrianism, which already possessed elaborate concepts of the resurrection, heaven, and hell.[9] Indeed, the Persian word *pairidaeza* (*firdaws* in Arabic), meaning "enclosed garden," is the basis for the word paradise.

The Zoroastrians of Persia, like the "Messiah" Cyrus the Great (see Chapter 8), believed in the existence of a bridge, known as the *Chinvat* bridge, that the souls of the dead cross to face judgment for their deeds in life, which are weighed on a scale. If a person is righteous, they will cross the bridge easily and enter into heaven at the hand of a beautiful maiden. But if a person is wicked, the bridge will become narrow and his wicked deeds will assume the form of demonic hag that pulls him from the bridge into an infernal fiery hell to be horrifically tortured for thousands of years.[10] Both heaven and hell are described in Zoroastrian texts in bodily terms, including the types of food eaten and other physical delights. Then, when the Day of Judgment arrives, the earth will be purged of all evil to bring about a new world and the souls of the dead will be reunited with their resurrected physical bodies for eternity. These "future bodies" will be pure and flawless, because they were resurrected after Ahura Mazda's final dispensation and live forever in the new creation.[11]

As it developed in the first century CE, Christianity thoroughly reflected the amalgamation of religious ideas that resulted out of the cross-cultural interaction of the time, namely, between Greek, Persian, and Jewish thought. Prior to Christianity, the pagan Greeks believed in an invisible, immaterial, and immortal soul (*psyche* in Greek), which contrasted with the corruptible flesh of the physical body.[12] Greek philosophers, such as Plato

(d. 347 BCE) and Pythagoras (d. 495 BCE), furthermore posited a connection between people's actions and their existence after death: good deeds result in bliss and wicked deeds result in punitive suffering.[13] The pagan concept of Hades, the Greek underworld named after its ruling deity, included a paradise for the righteous (especially heroic warriors) known as the Elysian Fields, a neutral intermediate realm, and a deep abyss of terrible punishment for the wicked, called Tartarus.

When the writings of the New Testament later took shape in Greek in the first century CE, they reflected the Jewish (Pharisaic) belief in the resurrection of the body and the different Greek realms of the next world infused with Persian elements (e.g., fires of punishment). For example, the Second Letter of Peter (2 Peter 2:4) uses the term Tartarus for hell, stating: "God did not spare the angels when they sinned, but condemned them to the chains of Tartarus and handed them over to be kept for judgment." In most cases, the New Testament refers to hell as *Gehennom*, meaning the Valley of Hinnom. This refers to an actual geographic location, a ravine outside of Jerusalem, where human sacrifices once took place before it was used as a dump by the Jews where garbage was continuously burned.[14] As the Gospel of Matthew states: "And if your eye causes you to sin, tear it out and throw it away; for it is better for you to live with one eye than with two eyes to be thrown into fiery *Gehennom*."[15]

The Christian understanding of heaven is most closely associated with the "Kingdom of Heaven," which the earliest Christians believed would arrive imminently on earth. When the Day of Judgment arrives with the return of Christ, the resurrection of the dead will occur and the final dispensation will cast people into either the paradise of the "kingdom" or the fires of hell. The Gospel of Matthew states:

> Just as weeds are collected and burned up with fire, so will it be at the end of the age. The Son of Man [i.e., Messiah] will send his angels, and they will collect out of his kingdom all who cause others to sin and all evildoers. They will throw them into the fiery furnace, where they will be wailing and grinding of teeth. Then the righteous will shine like the sun in the kingdom of their Father.[16]

The Gospel of John further suggests that heaven will include dwelling places for the righteous (14:2), stating: "[Jesus said:] In my Father's house there are many dwelling places. If there were not, would I have told you that I am going to prepare a place for you?"

This notion is affirmed in the Book of Revelation, which describes the descent of the new Jerusalem to earth with massive walls made of jasper, twelve gates of pearl, a sparkling flowing river with fruit-bearing trees on each side, and streets and dwellings of gold built on foundations of jasper, sapphire, chalcedony, emerald, sardonyx, carnelian, chrysolite, beryl, topaz, chrysoprase, hyacinth, and amethyst (see Rev. 21:9–21, 22:1–2). The Book of Revelation also relates that Christian martyrs will be the first people resurrected by Christ and they will reign by his side, stating:

> The souls of those who had been beheaded for their witness to Jesus and for the word of God, and who had not worshipped the beast or its image nor had accepted its mark on their foreheads or hands. They came to life and they reigned with Christ for a thousand years.[17]

The importance of martyrdom in Christianity was obvious from the very start. The Christian Messiah, the divine incarnation of Yahweh on earth, died, executed at the hands of the Roman Empire on the cross in brutal fashion. The central ritual of subsequent Christian worship, the Eucharist, commemorates this horrific event through the ceremonial ingestion of his martyred body and blood in the form of bread and wine, which literally becomes the blood and flesh of Christ during the ritual for the majority of the world's Christians (i.e., the doctrine of transubstantiation).

The early Christians, as related in the Acts of the Apostles, suffered martyrdom at the hands of the Jews and Romans for their beliefs. When Christianity rose to political power in the fourth century CE, Christian notions of martyrdom were reformulated for the soldiers of Christ on the march, righteously fighting against satanic pagans, infidels, and heretics.

The pagan Arabs during the time of *jahiliyyah* (see Chapter 3) did not believe in an afterlife or the resurrection of the body. The Arabs believed death was the end of human existence, and the gods and spirits of this world benefited human beings only in this life. Thus, when Muhammad began to preach to the Arabs of Mecca and the surrounding region about the essentially Judeo-Christian concept of the Day of Judgment and eternal life in heaven (*jannah*) or punishment in hell (*gehennom*), they scoffed and ridiculed what they considered to be a preposterous notion. Not only did Muhammad have to defend these beliefs against pagan criticism, but the concepts had to be tailored to appeal specifically to his desert-dwelling Arab audience.

The Delights of Heaven in the Qur'an

The Qur'an places great emphasis on the Day of Judgment (*Yawm al-Qiyamah*, *Yawm id-Din*, or *Yawm al-Akhira*), when the deeds of every person will be weighed on the scales, and the physical resurrection of the body will occur.

It relates countless verses describing the great rewards that await the righteous and the terrible fiery punishment that awaits the wicked in the afterlife.

The vivid Qur'anic imagery of the afterlife (heaven and hell) was expanded greatly by later Muslim traditions in the Hadith, textual commentaries (*tafasir*), and other popular religious literature, as well as the visual arts, over the centuries. Muslim understandings of these materials vary widely and range from literal to completely symbolic mystical readings. Adding to the interpretive debate, one commonly cited verse from Qur'an states: "For no soul knows what delights of the eye are hidden from them as a reward for what they have done."[18]

In the early Meccan *surahs* of the Qur'an, directed toward the pagan Arabs of Mecca that denied the existence of an afterlife, the concept of heaven or *jannah* ("garden") is described as a place where all wishes are fulfilled and lush green gardens, flowing streams of cool delicious water, grand thrones and cushions, ripe fruits and fowl, wine that does not intoxicate, and banquets with jeweled chalices are enjoyed by the righteous. In one such verse, the Qur'an states: "In a garden on high, they [i.e., the righteous] will hear no temptations; in it is a bubbling spring; in it are thrones raised high and chalices set out and cushions laid out in rows and carpets spread forth."[19]

The Meccan *surahs* also refer to the companionship of the *hur al-'ayn* (Houris), which have traditionally been identified as chaste heavenly maidens.[20] The literal meaning of the phrase *hur al-'ayn* refers to the contrast of the white of the eye with the blackness of the pupil, typically in reference to the large eye of the gazelle or the oryx.[21] The traditional Muslim interpretation of the phrase from the Qur'an is therefore understood in terms of the dark eyes of chaste heavenly maidens, although a small number of contemporary scholars, such as "Christoph Luxenberg" (*Die syro-aramäische Lesart des Koran*), have suggested alternative meanings on the basis of controversial linguistic analysis of the oldest existent Qur'anic manuscripts.

The later *surahs* of the Qur'an from the Medinan period (622–632 CE) generally depict paradise in a similar, but less worldly fashion, emphasizing *jannah* as the eternal abode of sustenance and peace where the pain of the world is forgotten, and families, including husbands and wives, are reunited, but the *hur al-'ayn* are no longer mentioned.[22] This is an interesting fact given that *Allah*'s permission for the Muslims to fight in war, and therefore the concept of battlefield martyrs (*shuhada*), came only during this period, yet the Medinan *surahs* do not refer to the *hur al-'ayn*. The term is exclusively Meccan, and even then it was used only sparingly. Nevertheless, references to righteous companions or spouses in the Medinan *surahs* are traditionally conflated with the *hur*, despite the explicit absence of the term, and this conflation is supported by later traditions.

The Hadith literature, recorded and compiled some two hundred years after the time of Muhammad, offers numerous new elements to Islam's vision of the afterlife, such as the eight gates of heaven, a special street that bestows beauty and fragrance on those who walk on it, a giant tree with seemingly infinite shade, giant tents made of pearl, and further elaborate details regarding the *hur* as the maidens of paradise.[23]

The specific tradition about the seventy-two virgins is surprisingly difficult to uncover in Islam's sacred texts. One such tradition is found in *Sunan al-Tirmidhi*, regarded as one of the six canonical collections of Hadith in Sunni Islam, compiled by the scholar Abu 'Issa al-Tirmidhi (d. 892 CE). The collection of al-Tirmidhi is ranked as the fourth most authoritative Hadith collection of the six, but is less commonly studied than other collections of Hadith (e.g., *Bukhari* or *Muslim*). The foremost authoritative collection of Hadith, *Sahih Bukhari*, as well as the second (*Sahih Muslim*) and third (*Sunan Abu Dawud*), do not contain the seventy-two virgins tradition, adding to its relative obscurity among Muslims prior to its popularity among contemporary extremists and among Western media outlets.

It is also interesting to note that the seventy-two virgins tradition related in *Sunan al-Tirmidhi* is classified as *gharib*, meaning "strange," "obscure," or even "weak," by the majority of Sunni scholars. This tradition, attributed to the Prophet Muhammad, reportedly states: "The smallest reward for the people of heaven is an abode where there are 80,000 servants and 72 wives, over which stands a dome decorated with pearls, aquamarine and ruby, as wide as the distance from al-Jabiyyah [a village in Damascus] to Sana'a [capital city of Yemen]."[24] This tradition is cited by the popular Athari-Hanbalite scholar and student of Ahmed ibn Taymiyyah (d. 1328 CE), Ibn Kathir, in his *tafsir* (exegesis) of the Qur'an. The reader will also note that the tradition does not refer to martyrs, but to the "people of heaven," which makes its usage by extremists even more tenuous.

To find an explicit connection between the seventy-two virgins tradition and Muslim martyrs, we must look outside of the six canonical collections of Sunni Islam to the more dubious *Musnad* of Ahmed Ibn Hanbal (d. 855 CE), the eponym of the Hanbalite *maddhab* (school of law) and a revered scholar among the Salafis and Wahhabites. The Wahhabite sect, dominant in Saudi Arabia, claims to practice *ijtihad*, but historically it is an offshoot of the Hanbalite school and affords great value to its texts. The *Musnad* tradition relates:

> The Messenger of *Allah*, peace and blessings be upon him, said: Verily *Allah* the Almighty will bestow upon the martyr (*al-shahid*) . . . a dignified crown of rubies better than anything in the world upon his head and the martyr

will be married to seventy-two maidens of paradise (*hur al-'ayn*) and intercede on behalf of seventy of his family members.[25]

There it is. Now that we have an explicit connection between the seventy-two virgins master narrative, explicitly using the term *hur al-'ayn*, and martyrdom, we will turn to the subject of martyrdom in Islam for further analysis.

The Qur'an states in the Medinan *surah*, *al-Imran*: "And if you are killed on the path of *Allah*, or you die, then forgiveness and mercy from *Allah* are greater than what they could possibly gather."[26] Such verses, along with a wealth of material found in the Hadith, directly inform Muslim conceptions of martyrdom. Islam, like its historical predecessors Judaism and Christianity, honors its martyrs with a special enthusiasm, as Muslims experienced the same type of persecution in Islam's early years that previously engendered martyrdom concepts among Jews and Christians.[27]

However, the concept of a martyr or *shahid* (literally "witness") in Islam, as expressed in both the Qur'an and the Hadith, encompasses a far broader range of circumstances than one might imagine, especially when analyzing the narrow usage of the concept in extremist writings. For instance, according to the collections of Hadith, a martyr is one who may, among other things, be killed by a plague, by disease of the stomach, by drowning, by a collapsing building, by fire, during childbirth, protecting his or her property, by being thrown from a horse or camel, from the sting of a poisonous creature, or one who dies defending his or her family.[28] These incidents, events, and accidents, of course, are all in addition to the more obvious traditional forms of martyrdom, namely, from persecution[29] or in a just war against the enemies of Islam.[30]

Islamic tradition points to Sumayyah bint Khayyat, the mother of Ammar ibn Yasir (d. 657 CE), as the first martyr of Islam in 615 CE.[31] It is reported that she was tortured and stabbed by Abu Jahl in Mecca after she refused to renounce Islam and return to the worship of the pagan gods of the *jahiliyyah* (see Chapter 3). The diverse notions of martyrdom evident in these traditions underscore the difficulty of understanding the concept of martyrdom in Islam. Put briefly, all of the above examples suggest that martyrdom in Islam encompasses essentially any unnatural or premature death that befalls a sincere believer (*mu'min*), and not simply a warrior fighting jihad. Nevertheless, the battlefield martyr is most certainly the core interest of Islamist extremists and it was historically the core interest of many Muslim empires interested in motivating their soldiers.

Before a martyr (*shahid*) can partake in the heavenly bounty of Islam's afterlife, he or she must endure the proceedings of the Day of Judgment along with the rest of humanity. But unlike non-martyrs, the *shuhada* (pl. of *shahid*) are spared the trials of the grave when the two angels, *Munkar* and *Nakir* (post-Qur'anic), interrogate the dead for their deeds and bypass the *barzakh* (intermediate existence) altogether.[32] According to some traditions, the souls of the martyrs immediately ascend into heaven and inhabit the bodies of green birds, flying about freely and eating from the fruits of paradise until the Day of Judgment when they will return to their earthly bodies for resurrection. These *shuhada*, being among the first to awake on the Day of Resurrection, will arise with their wounds intact.

A tradition recorded in *Sunan Abu Dawud* relates that "[i]f anyone is wounded in *Allah*'s path, or suffers a misfortune, it will remain on the Day of Resurrection as copious as possible, its color saffron, and its odor musk."[33] The martyr will then stand before *Allah*, having achieved the supreme sacrifice on the path of *Allah* (*fi sabil Allah*). He or she will then cross over the *Chinvat* bridge (or *al-Sirat*), which the reader will recall from Zoroastrian lore, to enter paradise for eternity and enjoy the delights contained therein.

The Seventy-Two Virgins Master Narrative in Extremist Discourse

The Seventy-Two Virgins master narrative, as frequently invoked by Islamist extremists, very clearly and explicitly expresses the desire (or intent) to die as a martyr in jihad on the path of *Allah* (*fi sabil Allah*) and to enter the blissful company residing in the gardens of paradise. But it also expresses a rebuke or rejection of the current world and any individual or any culture (e.g., American) attached to the material goods and temporal snares of worldly life, even to one's own family. The master narrative is a vivid example of what historian of religion Bruce Lincoln would associate with "religions of revolution." The stories expressed in the master narrative not only provide solace for suffering and oppressed peoples (as they perceive themselves to be), but challenge the priorities of ruling institutions in their societies and reject the right of the religion of the status quo to dictate normative values.[34]

Islamist extremists frequently juxtapose themselves to Westerners, or even "hypocrite" Muslims and their regimes, by stating that "we love death" (i.e., martyrdom) the way that "you" love life. This is a deliberate inversion of the normative ethical order. The Seventy-Two Virgins master narrative, in this context, is a proclamation of pious protest expressing the extremist preference for the next life with *Allah* over the current life, as well as the desire to achieve martyrdom and attain salvation.

For example, on January 11, 2010, the will of Hudhayfah Muhammad al-Hams, a teenage Palestinian militant killed by Israeli airstrikes in Gaza a few days prior, was posted on an extremist online forum in Arabic. Al-Hams was reportedly recruited by *Jaysh al-Ummah* ("Army of the Muslim Community"), a Palestinian Islamist group associated with al-Qaeda. Images of al-Hams, both alive and dead, were also posted online with the following statement:

> His will relates: Truthful was he [Prophet Muhammad] who said: "The martyr is special to *Allah*. He is forgiven from the first drop of blood [that he sheds]. He sees his throne in paradise, where he will be adorned in ornaments of faith. He will wed the wide-eyed virgins and will not know the torments of the grave and safeguards against the greater horror [hellfire]. Fixed atop his head will be a crown of honor, a ruby that is greater than the world and all it contains. And he will have seventy-two virgins and be able to offer intercessions for seventy of his relatives." The people are in need for a herald to shout at them that it is time to wake up and be attentive to what is happening around them, to look at the enemies around them, who are scheming and plotting against Islam and hatching one conspiracy after another. When are we going to wake up from our slumber?[35]

As the reader can see, the imagery articulated by al-Hams in his will is taken directly from the tradition found in the *Musnad* of Ahmed Ibn Hanbal discussed earlier in this chapter. His statement expresses a preference for the next world over the current world, which is dominated by infidel nations like Israel and the United States, and his desire to be a martyr and assume the role of a "herald" to "wake up" the Muslims from their "slumber."

On December 11, 2009, *Geo News TV*, an Urdu language twenty-four-hour satellite news network based in Karachi, Pakistan, reported the discovery of a Taliban base in the Nawaz Kot area of South Waziristan. The base reportedly included a school or training center where youths were instructed in the virtues of dying in battle as martyrs, specifically as suicide-bombers. The discovery received coverage throughout the world due to the disturbing images painted on the walls of the buildings. The paintings featured scenes of milk canals running through lush green gardens with tall trees, all depicted in bright colors that stood out vividly from the dusty mud brick structures they adorned. During training, the youths were reportedly told about the milk canals and other elements of heaven. Some of the paintings depicted women as *hur*, the maidens of paradise, and the youths were told to imagine themselves as being present in paradise and the *hur* waiting for them there.[36]

The use of such images, as a form of transmediation, is undoubtedly useful for extremists operating in a region where illiteracy remains very high. Indeed, it is quite similar to the way the medieval Church used images, such as stained-glass windows, to communicate their messages, including the rewards of heaven and terrors of hellfire, to uneducated European peasantry.

In yet another example, a forum participant on the extremist web site, Islamic Al-Fallujah Forums, posted a statement on August 22, 2009, announcing the release of a new extremist video entitled "Knights of Martyrdom 6." It featured three suicide-bombers making their final statements prior to carrying out attacks in Iraq. One of the bombers stated:

> Rush to the jihad fields with pure faith and intentions before Almighty *Allah*, everywhere and especially in Iraq. Rush to carry out martyrdom-seeking attacks, nowadays, these attacks are the most scary and hurtful to the enemy, and they are the fastest way to heaven. Brothers in Islam, the doors of the heaven are now open in the Land of the Two Rivers [i.e., Iraq], and each day a new groom is sent to the *hur* [virgins of paradise]. Are there any volunteers, O brothers? Whereas for you, my brothers the *mujahidin*, by God, He [God] has chosen you for a major mission and used you to support His religion and followers. Never leave your weapons and listen to the worldly people.[37]

In the final sentence of the statement, the extremist exhorts his audience "not to listen to the worldly people." This again is a juxtaposition of the Islamist extremist "believers" against the dominant sociopolitical order and its infidel culture. In this instance, the Seventy-Two Virgins master narrative is invoked in a fragmentary reference to convey an opportunity to act imminently and to reject or fight against the prevailing conditions of the world and escape to a new world in the afterlife full of delights and happiness.

Analysis of the Seventy-Two Virgins Master Narrative

The blissful solace promised by the Seventy-Two Virgins master narrative is certainly a vivid example of a noble sacrifice story form featuring the martyr archetype. The master narrative offers those willing to die for the Islamist cause the opportunity to identify with a holy martyr (*shahid*) who *Allah* will reward with a heavenly world and the companionship of dark-eyed maidens. By employing this framing device, a violent act that results in the death of the perpetrator is encoded as an act of holy martyrdom for *Allah* against the archetypal crusader and the forces of wickedness and unbelief in the world. Victory, the master narrative further tells us, belongs to the martyr regardless of whether or not the infidel enemy is defeated. The next world is far better than any one could imagine in the earthly realm. Even the most infallible and nominal Muslim can enjoy this saintly status by assuming the role of the martyr in the master narrative. All sins can be washed away by self-sacrifice and great honor (perhaps even intercession) will come to one's family and people for this courageous act of "true faith." At the same time, the martyr becomes an example to be emulated by others, and his or her life and decision to seek martyrdom for Islam will often assume narrative form itself (becoming part of a broader narrative system) and disseminated, sometimes through video-taped statements created prior to the act itself ensuring the persistence of the underlying master narrative.

CHAPTER 14

Master Narratives and Strategic Communication

The foregoing chapters describe thirteen master narratives of Islamist extremism, most based on stories from the Qur'an, but some with roots in more contemporary events. In each case, we have identified the narrative elements at work, as defined in Chapter 1. While up to this point we have focused on describing the master narratives, their evolution, and application in contemporary extremist discourse, there remains an open question about how extremists use the narratives strategically. In this concluding chapter, we look at the issue of how master narratives are used in communication by extremists to accomplish (or facilitate the accomplishment of) strategic goals.

We begin by identifying broad goals of Islamist extremism, and arguing that master narratives play a middle role in a system of vertical integration. Then we show how master narratives weave a rhetorical vision that provides a stock of story forms, archetypes, and emotional responses from which new narratives might be constructed. Next we show how master narratives and the rhetorical vision serve as resources for strategic rhetorical efforts to convince audience members to align their personal narratives in ways that serve the goals of Islamist extremism. We conclude by describing five strategies through which these functions of master narratives might be countered.

How is Narrative Strategic?

Strategic communication can be defined straightforwardly as communication intended to persuade an audience to support one or more specific goals. It is sensible, then, to begin by considering the strategic goals of Islamist extremists. While it would be a mistake to assimilate all Islamist extremist groups into a single unified set of specific goals, certain themes recur across the ideologies of these groups.[1] By drawing on them, we can identify three broad goals that would be supported by most, what might be called the three "R's" of Islamist extremism:

- **Resist**: Fight foreign invaders (especially the United States and its allies) who seek to destroy Islam and exploit Muslims and their lands, and internal enemies that seek to destroy the community from within.
- **Rebuke**: Discredit the oppressive "apostate" leaders of Muslim countries, who persecute their people and support the efforts of the foreign powers, including the United States.
- **Renew**: Reverse the decline of Muslim civilization by reestablishing the caliphate and reinstituting the rule of Islamic law.

As we will see, all of the master narratives discussed in this book support one or more of these goals and/or seek to place extremists in the vanguard of the effort to accomplish them.

In what way are master narratives persuasive? David Betz[2] answers this question by drawing upon Ann Swindler's continuum of cultural consciousness. She links *ideology* (an explicit belief and ritual system), to *tradition* (taken-for-granted cultural belief and practices), and to *common sense* (unself-conscious assumptions about how the world works).[3] Betz equates Swindler's "ideology" with a *cultural eschatological narrative* and her "common sense" with *local narratives*. He argues that *strategic narra*tives (analogous to her tradition) persuade by linking the latter with the former, creating *vertical integration*.

While we believe Betz's idea of vertical integration is important, we have three concerns about his formulation. First, while he is clear about what functions his strategic narratives perform, Betz is less clear about exactly what form they take. As an illustration of vertical integration, he gives the following example:

In one "night letter"[4] Afghan readers are told:

> Today once again your sons, clerics and Taliban and the faithful people in these circumstances are fighting against non-Muslims and are serving Islam. If you don't do anything else, at least support your Mujahedin sons and do not be impressed by the false propaganda of non-Muslim enemies.

In short, the letter effectively invokes an eschatological narrative in both Islam and Afghanistan's illustrious history in explaining the actions of the Taliban, parsimoniously places the non-Muslim enemy in context in a strategic narrative, and enjoins the reader individually to (at the very least) not support or believe the propaganda of the outsider.[5]

This would seem to be an example of a local narrative, because it expresses "ideas about what [people] should or should not do and what rewards or penalties they will incur from a particular course of action,"[6] and because it describes events that are happening in the here and now. The local story seems to invoke the higher cultural issues rather directly, without the aid of any explicit intermediary system of strategic stories. It would seem that it is *the rhetorical act* of telling a local story for persuasive purposes that is strategic, not the implied intermediate narratives.

Second, there seems to be inconsistency in Betz's mapping of his categories onto Swindler's in terms of level of consciousness/abstraction. For Swindler ideology is concrete, explicit, and self-conscious, whereas common sense is abstract, implicit, and unselfconscious. Yet Betz's eschatological narratives (which he likens to Swindler's ideology) are implicit and circulate in culture, while people directly deploy the local narratives (which he compares to Swindler's common sense) discourse. In other words, the mapping seems to be the reverse of what it should be.

Finally, "eschatological" is an equivocal term for describing the highest level of integration. Betz is undoubtedly using the word in Weber's sense, meaning a future "political and social transformation of this world."[7] But in theological usage, eschatology (deriving from the Greek *eschatos*, meaning "last things") refers to the events of the end times and the ultimate destiny of humanity or the universe. In the context of this book, the term risks confusion. Some of our master narratives relate directly to eschatology in this theological sense (e.g., the *Mahdi* master narrative). But many of the others, while theological in nature (e.g., the Pharaoh master narrative), do not.

So while we retain Betz's key insight about the importance of three-part vertical integration, we address these three concerns by offering the following reformulation of his terms and their relationships to each other and to strategic behavior (see figure 14.1). At the lowest level of abstraction are ***personal narratives***, which are systems of stories experienced, remembered, and told by individuals. As *homo narrans* (see Chapter 1), humans use these personal narratives to understand the world and their place in it, to frame events, and to plan and justify their actions. Donald Polkinghorne points out that

> [p]eople conceive of themselves in terms of stories. Their personal stories are always some version of the general cultural stock of stories about how life proceeds. As narrative forms, these stories draw together and configure events of one's life into a coherent and basic theme. One's future is projected as a continuation of the story, as yet unfinished.[8]

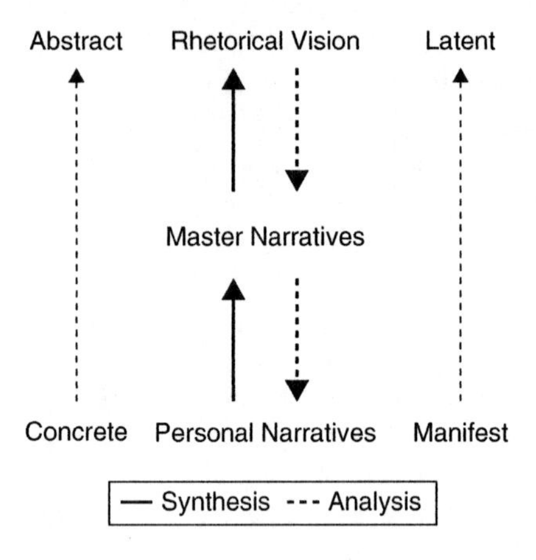

Figure 14.1 Vertical integration model

For example, the author of the night letter discussed above is telling a story (part of his personal narrative) about what the Taliban are doing, in order to justify their actions.

At the intermediate level of abstraction are *master narratives,* such as the ones described in this book. These are narratives whose component stories, by virtue of being widely shared and repeated across time, have become deeply embedded in a particular culture. Master narratives occupy this middle ground by virtue of the fact that their stories are sometimes explicitly recounted, but otherwise have a taken-for-granted character. They serve as common knowledge for members of a culture and provide a potential pattern for personal narratives, per Polkinghorne's quote above. They can be invoked without actually telling a story: calling some leader a "Pharaoh" is enough to establish (or at least imply) that he is a tyrant who deserves the wrath of God, and as we have shown, extremists do just that. It is not necessary to recount the actual details of the Pharaoh and Moses story to make the implication clear to someone who is part of the culture where the master narrative circulates.

At the highest level of abstraction, master narratives knit together to form a *rhetorical vision.* Ernest Bormann coined this term to refer to the way narratives chain together in a society to provide a universal resource for communication:

> Once such a rhetorical vision emerges, it contains *dramatis personae* and typical plot lines that can be alluded to in all communication contexts and

> spark a response reminiscent of the original emotional chain. The same dramas can be developed in detail when the occasion demands to generate emotional response.[9]

We can see a rhetorical vision as a context composed of master narratives, which share common story forms (Bormann's plot lines) and archetypes (his *dramatis personae*). A rhetorical vision, then, integrates the master narratives in an emotional and logical sense, and provides resources for constructing personal narratives and developing goals for actions and behavior.

In this scheme, master narratives themselves are not strategic. Growing as they do by accretion, we cannot say that someone formulated them for the purposes of advocating a particular course of action at a particular time. Instead, the strategic act is a rhetorical one, namely, using the master narratives as a persuasive resource in the service of goals. Islamist extremists use *arguments* to convince members of their audience to adopt particular personal narratives, using the master narratives as a pattern.

This usage is evident in the night letter example. It evokes master narratives (e.g., Crusader and Tatar) in which the community is faced with a threat by invading forces, demanding a response by a champion who repels the invasion. It asks the reader to see the Taliban as the champion, and to support their goal of offering resistance. The audience can do this if not by directly contributing to the efforts then by staying out of the way and resisting efforts to persuade them to interpret the situation differently. The argument is effective because the audience already understands and subscribes to the master narrative, making the argument seem natural and the request reasonable (not to mention the implied threat of consequences for doing otherwise). Collective memories of the dire consequences of invasion contained in the rhetorical vision also produce an emotional (fear) appeal.

Knitting a Rhetorical Vision

In the scheme just proposed, master narratives collectively constitute the rhetorical vision. Whereas the preceding chapters went into the specific details of the master narratives, in this final chapter we back away from these details to get a better view of the "big picture" that they construct. Table 14.1 summarizes the main features of the thirteen master narratives, as defined by the method outlined in Chapter 1. By examining these elements, we can see how the master narratives are integrated by common elements of story forms and archetypes.

Table 14.1 Summary of master narrative elements

Master narrative	*Story form*	*Archetypes*
Pharaoh	Conflict with God (deity)	Tyrant, deity, prophet
Jahiliyyah	Deliverance	Deity, prophet, martyr, pagan
Battle of Badr	Deliverance	Prophet, pagan, champion
Hypocrites	Ruse	Imposter, prophet
Battle of Khaybar	Betrayal	Traitor, trickster, prophet
Battle of Karbala	Noble sacrifice	Martyr, tyrant, imposter
Shaytan's handiwork	Ruse	Trickster, deity, prophet
Seventy-two virgins	Noble sacrifice	Martyr, imposter, crusader
Mahdi	Deliverance	Savior, imposter
Crusader	Invasion	Crusader/colonizer, champion
Tatar	Invasion	Barbarian, imposter, champion, sage
1924	Ruse	Imposter, traitor
Nakba	Deliverance	Crusader/colonizer, martyr

Story Forms

As described in Chapter 1, story forms are generic frameworks for stories, identifying the entities (usually, but not necessarily people) that are involved, the actions they take, and how these actions relate to one another. Though many of the master narratives invoke more than one story form, one is always predominant, with the others furnishing *supplementary events.*[10] The latter are important stories, but without them the basic narrative would remain intact. For example, the Tatar master narrative invokes the ruse story form, describing Ghazan Khan as a *poseur* (imposter) who publicly converted to Islam but refused to rule according to its dictates. Though this is an important contextual detail, the Invasion story of the Mongols (Tatars) would have still taken place and had its ill effects on the Muslims even if the ruse had never happened.

One of the most prominent story forms in the master narratives is the *Ruse.* Here a deceiver executes a plan designed to mislead an individual or community, and the plan is sometimes foiled. This form appears in the Hypocrites, 1924, and *Shaytan*'s Handiwork master narratives. All three pit the believers as dupes against an imposter or trickster as deceiver, and create a desire to foil the plot that underlies the ruse. The Hypocrites master narrative, especially the stories of the hypocrites of Medina, shows that with sufficient vigilance and assistance from God, the deceivers can be exposed and their plots foiled. The 1924 master narrative, on the other hand, can be used to argue that without vigilance the deceivers' plots can succeed, with disastrous consequences for the faith. *Shaytan*'s Handiwork can show that ruses are not exceptional cases or historical anomalies. Rather, the threat of deception is omnipresent in the mundane details and decisions of everyday life.

These three master narratives provide resources to paint the world as a dangerous place where enemies are always on the lookout for opportunities to undermine Islam by deception. Moreover, in these master narratives the threat comes from forces within—be it within the community of (supposed) believers or within the minds of individuals. The narrative trajectory from the conflict to the resolution of the desire is eternal vigilance against internal threats and living one's life in the path of God (*fi sabil Allah*) in order to gain His assistance in uncovering and thwarting the plots and avoiding snares along the way. Given the omnipresent threat of deception, this is the only hope for avoiding the disastrous consequences that can ensue—and have ensued in the past.

It is worth noting that other master narratives are related to this theme. While the Battle of Khaybar invokes a betrayal rather than a ruse story form, it, too, is an example of treachery by a supposedly allied group in the same (physical) community. The Pharaoh master narrative presents tyrannical rulers of the community as deserving targets of God's wrath, and shows that the actions of vigilant believers can and should help bring about their downfall. The *Jahiliyyah* master narrative likewise relates that failure by Muslims to be vigilant against religious decline has (in part) led to disastrous consequences for the community.

Another prominent story form is the *invasion*. While it appears in only two of the master narratives, they are by far the most commonly invoked in contemporary extremist rhetoric. For example, we have collected a database of over 500 extremist texts, consisting of writings, public statements, and media interviews by members of al-Qaeda and other extremist groups. Use of the word "crusade" (and its forms) grew steadily from rare occurrences in the year 2000 to an astonishing average of *eleven times per text* in 2008. The *Nakba* master narrative also contributes to the prominence of this theme. While it does not invoke the invasion story form directly, it has inherent connections to it because the loss of Palestine has clear ties to British colonialism, and it was imposed by Western powers against the Arab inhabitants over their objections.

In the Invader story form, a powerful foreign force conquers the lands and cities of a victim group, destroying and desecrating it, and killing many in the process. Then a champion emerges who defeats the invaders and initiates a reversal of fortunes that restores the original social order. Narratives based on this form serve a dual purpose. First, they can be used to establish an ongoing threat to the community, not from within as in the ruse narratives, but from external enemies. The recurrence of these invasions over the course of history proves the need, again, for constant vigilance against the threat. But at the same time, they can hold out the promise that the invading forces will be defeated by heroes who—by virtue of their faith and the assistance of God, and despite the seeming strength of the enemy—emerge to restore the community to its rightful place and order. This establishes a promise that the desire to defeat and expel the invaders can be realized by sacrifice, endurance, and effective resistance.

Two of the other story forms support this promise. The *noble sacrifice* story form in the Battle of Karbala and Seventy-Two Virgins master narratives establishes the importance of self-sacrifice on the part of the believers in the struggle against the enemies of Islam. Though the sacrifice may result in death, it fulfills God's Will, serves the community, and the act is rewarded in the afterlife. The nobility of the act establishes a motivation to fight even when the odds seem overwhelmingly unfavorable, because acts of martyrdom serve the long-term interests of the believers and they are rewarded and honored.

Deliverance is the other supporting story form. It describes a situation in which an unfortunate victim is menaced by a threatening foe that is later defeated by a heroic rescuer, restoring the safety and well-being of the unfortunate. In two of the master narratives, this story plays out in complete form owing to miracles involving the Prophet Muhammad. In the classical *jahiliyyah*, Muhammad delivered the Arabs from an age of pagan barbarity and ignorance by bringing them revelations from God. In the Battle of Badr, the prophet leads a small army to victory over a force more than three times its size when God and His angels intervene.

Together the noble sacrifice and deliverance story forms help define the logic of the struggle (jihad) against the enemies of Islam. Since humans cannot fathom God's ways, they cannot know whether He will see any particular struggle as the right time to deliver victory. But the combined deliverance and noble sacrifice forms create a win-win situation for the holy warrior (*mujahid*): Either he (or she) will be martyred in battle and enjoy the bliss of the afterlife, or he will become God's glorious agent, helping to deliver the community from oppression. The rational course of action is for the believers to do God's Will by going into battle, leaving the outcome up to God.

Importantly, the deliverance story form does not only function as a means of rationalization. In the Battle of Badr and the *Jahiliyyah* master narratives, the entire story form appears, ending in deliverance. But unlike all of the other master narratives we have analyzed, the *Nakba* and *Mahdi* master narratives leave the deliverance story incomplete. While they establish the identities of the unfortunate and threatening foe, the rescuer has yet to come along. Indeed, his identity is not even known (except perhaps among the Twelver Shi'ites in the *Mahdi* master narrative).

The effect of this omission not only acts as a way to create the desire for relief from tribulation, *but also a desire for a rescuer to appear to deliver it.* In the case of the *Mahdi* master narrative, this can clearly be seen in the case of Twelver Shi'ites who routinely anticipate the return of the Hidden Imam in their rhetoric, and in the meantime invest his agency in a mortal leader through the doctrine of *velayat-e faqih* (see Chapter 8). In the Sunni tradition, the desire is reflected in the case of Muhammad Ahmad of the Sudan, who styled himself as the *Mahdi* and attracted a large following in his war against the British and Egyptians.

The *Nakba* master narrative, as well as the modern *jahiliyyah* articulated by Qutb, carries even more uncertainty about who the rescuer will be and focus entirely on the threatening foe and the suffering of the believers. In Qutb's utilization of the *Jahiliyyah* master narrative, the unfortunate victim is the *ummah.* The threatening foe takes the form of creeping decline of the religion, brought on by a combination of languid practice by believers, corruption by nonbelievers, and tyrannical actions of apostate rulers. In the *Nakba* master narrative, the unfortunate victim has a more specific identity, the Palestinian people, for whom other Muslims feel sympathy. The threatening foe is represented by Israel (or Zionism) and its allies in the western world (chiefly the United States) who expelled the Palestinians from their sacred land. They continue this tyranny with additional land seizures and other oppressive treatment. These incomplete stories of the modern *Jahiliyyah* and *Nakba* master narratives lack closure and thus cry out for a rescuer to emerge on the scene.

Archetypes

As described in Chapter 1, archetypes are standard characters that one might expect to find in a story, which unlock motives and operate as shorthand terms for situations in which characters might find themselves. Table 14.1 (above) lists the archetypes featured in the master narratives in this book. Some of these archetypes are closely tied to the story forms just discussed. Indeed, they are canonical: certain story forms *require* certain kinds of characters. The ruse story form requires a deceiver, so we always see the imposter or trickster archetypes in these narratives. The invasion story form requires a belligerent force, a role fulfilled by the crusader/colonizer or barbarian archetypes. Conflict with God requires an immortal, played by the deity archetype (sometimes represented by an agent of the deity, such as an archetypal prophet), and a mortal who incurs the deity's wrath, such as the tyrant.

However, in many of the master narratives that we have reviewed, there are other archetypes present that are not canonical to the story form. We find the imposter in many narratives where he is not technically required. An imposter appears in the Battle of Karbala master narrative even though there is no need for an imposter in order for a noble sacrifice to take place. Likewise, there is nothing about an Invasion story form that requires the presence of an imposter or sage, yet these archetypes are present in the Tatar master narrative. The deity appears in the *Shaytan*'s Handiwork master narrative even though a ruse can be perpetrated without the involvement of a deity.

In these cases the archetypes contribute important supplementary information. For example, in the Karbala master narrative, the imposters are Shimr and the Umayyad troops. Without knowing that, it would be hard to understand what the underlying conflict—the one calling for a noble sacrifice—was all about. Likewise, in the *Shaytan*'s Handiwork master narrative, the deity is important in explaining the origin of the trickster *Shaytan*. These "supplementary" archetypes establish the context of the master narratives, and therefore serve as another means by which a rhetorical vision is integrated.

Figure 14.2 visually depicts relationships between the archetypes. Two archetypes are connected by a line if they jointly appear in one or more of the master narratives. The lines are thicker if the two archetypes coappear in more than one master narrative. The "good guy" archetypes are shown in white boxes, while the "bad guy" archetypes are shown in black boxes. The size of the boxes indicates the centrality of a particular archetype in the network—how much it ties together elements of the system.[11]

One notable feature of this network is that there are more "bad guys" than there are "good guys," and two of the "good guys," the savior and sage, are peripheral in the network. The most central "bad guy"—by far—is the imposter, someone who lies about his true identity or intentions in a calculated fashion. All of the imposters in the master narratives we have reviewed mislead people to believe that they are either true believers or they are on the side of the believers. Considering the predominance of the ruse story form, as already discussed, a key feature of the rhetorical vision of Islamist extremists appears to be the belief that their world is plagued by internal threats. The connections of the imposter archetype to the crusader and barbarian archetypes further indicate the idea that the imposters facilitate or serve external enemies in undertaking their evil machinations.

The second most central archetype is the *prophet*. That this "good guy" is a central archetype is not surprising. Many of the master narratives have

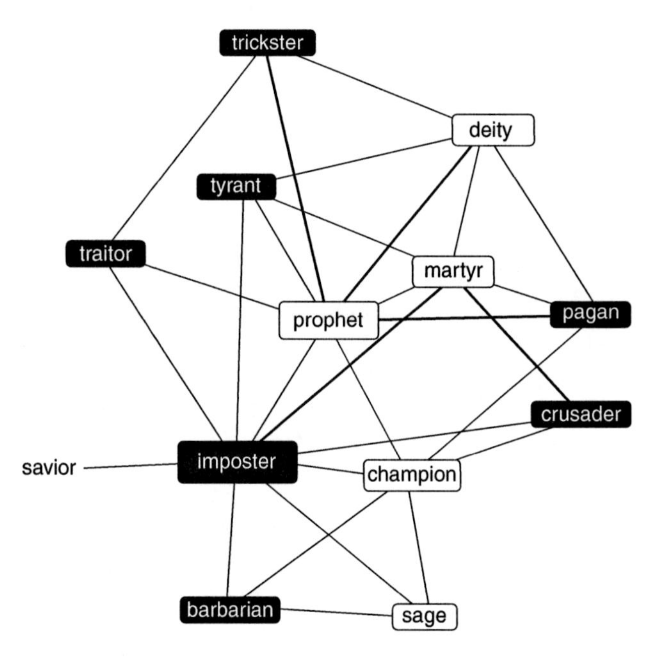

Figure 14.2 Relationships among archetypes

close connections to the Qur'an and Hadith, which either relate revelations to Muhammad or tell stories of his life. At the same time, none of the story forms, except perhaps "conflict with God," require the presence of a prophet, so this archetype is primarily important in establishing context for the narratives. The connection to the imposter shows that even the prophet (or agent of the deity) is vulnerable to treachery in the form of deception.

The next most prominent "good guy" archetype is the *champion*. It makes sense that the champion is primarily connected to the external invader "bad guys" and the imposter. As a heroic leader capable of surmounting great and deadly challenges, including battles, this archetype provides the community's essential means of defense against threats. The *martyr*, who sacrifices his or her life in a just and righteous cause, is only slightly less central than the champion. This archetype has similar motives to the champion and functions in a similar way; indeed would-be champions who do not succeed in surmounting their deadly challenges are usually treated as martyrs, and, except in the case of a suicide ("self-martyrdom"), a person cannot know what he or she will be until after the fact.

The big picture

Together, the master narratives, their story forms, and archetypes, constitute a rhetorical vision of a dangerous world for Islam. Imposters who pretend to be believers (or allies of the believers) lurk around every corner, poised to take actions that erode the strength of Islam and destroy the *ummah*. There are enemies at the gates too, in the form of crusaders (or colonizers), and barbarians. The imposters collude with these external enemies in their treachery, serving as vectors inside the body politic, and compromise the immune system that would ordinarily enjoy strength from pious devotion to Islam. Stories of this tribulation go all the way back to the days of the prophet; even he was not immune to the influences of such enemies. These stories have continued unabated across history, proving the need for eternal vigilance and active defense of the religion.

History has shown that the only hope of defense comes from that action of heroes in the form of champions and martyrs. They are prepared to make noble sacrifices for the sake of the community, risking their lives to defend the *ummah* against its enemies. In some cases, with the help of God, they succeed and live, and reap worldly rewards and glory. In other cases, they die and they are paid the wages of martyrdom in the afterlife. In all cases, they are doing God's Will, so victory is assured and they cannot lose.

Nevertheless, the present day situation is dire. The *ummah* continues to suffer through a centuries-long decline, according to some (such as Qutb) since the time of the Prophet and his companions. External enemies, with the collusion of apostates who rule the Muslim world, have managed to destroy what vestiges of divine sovereignty were left. These enemies continue their assault to this day, seizing sacred land, and leading armies to invade, subjugate, and exploit Muslim countries. In the past, champions and martyrs emerged to meet such challenges, but today they have not—at least not in sufficient numbers. Someone must step up and take on these roles before it is too late.

Strategic Use of Master Narratives

The preceding section explained how master narratives relate to one another to create a rhetorical vision. This is one source of vertical integration in Betz's sense: The rhetorical vision gives the master narratives an underlying unity of story forms and archetypes that can be used to create new stories. It also establishes the legitimacy of an emotional response to the stories in members of a community.

The other aspect of vertical integration links the master narratives to personal narratives of people in the audience. As we argued above, master narratives are themselves not strategic in the sense that they were not created for a particular purpose. Instead, they are *used strategically* in rhetorical acts that seek to persuade audiences to align their personal narratives in support of particular goals, in this case the three "R's" of Islamist extremism. This section asks the question: How are master narratives used in this strategic sense by extremists?

The short answer is that they usually depend on a class of arguments that Gerald Smith, George Benson, and Shawn Curley call *observational arguments.*[12] Three closely related argument types make up the class. One is *argument from sign*, where a known causal process produces symptoms that can be used to diagnose the cause. For example, smoke, fire, and ash suddenly spewing from the top of a mountain are signs of a volcano. A second is *argument from analogy*, wherein a target and analogue are shown to have similar properties, supporting a conclusion that the target must also have a property of the analogue that is not immediately apparent. For instance, philosopher William Paley used what has come to be known as the "watchmaker analogy" as an argument that there must be a Creator.[13] A watch is an exceedingly complex thing. Things of such complexity do not appear by chance, they have a creator. The Earth is also a complex thing. Something of such complexity could not have occurred by chance, therefore the Earth—like the watch—must have a creator. A third is *argument from parallel case*, which claims that a current situation is similar to a past situation, and can therefore be assumed to have similar attributes and outcomes. During the worst days of the second Iraq war, parallels were frequently drawn to the Vietnam war[14] as a way of arguing that things would end badly and that the United States should cut its losses before things get any worse.

The differences between these argument types are technical,[15] mainly having to do with the degree of certainty about the attributes of the target and the nature of the things compared. The important thing for our purposes here is that they operate cognitively in similar ways. They do not rely on incontrovertible logic or deduction, but rather "on available data and relatively superficial relationships [between attributes], ultimately underwritten by assumed structural regularities."[16] All such arguments work by using analogical reasoning to establish similarity between a present target case and some known situation. In Islamist discourse, the known situations are those described in the stories of the master narratives, and the strategic objective is to establish similarities between them and current events. The importance of this rhetorical move cannot be overestimated, especially in Muslim culture. As Rosalind Gwynne notes, "[C]omparison is an activity of the intellect fundamental to humans' understanding and evaluation of the world; and it is one of the principal means used in the Qur'an to teach moral and spiritual discernment."[17]

The Pharaoh master narrative is used by Islamist extremists to reflect their struggles against corrupt regimes (internal enemies) and foreign nations (external enemies) they deem to be irreligious. It creates desire to rid the religion of corrupting influences, meaning that it primarily serves the Rebuke goal. By strategically applying this narrative, an analogy is drawn between the Pharaoh and the despised rulers (or foreign enemies) on the one hand, and the Prophet Moses (God's agent) and the extremists on the other. This analogy casts the extremists and their supporters as God's agents who seek to smite the rulers/enemies on God's behalf. Invoking the Pharaoh master narrative argues that the audience should see their own stories as part of the same narrative. There could hardly be more convincing evidence of the effectiveness of this argument than Lt. Khalid al-Islambouli shouting "I have killed the Pharaoh!" after the assassination of Anwar Sadat (see Chapter 2).

The modern variant of the *Jahiliyyah* master narrative is based on an explicit analogy drawn by Sayyid Qutb between the present circumstances and those that existed before the revelations to Muhammad. After noting the state of ignorance that existed before Islam, he said: "It is now not in that simple and primitive form of the ancient *jahiliyyah*, but takes the form of claiming that the right to create values, to legislate rules of collective behavior, and to choose any way of life rests with men, without regard for what God has prescribed."[18] Extremists invoke this master narrative primarily in service of the Renew goal, suggesting, as it does, a need to reverse the decline and get things back to the way they were during the time of the Prophet in Medina. As discussed above, it is a deliverance story form that lacks closure, establishing the need for a rescuer to come along to deliver the unfortunates. Invoking it positions the extremists as the champions in the present-day story, and suggests to the audience that they too can be rescuers by becoming extremists or by supporting their efforts.

The Battle of Badr master narrative operates analogically on several levels. Modern day invocation of the *ummah* argues in favor of transcending modern day "false" nationalist categories, just as the warriors of Badr transcended their tribes, and working together against a foe. Doing so will result in divine sanction and assistance in the efforts, just as it did then. This argument primarily serves the Resist goal, but also the Restore goal: 'Abdullah Azzam saw the Afghan jihad against the Soviets as the gathering point of Qutb's vanguard (see Chapter 4). His accounts of battles in the Afghan war against the Soviets are patterned directly on the Badr master narrative, down to the appearance and assistance of angels on the battlefield.

Drawing comparisons to Badr invites the audience to see themselves as part of a unified global community for which they are obligated to fight against the unbelievers, and to recognize that efforts to support that fight are divinely sanctioned and likely to benefit from divine intervention.

The Hypocrites master narrative is invoked to claim similarity between various internal enemies—such as insufficiently supportive Islamist groups (e.g., the Muslim Brotherhood), apostate regimes, and a complacent clergy—and the hypocrites of Medina. It serves the Rebuke goal of purging the *ummah* of these "near" enemies who interfere with its duty of self-defense and restoration, and shill for external "far" enemies who seek to destroy it outright. Invoking this master narrative tells the audience that they should view any person or group who is unsupportive of the extremists' cause as dangerous and take it as their duty to remain vigilant against these corrupting influences.

The Battle of Karbala master narrative depends on an analogy between present-day circumstances and the classical story in which Husayn, his family, and his supporters were slaughtered in a heroic battle against the army of the evil tyrant, Yazid. In the Iran-Iraq war, Ayatollah Khomeini symbolically positioned himself as Husayn and Saddam Hussein as Yazid to inspire outgunned Iranian forces to sacrifice themselves in battle. For Shi'ites, using this master narrative serves the Resist goal by arguing that the audience should follow the example of Husayn and his supporters, and not fear death in battle because they will be rewarded in the afterlife as martyrs.

The *Mahdi* master narrative tells deliverance stories of a Savior that will come to restore Islam throughout the world and destroy the wicked nations following a period of great turmoil. Invoking it serves the Restore goal by indicating a divine plan for deliverance of the world, and urging the faithful to take part in the plan. While there is no direct similarity between the *Mahdi* and current events, there have been instances where people have claimed to represent him, and Twelver Shi'ites who follow *velayat-e faqih* treat the Grand Ayatollah as his agent on Earth. There have also been claims about signs of his presence in the Iraq conflict and in the 2006 war between Israel and Hezbollah (see Chapter 8).

The Crusader and Tatar master narratives serve the Resist goal by recounting historical events that are themselves treated as parallel cases, and arguing that current events fit the same pattern. Qutb drew a direct comparison by saying that there is a common "crusading spirit." These master narratives construct a conflict between the *ummah* and unbelieving foreign forces that seek to dominate and exploit them. The analogy with the Crusader and Tatar cases also promises that, just as in the past, Muslims can prevail against external enemies through vigilance and the grace of God, despite inferior numbers. Invoking these master narratives argues that the audience should see itself as part of the resistance, to serve as the rescuer that will repel the external enemy and restore the proper order of the world.

The *Shaytan*'s Handiwork master narrative has some elements of comparison in extremist discourse. For example, we noted in Chapter 10 that the Ayatollah Khomeini likened the United States to the "Great Satan," implying to his audience that its temptations should be resisted in a similar manner. For the most part, though, this master narrative plays a supporting role to the others, reminding people that corruption creeps into the mundane activities of everyday life, drawing believers away from a life in the path of God. Over time, these deviations can accumulate, leading to corruption, tyranny, and hypocrisy, and the possible collapse of communities, as some extremists argue is the case with Bahrain. Invoking this master narrative therefore serves all the three "R's" of Islamist extremism: the Resist goal by demonstrating the need for vigilance against internal forces of corruption, the Rebuke goal by implying that internal enemies are under the influence of the *Shaytan*, and the Restore goal by suggesting that the evils that have accumulated over time must be purged to restore the *ummah* to its former glory. It is used to argue that audiences must actively work to recognize evil, even in mundane situations, and do everything possible to resist *Shaytan*'s efforts to draw them off the path of God.

The 1924 master narrative is invoked to draw parallels between the actions of foreign enemies (especially Israel and its allies), and those of Atatürk, the supposed "secret Jew" who destroyed the Ottoman Caliphate in the 1920s. For example, Islamist extremists have likened President Barack Obama to Atatürk in an effort to discredit his overtures to the Muslims world, and, among other instances, have claimed that the Algerian presidential elections in 2009 were a Jewish/Christian plot to destroy Islam. Strategic use of this master narrative serves the Rebuke goal by persuading audiences of the need to destroy internal enemies, and the Resist goal by establishing the need for someone to take on the role of the rescuer to deliver the community from treachery. Like the other "incomplete" master narratives containing the deliverance story form, it makes an especially strong appeal for a champion to step forward. This is a role the extremists are only too happy to claim and they urge others to support them, if not join them, in their efforts.

The *Nakba* master narrative, like the 1924 master narrative, reminds Muslims of the catastrophes that can result from failure to be vigilant against one's enemies—in this case external ones. As we noted earlier, it has strong connections to the invasion themes of the Crusade and Tatar master narratives, as the Israeli state was created on Palestinian land by invading Western powers over the objections of the Muslim (and Christian) Arab inhabitants. Hamas leaders have made this comparison to other foreign invasions explicit (see Chapter 12). Similar to the 1924 master narrative, the *Nakba* master narrative serves the Resist goal by reminding the audience of the disastrous consequences of the failure to remain vigilant against enemies, and constitutes an incomplete narrative where there is the need for a champion to rectify the situation, a role that can be played by Islamist extremists and their supporters.

Finally, the Seventy-Two Virgins master narrative contains implicit comparisons to all the other instances in Islamic history where Muslims have laid down their lives for the sake of the community. But its main rhetorical function is to convince the audience to willingly die for the cause by establishing the certainty of rewards for their efforts in the afterlife through an argument from first principles. The Qur'an and Hadith glorify the martyr and accord him (or her) and his family special consideration in judgment, making this a divinely ordained archetype that any believer would seek to emulate. In this way, the master narrative (along with others like the *Jahiliyyah*) serves a significant ideological function of naturalizing[19] the idea of violent resistance.

Countering Islamist Master Narratives

Thus far in this chapter, we have introduced a reformulation of Betz's idea of vertical integration, where master narratives occupy the intermediate position. On the one hand, they fit together to create a rhetorical vision of an *ummah* constantly under attack by internal and external enemies manifested in a range of archetypes, creating the need for champions and martyrs to offer resistance.

On the other hand, master narratives serve as resources for strategic rhetorical acts that are invoked in hopes of persuading audiences to frame events in their terms and align personal narratives in the service of their specific goals. It is beyond the scope of this book to offer specific communicative tactics to counter these strategies; however, we are in a position to conclude in this section by suggesting five strategic principles on which such efforts might be based.

But first, it is important to note that there is little profit in trying to contest the master narratives themselves, or the rhetorical vision that they weave. Master narratives develop over long periods of time and are deeply embedded in a culture. Accordingly, the same is true of the rhetorical vision they create. It is no more feasible to convince Muslims that they have no internal and external enemies than it is to convince Americans that they live in the land of the enslaved and the home of the cowardly. In both cases, these ideas are too deeply ingrained to be disrupted, and efforts to do so would be seen as ridiculous. Strategic efforts to contest the master narratives of Islamist extremism must therefore focus on the bottom end of the vertical hierarchy, where the master narratives are invoked in rhetorical acts—arguments—that make them relevant to the personal narratives of the audience.

Avoiding reinforcement

One strategy for dealing with the master narratives is to avoid reinforcement through communication and other behavior that tends to support them. This would appear to be obvious, but appearances can be deceiving. With respect to the Crusader master narrative, there is the infamous statement by U.S. President George W. Bush in 2001: "And the American people are beginning to understand. This *crusade*, this war on terrorism, is going to take a while. And the American people must be patient" [20] (emphasis added). While this statement used the vernacular form of the word "crusade," foreign audiences—especially Muslim ones—could not be expected to understand this, and extremists seized on Bush's words as proof that American efforts were what some U.S. critics dubbed a "tenth Crusade."[21]

One would think that this incident might have taught Westerners to be careful about using symbols that might benefit their adversaries. Alas, this seems not to be the case. We have reliable reports that active-duty military personnel from (at least) the United States and Denmark serving in Muslim countries are wearing the patch shown in figure 14.3 on their uniforms. It proudly labels the wearer a "pork eating crusader" in both English and Arabic, and features an image of a crusader knight with a red cross on his chest eating said meat. While we understand that military personnel have a tradition of wearing symbols of this kind as a way of promoting *espirit de corps*, this particular symbol clearly undermines their mission by literally labeling Western forces as Crusaders.

There is also the recently discovered fact that a U.S. weapons manufacturer was embedding Bible references in the serial numbers of gun sights that they manufacture for the United States and other Western countries. These sights are used by the military in battle in Iraq and Afghanistan, meaning that their weapons are inscribed with Christian verses of scriptures, echoing the religious nature of the Crusaders. Perhaps worse, these sights were even used on weapons used to train unwitting Afghan Muslim troops. As Haris Tarin, director of the Muslim Public Affairs Council, correctly

Figure 14.3 Pork eating crusader patch

pointed out, this "provides propaganda ammo to extremists who claim there is a 'Crusader war against Islam' by the United States."[22]

Beyond these direct inferences, there is the simple fact that Western forces have conducted military operations in Muslim countries for years. While the stated intention of these forces is not to capture or govern these territories in the long run, extremists focus on the deed rather than words to make the case that the forces are analogues of the Crusaders. This is why withdrawing troops out of Muslim countries, as the United States seems to be doing at present in Iraq, is essential.

Yet not all of the reinforcement problems lie with the West. Corruption and bad behavior by Muslim governments also support extremist master narratives by enacting the Tyrant and/or Imposter archetypes. *New York Times* reporter Dexter Filkins has recently reported on corruption in the Afghan government, stating:

> The Afghan government is corrupt from top to bottom. At the very top, you have the people around President Karzai, his brothers, who are allegedly . . . involved in the drug trade in that country, which of course is fueling the Taliban. And all the way down at the bottom, with the police on the streets who collect bribes. To become a police chief in a province is said to cost \$50,000 or \$100,000. You can make that back, of course, when you become the police chief. And so the picture that emerges from that—and the troubling questions that raises—are What are the Americans fighting for and who are they defending?[23]

There have also been reports that "hundreds of Sunni men disappeared for months into a secret Baghdad prison under the jurisdiction of [Shi'ite] Prime Minister Nouri al-Maliki's military office, where many were routinely tortured."[24] Such reports lend credibility to the Pharaoh and Hypocrites master narratives, and they cast aspersions on Western countries that support the Iraqi government, validating principles in the extremists' rhetorical vision of collusion between internal and external enemies. It is crucial that these kinds of reinforcing events be avoided if there is to be any hope of diminishing the power of rhetoric based on master narratives.

Contesting analogies

Another counterstrategy is to attempt to disrupt the analogical reasoning that establishes similarity between the elements of the master narratives and contemporary situations. As we have shown, almost all of the master narratives depend on this observational move in one way or another to gain persuasive force.

Shelley[25] offers a scheme of four different types of analogy counterargument. Choosing among them depends on the answers to two questions: (1) Is the underlying analogy valid or not, and (2) Is the goal to simply dissolve the existing analogy or replace it with a different one? The appropriate strategies, given answers to these questions, are shown in table 14.2.

Table 14.2 Analogy counterarguments (adapted from Shelley)

Analogy is	*Invalid*		*Valid*	
Goal is to	Dissolve	Replace	Dissolve	Replace
Strategy	False analogy	Misanalogy	Disanalogy	Counteranalogy
Counterargument	The analogy seems correct on the surface, but falls apart on further examination.	The analogy is wrong, and there is a different one that is right.	The analogy seems to be true, yet the facts do not obey its structure.	The analogy seems to be true, but there is a better analogy for explaining the same situation.
Objective	Make the audience struggle to map things that aren't similar.	Create a new, more coherent analogy with a conclusion that undermines the original one.	Identify characteristics that the analogue and target should share, but do not.	Use a different analogue to make a claim about the target that is incompatible with the original claim.

As mentioned above, the analogy between current events and those of the Crusades is the one most commonly deployed in extremist arguments. While there are a number of similarities between the situations, there are also a number of important differences that might be used to argue that the analogy is invalid.

For example, the First Crusade was carried out by Roman Catholic forces of Europe and initiated by a request from the Byzantine Emperor Alexios I, whose empire was beleaguered by war with the Seljuk Turks over control of land (Anatolia). The current conflict, in contrast, was initiated after Islamist extremists (who do not represent any political entity) attacked a faraway nation-state, not for the purposes of controlling holy land,[26] but to disrupt its political system and economy. The country that responded to attack, while majority Christian, is secular by its constitution (reflecting post-Reformation Enlightenment ideals) and does not recognize the leadership of the Catholic Pope. The Crusaders were promised forgiveness of sins and other indulgences by the Roman Church; Western soldiers (from a multitude of religious traditions) have received no such promises by the federal government, and any such promises would be treated as insane. Furthermore, the objective of the Crusades was to capture and permanently occupy Muslims lands, especially the city of Jerusalem. The United States has demonstrated that this is not its intent; as we write this book, the administration of President Barack Obama is withdrawing forces from Iraq. The American public favors withdrawal and the cessation of enormous ongoing military expenditures for the campaign.

An example of a possible counter-analogy to the Crusader master narrative is the story of the Wahhabi rebellion in Arabia that was crushed by the Ottoman Caliphate in 1818. The emergence of violent extremists—known to outsiders as Wahhabis—in Arabia (now Saudi Arabia) during the eighteenth century ultimately required an international military campaign from 1811 to 1818 led by the Albanian ruler of Egypt, Muhammad 'Ali Pasha, to crush it. The Wahhabis launched a violent campaign against other Muslims in Arabia and Iraq who they declared to be unbelievers. The Wahhabis also destroyed traditional Muslim holy sites, especially tombs and shrines (including Shi'ite holy sites in Karbala) that they deemed idolatrous, and sought to create their own "Islamic state." The Ottoman campaign, under the Caliph Mahmud II, echoed the events of an older narrative that took place during the time of the Caliph Abu Bakr in the seventh century. Abu Bakr launched a campaign against a self-styled prophet in Arabia called Musaylimah, also known as *al-Kadhab* ("the Liar") in Muslim sources, and defeated his rebellion. When the Ottoman campaign under Mahmud II succeeded, the leader of the Wahhabi extremists was beheaded and his head was taken back to Istanbul as a heretic. Turkey's membership in NATO obviously provides a useful analogy to the Ottomans and their campaigns.

The related arguments based on sign and parallel case can be contested in similar ways. In all cases the strategy is to dispute the similarities on which the comparisons are based, and possibly to also propose an alternate set of similarities (i.e., argue that the signs indicate some other process, or that other cases provide a better parallel) to explain the observed facts. Which of these arguments are most likely to succeed is a tactical decision, but we have established that the move is plausible.

Decompressing time

In their analysis of the ideological basis of religious extremism in *Strong Religion*, Gabriel Almond, R. Scott Appleby, and Emmanuel Sivan[27] argue that extremism depends on the maintenance of an "enclave culture" that perceives itself as continuously under attack from the outside. They note that this perception depends on a particular perspective on historical time:

> Historical time is the cosmological element most readily accessible to the analyst in that it relates directly to the primal impulse—the diagnosis—which the enclave feeds on. Its time perspective tends to be somewhat shrunken, collapsed, and condensed. The past is reduced to a few key eras, closely related to the enclave's notion as to what accounts for the glory and decline of the tradition; it is, hence, intensely relevant for the present. The future perspective is likewise rather short; the more radical the enclave, the shorter it is. Its overall bent is pessimistic, if not doom-laden.[28]

David Hackett Fischer[29] describes a narrative fallacy that underlies this perspective, which we believe is particularly important in the case of Islamist extremists. It is the *fallacy of presentism*:

> In which the antecedent in a narrative series is falsified by being denied or interpreted in terms of the consequent . . . [I]t is the mistaken idea that the proper way to do history is to prune away the dead branches of the past, and to preserve the green buds and twigs which have grown into the dark forest of our contemporary world.[30]

A possible communication strategy for dealing with this compression of time is to put back the dead branches that were pruned away. In other words, time can be uncompressed by surfacing "inconvenient details" from history that disrupt the interpretation of the present in terms of selective and favorable facts from the past. For example, in the Crusader master narrative, the archetypal champion, Saladin, did not lead the Islamic world in a monumental binary "clash of civilizations" against Christendom. As discussed in Chapter 9, Saladin actually undertook the capture of Jerusalem at the same time he was allied with the Byzantine Christians against their shared foes, the Roman Catholic Crusaders and the Sunni Muslim Seljuk Turks. Saladin was an adherent and patron of the Ash'arite school of Sunni theology, a school that contemporary Salafis and Wahhabis, like Usama Bin Laden and Mullah Omar, consider to be a blasphemous heresy.

These sorts of verifiable historical details begin to create "wedges" that immediately weaken and disrupt the parallels and compression of the narrative. The Ash'arite school has its origins with the tenth-century theologian, Abul-Hasan al-Ash'ari. In the centuries thereafter, Western Christendom experienced its most dramatic theological division in the form of the Protestant Reformation. The emergence of Protestant rebellions against the Roman Church is a significant "wedge" that distances predominately Protestant nations, such as the United States, from the institution that organized and led the medieval Crusades. Rhetorically, it may be possible to cast the heirs of the Reformation (e.g., the United States) as mutual victims of Papal tyranny and military campaigns, such as the Crusades.

Deconstructing binaries

One prominent characteristic of the master narratives is their dependence on binary oppositions. These sorts of binary oppositions are evident in master narratives such as the Battle of Karbala. The conflict is easily reduced to one of good versus evil. On one side is the righteous Imam Husayn (i.e., good) and on the other side is the wicked tyrant Yazid (i.e., evil). Other instances where binary oppositions are evident include the Pharaoh and Moses, the Muslims and the pagan Meccans at Badr, or the Mamluks and the barbaric Tatars at 'Ayn Jalut. These binaries provide easy analogies or framing devices through which participants in current day conflicts can quickly understand their roles, duties, and goals in straightforward ways. But the extremist analogies often obscure details and points of difference ("inconvenient details") in order to make different events "fit" together.

Given the importance of these binaries, a strategy that disrupts or puts them in tension can possibly reduce their rhetorical effectiveness. For example, when President Barack Obama accepted the Nobel Prize in 2010, he complicated the binary of war/peace by showing that the two concepts were inextricably linked throughout human history.[31] He suggested that instead of thinking about the relationship between peace and war as binary opposites, we should think of them as aspects of a common process—in the same way we now consider reason and emotion. In other words, he used a both/and strategy to complicate the either/or formation of the binaries.

For Barack Obama, this complication involves engaging in a "necessary" or "just" war in order to obtain peace and stability, despite the fact that peace—regardless of the sacrifices required to obtain it—is never itself sustainable. Once that inherent connection between peace and war is established, the binary opposites become associated with what communication theorist Leslie Baxter calls "dialectical tensions," or the back and forth tug of two seemingly opposite emotions that must be understood together rather than separately.[32]

Although no one would accuse President Obama of being a postmodernist, his rhetorical strategy is very much like Jean Francois Lyotard's attack on "grand narratives" (1980).[33] For Lyotard, the problem with any large-scale narrative that attempts to characterize history as a constant progressive urge defined by one idea—say, for example, the "class struggle" of Marx, the "scientific enlightenment" embraced by many in the West or, for our purposes, the "good/evil" and "believer/unbeliever" binaries that structure many Islamist master narratives—ignores, represses, or obscures the diverse "micronarratives" that were a real part of history and that resist(ed) or contested such a characterization of "what happened." It would no doubt be difficult—perhaps impossible—to challenge the authority of Islamist master narratives on that basis by, say, rearticulating "lost" historical resources or the perspective of Muslims who did not agree with the characterization of events as posited by radicals. But it might complicate the received wisdom of such narratives with Muslims who may yet be persuaded not to accept them at face value.

The anthropologist Jack Goody, a critical theorist who has written about binary oppositions from a post-structural perspective, suggests that the problem with binaries is that they are "often value-laden and ethnocentric," presenting a sense of social or political order that is both illusory and superficial.[34] He argues for a deep deconstruction of binary opposites that questions their objective basis in reality, which have been so much a part of feminist critiques of male/female binaries and the whole of critical race theories. Here again we confront the stubborn nature of master narratives as received cultural wisdom and the continuing challenge to find ways into discussions of those narratives that call into question their historical facts.

While extremists will no doubt resist giving up their precious binaries, strategic communication practitioners might establish a new goal of questioning at least one or two of those binary oppositions, thereby reframing them as dialectical tensions that, like Obama's war and peace, could be offered as alternative interpretations to a wide variety of audiences. It is a worthy goal, because if communication theories are correct, once dialectical tensions are established, it is possible for those understanding them to move on to genuine *dialogue*.

Recasting archetypes

A final strategy for countering master narratives is recasting contemporary actors in different archetypal roles that are already part of the rhetorical vision. As noted above, certain archetypes like the imposter and champion are especially strong. One way this existing strength can be turned against extremists is through casting them into unfavorable, rather than favorable roles. For instance, if Usama Bin Laden is assuming the role of the champion in a narrative, one strategy would be to shift his role to that of the archetypal prophet.

This strategy may sound odd at first, but readers should note that Muslims regard Muhammad as the "Seal of the Prophets" and anyone who claims prophethood after him is a liar, heretic, and imposter, akin to the seventh century false prophet, Musaylimah (*al-Kadhab*), who was killed in battle against Muhammad's political successor, the Caliph Abu Bakr. At present, it is difficult to definitively brand a Muslim figure as a heretic due to the absence of significant institutional authority in Islam. However, one of the quickest and most powerful ways to do so is through depicting someone as a self-proclaimed prophet.

If one has any questions about the hostility such notions evoke, simply look at the persecution of the Baha'i or Ahmadiyya in the Muslim world. In both instances, followers are accused of being infidels due to claims that the founders of these traditions or sects were new prophets of God after Muhammad. If Bin Laden or Mullah Omar could be accused of similar allegations with significant narrative reinforcement that gained traction in the Muslim world, the results could be considerably damaging to the extremist cause.

Another way to cast figures like Bin Laden is through the story of the Kharijites (*khawarij*), the first extremist offshoot in Islamic history. Their origins are attributed to a rebellion of Arab Muslims against the leadership of the Rightly Guided Caliph, 'Ali, during the Battle of Siffin in 657 CE. Following the battle, the Kharijites separated themselves from the *ummah* and waged war against both the Caliph 'Ali and his opponent at Siffin, Muawiyyah. In 661, a Kharijite assassinated 'Ali. Since that time, Kharijites have been defined as anyone who rebels against the legitimate *imam* ("leader") accepted by the people of any time period. They are particularly known for adhering to the practice of *takfir*, or declaring other Muslims to be infidels (thus they killed 'Ali, calling him an infidel). Due to their judgmental nature, they fragmented into many different groups over differences. *Takfir* is a heresy in mainstream Sunni Islam, and 'Ali is revered as the fourth Rightly Guided Caliph. To the Shi'ites, 'Ali is the first Holy Imam, and the father of the second and third Imams. Thus, Kharijites are rejected by Sunni and Shi'ite Muslims as fanatical and murderous rebels that must be defeated. Numerous revolts by Kharijite groups occurred for centuries, especially in the seventh and eighth centuries. Contemporary extremists share many characteristics with the Kharijites, including the practice of *takfir*, preoccupation with rigid outward practice (over spirituality), and rebellion against Muslim leaders. According to local Afghan tradition, the Rightly Guided Caliph, 'Ali, is entombed at the "Blue Mosque" in Mazar-e Sharif in northern Afghanistan, making it a major site of Afghan Muslim pilgrimage. However, for the majority of the world's Muslims, 'Ali is entombed in Najaf, Iraq. The historical descendants of the original Kharijites are the Ibadis of Oman, but they have significantly reformed their teachings over the centuries.

Another option is to question the *competence* of extremists as occupants of archetypal roles. For example, champions are designated as such because of the success and victories they achieve. But what have Usama Bin Laden or Ayman al-Zawahiri achieved aside from death, destruction, and further suffering on the part of Muslims? The defeat of the Soviets is still hailed as a victory claimed by Bin Laden and others, but the truth of the matter is that Afghanistan lies in ruins, squalor, and poverty. The countryside is filled with landmines and rubble. Compared to Afghanistan in the 1950s, the Islamists have brought nothing to the country, certainly nothing worthy of a "champion." In contrast, the great champions of the master narratives described in this book, such as Saladin or Qutuz, all delivered tangible and lasting results that benefited the Muslim community.

Finally, it is plausible to refigure the kind of behavior that might qualify for the archetype. Due to the violent nature of Islamist extremists, the master narratives they employ in their rhetoric often carry militant connotations. The archetypal champions featured in the master narratives are great warriors who triumphed on the battlefield. However, counter-narratives that offer alternative understandings of archetypal roles can help to disrupt or weaken extremist designations. For example, Martin Luther King Jr. is understood to be a nonviolent champion in the master narratives of the United States. In a similar fashion, the promotion of narratives about Muslim figures such as Abdul-Ghaffar Khan can function in a similar manner. Khan, an ethnic Pashtun, founded the Khudai Khidmatgars, or the

"Servants of God." The Servants of God were a disciplined "army" of non-violent soldiers who struggled against British colonial rule and worked for the education and advancement of the Pashtun tribal peoples in Afghanistan and Pakistan. At its peak, the Servants of God included 100,000 Muslims, each of which took an oath pledging service to God by serving humanity, by forgiveness, and by refraining from violence and revenge. Such narratives provide alternative understandings of archetypal roles traditionally associated exclusively with militant or violent figures in extremist rhetoric.

Summary

In this chapter we have argued that master narratives serve as the bridge between a rhetorical vision at the most abstract level of culture and concrete personal narratives of members of extremists' audience. They use master narratives as resources for strategic arguments that support their goals, the three "R's" of Islamist extremism. These arguments primarily seek to establish similarity between the stories that make up the master narratives and contemporary events.

The objective is to persuade audiences to align their personal narratives to be consistent with story forms and archetypes contained in the rhetorical vision. That vision paints a world where Islam and its believers are under constant attack from the inside and outside, requiring champions to step up and thwart the efforts of imposters and various kinds of invaders. This allows extremists to frame themselves as the champions and urge their audience to support their efforts.

The framework we have developed suggests five possible strategies for countering extremists' use of the master narratives. The simplest and most direct strategy is for Western forces and Muslim government to stop taking actions that evoke the "bad guy" archetypes in the rhetorical vision. Strategies for directly countering their arguments involve challenging the analogical reasoning used in extremist arguments and upsetting the time compression on which their rhetorical vision depends. Finally, it seems plausible to turn roles in the master narratives against the extremists by associating them with "bad guy" archetypes, questioning their competence as inhabitants of "good guy" archetypes, and recasting archetypes like the champion in nonviolent terms.

APPENDIX

Selected Archetypes and Story Forms

Barbarian a savage warrior who conquers and destroys for the sake of destruction.

Betrayal Story Form an ally or friend of the protagonist betrays his or her relationship with the protagonist for selfish ends, advantage, or political expediency and must pay for it.

Champion a heroic leader capable of surmounting great and deadly challenges, including battles.

Conflict with God (Deity) Story Form the conduct of an antagonist is in conflict with a deity who must humble the arrogant antagonist through an assertion of divine power or sovereignty.

Crusader a Western occupier who conquers lands to subjugate and inhabit them; often conflated with **Colonizer**.

Deity a god, goddess, or transcendent being.

Deliverance Story Form the community, people, or nation of the protagonist struggles in a precarious existence and must be delivered from those conditions.

Imposter one who lies about his or her true identity or intentions in a calculated fashion.

Invasion Story Form a belligerent foreign force conquers the land of the protagonist and must be fought, defeated, or expelled.

Martyr one who sacrifices his or her life in a just and righteous cause.

Noble Sacrifice Story Form a protagonist sacrifices his or her life in a just and righteous cause in a manner that ultimately benefits his or her community, people, or nation.

Pagan one who follows false man-made idols and backward traditions.

Prophet a mortal agent of a deity who conveys the message of the deity or enacts divine commands.

Ruse Story Form an antagonist enacts an elaborate plot to fool or mislead people by misrepresenting or hiding his true identity or intentions.

Sage an elder figure of great knowledge who advises or teaches others.

Savior a remarkable and rare leader who appears at a critical and precarious time to rescue or redeem a people or nation.

Traitor one who betrays an alliance or personal bond for personal gain or selfish ends.

Trickster one who purposely misguides others in order to lead them into misfortune.

Tyrant an arrogant and cruel ruler who oppresses his people.

Notes

Introduction

1. William D. Casebeer and James A. Russell, “Storytelling and Terrorism: Towards a Comprehensive ‘Counter-Narrative Strategy,’” *Strategic Insights*, Vol. IV, No. 3 (March 2005): 1.
2. See Akbar S. Ahmed, *Islam Today: A Short Introduction to the Muslim World* (New York: I. B. Tauris, 1999).
3. Bruce Lincoln, *Holy Terrors: Thinking about Religion after September 11* (Chicago: University of Chicago Press, 2003), 6.
4. David Betz, “The Virtual Dimension of Contemporary Insurgency and Counterinsurgency,” *Small Wars and Insurgencies*, Vol. 19, No. 4 (2008): 510–540.

Chapter 1

1. Jeffry R. Halverson, *Theology and Creed in Sunni Islam: The Muslim Brotherhood, Ash'arism, and Political Sunnism* (New York: Palgrave Macmillan, 2010), 60–65.
2. Alasdair MacIntyre, *After Virtue: A Study in Moral Theory* (South Bend, IN: University of Notre Dame Press, 1984), 8.
3. The following synopsis of al Qaeda's narrative is drawn from two principal sources: Sebastien Gorka and David Kilcullen, “Who's Winning the Battle for Narrative? Al Qaeda versus the United States and its Allies,” in *Influence Warfare: How Terrorists and Governments Fight to Shape Perceptions in a War of Ideas*, ed. James J. F. Forrest (New York: Praeger Security International, 2009), 229–240; and Tom Quiggin, “Understanding Ideology for Counter-Narrative Work,” III, 2, available online at: http://www.terrorismanalysts.com/pt/index.php?opt ion=com_rokzine&view=article&id=77&Itemid=54. (Last accessed on September 2, 2010).
4. Joseph Campbell, *The Power of Myth* (New York: Anchor, 1991).

5. Walter R. Fisher, *Human Communication as Narration: Toward a Philosophy of Reason, Value, and Action* (Columbia: University of South Carolina Press, 1989).
6. Clifford Geertz, "Thick Description: Toward an Interpretive Theory of Culture," in *The Interpretation of Cultures* (New York: Basic Books, 1973).
7. See Max Weber, "Objectivity in Social Science and Social Policy," in *The Methodology of the Social Sciences*, ed. and trans. E. A. Shils and H. A. Finch (New York: Free Press, 1904/1949).
8. So, for example, while the Southern Baptist Convention may select texts from its holy scripture to "prove" that women are lesser beings and to condone violence against them, one of its more prominent members, Deacon Jimmy Carter, can point to the same text and use his interpretation of it to divorce himself from the SBC in a public statement (see http://www.guardian.co.uk/commentisfree/2009/jul/12/jimmy-carter-womens-rights-equality). (Last accessed on September 2, 2010).
9. Kenneth Burke, *On Symbols and Society*, ed. Joseph Gusfield (Chicago: University of Chicago Press, 1989).
10. Translated into English by James Murphy.
11. H. L. Goodall, Jr., "Blood, Shit, and Tears: The Terrorist as Abject Other," paper presented at the "Managing and Legislating Workplace Abjection," University of York, United Kingdom, September 23, 2009. For an elaboration of the Crusader/Infidel binary, please see Jeff Sharlet, "Jesus Killed Mohammad," *Harper's* (May 2009): 31–43.
12. Octavio Paz, *In Search of the Present: 1990 Nobel Lecture* (San Diego: Harcourt Brace Jovanovich, 1990).
13. Anthony Giddens, *The Constitution of Society* (Cambridge: Polity Press, 1984).

Chapter 2

1. Ulrich H. Luft, "Religion," *The Oxford Encyclopedia of Ancient Egypt*, ed. Donald B. Redford. (New York: Oxford University Press, 2005); *The Oxford Encyclopedia of Ancient Egypt*: (e-reference edition). Oxford University Press. Arizona State University, 16 October 2009. http://www.oxfordancientegypt.com/entry?entry=t176.e0615.
2. Arielle P. Kozloff, Karol Myśliwiec, Roland Tefnin, Angélique Corthals, and Julia Harvey, "Sculpture," *The Oxford Encyclopedia of Ancient Egypt*, ed. Donald B. Redford (New York: Oxford University Press, 2005); *The Oxford Encyclopedia of Ancient Egypt*: (e-reference edition). Oxford University Press. Arizona State University, 16 October 2009. http://www.oxford-ancientegypt.com/entry?entry=t176.e0640.s0002.

3. A. J. Wensinck, "Fir'awn," *Encyclopedia of Islam*, Vol. 2, ed. Bernard Lewis, Charles Pellat, and Joseph Schacht (Leiden: E. J. Brill, 1991), 917.
4. Ibid.
5. Ibn Kathir, *Stories of the Prophets*, trans. Sayed Gad (El-Mansoura, Egypt: Dar al-Manarah, 2000), 275.
6. Ibid., 284.
7. Ibid., 287.
8. Ibid., 291.
9. Ibid., 294.
10. Gilles Kepel, *Muslim Extremism in Egypt: The Prophet and Pharaoh*, trans. Jon Rothschild (Berkeley: University of California Press, 2003), 192.
11. Usama Bin Laden quoted in Henry Shuster, "Al Qaeda-linked Web site posts bin Laden tape text," *CNN.com* (November 14, 2002); Retrieved from http://archives.cnn.com/2002/WORLD/meast/11/14/binladen.tape/index.html.
12. Translation by Open Source.Gov; Retrieved from https://www.opensource.gov/portal/server.pt/gateway/PTARGS_0_0_200_240_51_43/content/Display/10802690?highlightQuery=eJzTcPcNMDIwsDQwM7IwNDYzMDDWBAAp9AP%2B&fileSize=467198.
13. "The Propaganda War: War of Words," *Islamist Magazine* (January 2009); Retrieved from http://www.scribd.com/doc/10101469/Islamist-Magazine-Final-Muharram-1430-January-2009.
14. Abu Salman Faris ibn Ahmad al-Shuwayl az-Zahrani, *The Game of the Pharaohs* (1424 AH), 13.

Chapter 3

1. Martin Lings, *Muhammad: His Life Based on the Earliest Sources* (Cambridge, UK: The Islamic Texts Society, 1991), 15.
2. Mehmed A. Simsar, "Review: The Book of Idols or The Kitab al-Asnam by Nabih Amin Faris; Hisham ibn-al-Kalbi," *Speculum*, Vol. 28, No. 1 (Jan., 1953), 167.
3. See, e.g., Leila Ahmed, *Women and Gender in Islam: Historical Roots of a Modern Debate* (Hartford, CT: Yale University Press, 1993).
4. *Sahih al-Bukhari*, Vol. 2, Book 24, No. 489. Retrieved from http://www.usc. edu/schools/college/crcc/engagement/resources/texts/muslim/hadith/bukhari/024.sbt.html#002.024.488.
5. Sayyid Qutb, *Milestones*, trans. Anonymous (New Delhi: Islamic Book Service, 2002), 9.
6. Ibid., 82.
7. Ibid., 10–11.

8. Shahrough Akhavi, "Sayyid Qutb," *The Oxford Encyclopedia of the Modern Islamic World*, Vol. 3, ed. John L. Esposito (New York: Oxford University Press, 1995), 402.
9. Qutb, *Milestones* (2002), 15.
10. Ibid., 17.
11. Ibid.
12. Qutb naively assumes that the people during the lifetime of the Prophet and the *sahabah* somehow managed to remain completely isolated or immune (on a conscious and subconscious level) to the influence of neighboring communities, religions, and cultures. This is not at all the case.
13. Qutb, *Milestones* (2002), 20.
14. Ibid., 21.
15. Ibid., 33.
16. Ibid., 12.
17. Ibid., 38.
18. Ibid., 46–47.
19. Ibid., 95.
20. Ibid., 104.
21. Ibid.
22. Ahmad S. Moussalli, *Radical Islamic Fundamentalism: The Ideological and Political Discourse of Sayyid Qutb* (Beirut: American University of Beirut Press, 1992), 156.
23. Qutb, *Milestones* (2002), 107.
24. Ibid.
25. Ibid., 118–119.

Chapter 4

1. Safi ur-Rahman al-Mubarakpuri, *Ar-Raheeq al-Makhtum (The Sealed Nectar): Biography of the Noble Prophet* (Riyadh, SA: Maktaba Dar-us-Salam, 1995), 210.
2. Ibid.
3. Ibid., 212.
4. Ibid., 215.
5. *Sahih Bukhari*, Vol. 5, Book 59, No. 330; Retrieved from http://www.usc.edu/schools/college/crcc/engagement/resources/texts/muslim/hadith/bukhari/059.sbt.html#005.059.330.
6. This is a famous story in Islamic tradition. For a more detailed account, see Martin Lings, *Muhammad: His Life Based on the Earliest Sources* (Cambridge, UK: Islamic Texts Society, 1991), 59.

7. al-Mubarakpuri, *Ar-Raheeq al-Makhtum*, 223.
8. Ibid., 224.
9. Ibid., 226.
10. Ibid., 229.
11. Gilles Kepel, *Jihad: The Trail of Political Islam*, trans. Anthony F. Roberts (New York: I. B. Tauris, 2002), 145.
12. "Biography of Sheikh Abdullah Azzam (Shaheed)" in Abdullah Azzam, *Defense of Muslim Lands: The First Obligation after Iman,* trans. unknown (2002); Retrieved from http://www.religioscope.com/info/doc/jihad/azzam_defence_2_intro.htm.
13. Translated by Open Source.Gov; Retrieved from https://www.opensource.gov/portal/server.pt/gateway/PTARGS_0_0_916_314_0_43/content/Display/4023449?highlightQuery=eJxVzsEOgyAMBuBX4ag3 WoGuxyU67EFdpsne%2F01WkCylvZAvf%2FMzDO58vtF70H14HUJ3fP446eoAF8zbqyEVC10ytGToEHxFsBjruT46BIN5uzFhRaKC0pIMqSbJJhmh9sQeoyJCskWMfP%2FJJPW2FOGEbnRfuVbZnex5Oa9llnn8Aar7Pw8%3D&fileSize=74409.
14. Ayman al-Zawahiri, "Allegiance and Disavowal" (December 2002); Retrieved from https://hdshcresearch.asu.edu/aqp/servefile.php?id=528&type=html.
15. Olivier Roy, *Globalized Islam: The Search for a New Ummah* (New York: Cambridge University Press, 2004), 296.
16. Abdullah Azzam, *Signs of Ar-Rahman from the Jihad in Afghanistan*, ed. A. B. al-Mehri (Birmingham, UK: Maktabah, n.d.), 33.
17. Ibid., 36–37.
18. Ibid., 38.
19. "Timeline: Soviet War in Afghanistan," *BBC News* (February 17, 2009); Retrieved from http://news.bbc.co.uk/2/hi/south_asia/7883532.stm.
20. Roy, *Globalized Islam*, 296.
21. Ibid., 297.
22. Ibid.; Tim McGirk, "Asian Journey—Moscow's Graveyard," *Time.com* (August 2005), 2; Retrieved from http://www.time.com/time/asia/2005/journey/afghan2.html.
23. Translated by Open Source.Gov; Retrieved from https://www.opensource.gov/portal/server.pt/gateway/PTARGS_0_0_916_314_0_43/content/Display/4023449?highlightQuery=eJxVzsEOgyAMBuBX4ag3 WoGuxyU67EFdpsne%2F01WkCylvZAvf%2FMzDO58vtF70H14HUJ 3fP446eoAF 8zbqyE8zbqyEVC10ytGToEHxFsBjruT46BIN5uzFhRaKC-0pIMqSbJJhmh9sQeoyJCskWMfP%2FJJPW2FOGEbnRfuVbZnex5Oa9llnn8Aar7Pw8%3D&fileSize=74409.

Chapter 5

1. Exodus 32: 26–29.
2. Martin Lings, *Muhammad: His Life Based on the Earliest Sources* (Cambridge, UK: Islamic Texts Society, 1991), 108.
3. Ibid., 108, 129.
4. Daniel C. Peterson, *Muhammad: Prophet of God* (Cambridge, UK: William B. Eerdmans, 2007), 109.
5. Lings, *Muhammad,* 129.
6. Ibid., 174.
7. Peterson, *Muhammad,* 113.
8. Lings, *Muhammad,* 197.
9. Safi-ur-Rahman al-Mubarakpuri, *Ar-Raheeq Al-Makhtum (The Sealed Nectar): Biography of the Noble Prophet* (Birmingham, UK: Maktaba Dar-us-Salam, 1995), 302–304.
10. Ibid., 336.
11. Translated by Open Source.Gov; Retrieved from https://www.opensource.gov/portal/server.pt/Gateway/PTARGS_0_0_200_240_151207_43/content/Display/11429127? highlightQuery=eJzTyKgsyE8uyixJLdYEAB4CBJw%3D&fileSize=60556.
12. Translated by Open Source.Gov; Retrieved from https://www.opensource.gov/portal/server.pt/gateway/PTARGS_0_0_200_240_151207_43/content/Display/11411484?highlightQuery=eJzTyKgsyE8uyixJLdYEAB4CBJw%3D& fileSize=257862.
13. Retrieved from http://www.al-faloja.info/vb/showthread.php?t=39334 [No longer active].
14. Translated by Open Source.Gov; Retrieved from https://www.opensource.gov/portal/server.pt/gateway/PTARGS_0_0_200_240_151207_43/content/Display/11411137?highlightQuery=eJzTyKgsyE8uyixJLdYEAB4CBJw%3D&fileSize=5011.
15. Ibid.
16. Translated by Open Source.Gov; Retrieved from https://www.opensource.gov/portal/server.pt/gateway/PTARGS_0_0_8423_240_0_43/content/Display/11311071?highlightQuery=eJzTUKrOysxITMksLlEoT00qzixJLa5VUgj3DPHw9FMI9g8NcnbVVPDzD1HQUHDzD%2FVX8A9ScHN1VNAEMTRQNSsQrxsAmBsi4A%3D%3D&fileSize=6556.

Chapter 6

1. Robert Michael, *History of Catholic Antisemitism: The Dark Side of the Church* (New York: Palgrave Macmillan, 2008), 14–15.

2. Ibid., 2.
3. Ibid., 3, 18.
4. Alfred Guillaume, *The Life of Muhammad: A Translation of Ishaq's Sirat Rasul Allah* (Karachi: Oxford University Press, 1955), 231–233; Retrieved from http://www.constitution.org/cons/medina/con_medina.htm.
5. Daniel C. Peterson, *Muhammad: Prophet of God* (Cambridge, UK: William B. Eerdmans, 2007), 109.
6. Ibid., 116–118.
7. Martin Lings, *Muhammad: His Life Based on the Earliest Sources* (Cambridge, UK: Islamic Texts Society, 1997), 215.
8. Peterson, *Muhammad,* 121.
9. Ibid., 125.
10. *Sahih Muslim*, Book 19, No. 4370; Retrieved from http://www.usc.edu/schools/college/crcc/engagement/resources/texts/muslim/hadith/muslim/019.smt.html#019.4370.
11. Lings, *Muhammad,* 229.
12. Peterson, *Muhammad,* 126.
13. *Sahih Muslim*, Book 19, No. 4370; Retrieved from http://www.usc.edu/schools/college/crcc/engagement/resources/texts/muslim/hadith/muslim/019.smt.html#019.4370.
14. Lings, *Muhammad,* 232.
15. Safi-ur-Rahman al-Mubarakpuri, *Ar-Raheeq Al-Makhtum (The Sealed Nectar): Biography of the Noble Prophet* (Riyadh, SA: Maktaba Dar-us-Salam, 1995), 349.
16. Peterson, *Muhammad,* 136.
17. Ibid.
18. *Sahih al-Bukhari*, Vol. 4, Book 52, No. 195; Retrieved from http://www.usc.edu/schools/college/crcc/engagement/resources/texts/muslim/hadith/bukhari/052.sbt.html#004.052.195.
19. al-Mubarakpuri, *Ar-Raheeq Al-Makhtum,* 370.
20. Ibid., 371.
21. Peterson, *Muhammad,* 137.
22. al-Mubarakpuri, *Ar-Raheeq Al-Makhtum,* 372; Peterson, *Muhammad,* 138.
23. Peterson, *Muhammad,* 138.
24. *Sahih al-Bukhari*, Vol. 3, Book 44, No. 678; Retrieved from http://www.usc.edu/schools/college/crcc/engagement/resources/texts/muslim/hadith/bukhari/044.sbt.html#003.044.678.
25. See Patricia Crone, *Hagarism: The Making of the Islamic World* (Cambridge: Cambridge University Press, 1977).
26. Deborah J. Gerner, *One Land, Two Peoples* (Oxford: Westview, 1994), 124–125.

27. Ibid., 127.
28. http://www.ynetnews.com/articles/0,7340,L-3286431,00.html.
29. Sayyed Hassan Nasrallah, *Voice of Hezbollah: The Statements of Sayyed Hassan Nasrallah,* ed. Nicholas Noe, trans. Ellen Khouri (New York: Verso, 2007), 188.
30. Ibid., 189–190.
31. Translated by Open Source.Gov; Retrieved from https://www.opensource.gov/portal/server.pt/gateway/PTARGS_0_0_200_240_51_43/content/Display/11349078?highlightQuery=eJzTyM5IrExKLFJw9HNRyEotL9YEADnlBgA%3D&fileSize=43466.
32. Translated by Open Source.Gov; Retrieved from https://www.opensource.gov/portal/server.pt/gateway/PTARGS_0_0_200_240_51_43/content/Display/11331110?highlightQuery=eJzTyM5IrExKLFJw9HNRyEotL9YEADnlBgA%3D&fileSize=12893.

Chapter 7

1. See Kamran Scot Aghaie, *The Martyrs of Karbala: Shi'i Symbols and Rituals in Modern Iran* (Seattle: University of Washington, 2004).
2. Willard G. Oxtoby, "The Christian Tradition," in *World Religions: Western Religions,* ed. Willard G. Oxtoby (New York: Oxford University Press, 2002), 215.
3. Ibid.
4. Stephen L. Harris, *Understanding the Bible: Fifth Edition* (Mountain View, CA: Mayfield Publishing, 2000), 419–420.
5. *Nahjul Balagha: Peak of Eloquence,* trans. Sayed Ali Reza (Elmhurst, NY: Tahrike Tarsile Qur'an, 1985), 411.
6. Aghaie, *Martyrs of Karbala,* 92.
7. Ibid.
8. Ibid., 91.
9. Mahmoud Ayoub, *Redemptive Suffering in Islam* (New York: Mouton Publishers, 1978), 96.
10. John J. Donohue and John L. Esposito, eds. *Islam in Transition: Muslim Perspectives* (New York: Oxford University Press, 1982), 315.
11. Ruhullah Khomeini quoted in John L. Esposito, *Voices of Resurgent Islam* (New York: Oxford University Press, 1983), 154–155.
12. Maziar Bahari, "Iran's President Bush," *Newsweek* (June 3, 2009); Retrieved from http://www.newsweek.com/id/200236.
13. Ibid.
14. Kevin Sim, *Pilgrimage to Karbala: Iran, Iraq, and Shia Islam,* PBS Video (2007).

15. Gilles Kepel, *Jihad: The Trail of Political Islam*, trans. Anthony F. Roberts (New York: I. B. Tauris, 2003), 87.
16. The Arabic term for a self-martyr, *istishhadi*, is a variation of the verb *yustashhid* meaning "to become a martyr." *Istishhadi* literally means "one who martyrs himself."
17. Amal Saad-Ghorayeb, *Hizbu'llah: Politics and Religion* (London: Pluto Press, 2002), 131; Hala Jaber, *Hezbollah: Born with a Vengeance* (New York: Columbia University Press, 1997), 75.
18. Saad-Ghorayeb, *Hizbu'llah*, 131.
19. Jaber, *Hezbollah,* 19.
20. Deborah J. Gerner, *One Land, Two Peoples* (Oxford: Westview, 1994), 124–125.
21. Ibid., 127.
22. Particularly U.S. and French forces stationed in Lebanon as UN peacekeepers.
23. Joyce M. Davis, *Martyrs* (New York: Palgrave Macmillan, 2003), 46.
24. Valerie Saturen, "Divine Suffering in Shiism: Origins and Political Implications," *Iran Analysis Quarterly,* Vol. 2, No. 4 (July-September 2005), 38.
25. Saad-Ghorayeb, *Hizbu'llah,* 127.
26. See, e.g., Acts 20:28, Rom. 3:24–26, 1 Pet. 1:18, and Heb. 10:10–13 for Christian notions of the redemptive suffering of Christ.
27. Saad-Ghorayeb, *Hizbu'llah*, 133.
28. See, e.g., the outbreak of the U.S.-led war against Iraq in March 2003.
29. Jaber, *Hezbollah,* 86.

Chapter 8

1. NIV translation of 2 Samuel 7:12–16; Retrieved from http://www.biblegateway.com/passage/?search=2%20Samuel%207&version=NIV.
2. Stephen L. Harris, *Understanding the Bible: Fifth Edition* (Mountain View, CA: Mayfield Publishing, 2000), 567.
3. NIV translation of Isaiah 45:1–13; Retrieved from http://www.biblegateway.com/passage/?search=Isaiah+45&version=NIV.
4. Quoted and translated in Alan F. Segal, "The Jewish Tradition," in *World Religions: Western Religions*, ed. Willard G. Oxtoby (New York: Oxford University Press, 2002), 101.
5. Harris, *Understanding the Bible*, 317.
6. Segal, *World Religions*, 69.
7. NIV translation of John 18:36; Retrieved from http://www.biblegateway.com/passage/?search=John%2018:36&version=KJ21.

8. Harris, *Understanding the Bible*, 332.
9. Roger Beck, *The Religion of the Mithras Cult in the Roman Empire: Mysteries of the Unconquered Sun* (New York: Oxford University Press, 2006), 5.
10. Harris, *Understanding the Bible*, 333–334.
11. Ibid., 330.
12. NIV translation of Revelation 19:12–16; Retrieved from http://www.biblegateway.com/passage/?search=Revelation+19&version=KJ21.
13. Ibn Kathir, *Stories of the Prophets*, trans. Sayed Gad (El-Mansoura, Egypt: Dar al-Manarah, 2000), 259.
14. David Cook, *Martyrdom in Islam* (Cambridge: Cambridge University Press, 2007), 49.
15. Ibn Kathir, *Stories of the Prophets*, 262–263.
16. Jan-Olaf Blichfeldt, *Early Mahdism: Politics and Religion in the Formative Period of Islam* (Leiden: E. J. Brill, 1985), 2.
17. Yann Richard, *Shi'ite Islam: Polity, Ideology, and Creed*, trans. Antonia Nevill (Oxford: Blackwell, 1995), 41.
18. Ibid., 42.
19. Ibrahim Amini, *Al-Imam al-Mahdi: Just Leader for Humanity*, trans. Abdulaziz Sachedina (Ahlul Bayt Digital Islamic Library Project, n.d.); Retrieved from http://www.al islam.org/mahdi/nontl/Chap-10.htm.
20. Blichfeldt, *Early Mahdism*, 9.
21. Amini; Retrieved from http://www.al-islam.org/mahdi/nontl/Chap-11.htm.
22. Blichfeldt, *Early Mahdism*, 9.
23. *Sunan Abu Dawud* Book 36, No. 4269; Retrieved from http://www.usc.edu/schools/college/crcc/engagement/resources/texts/muslim/hadith/abudawud/036.sat.html#036.4269.
24. *Sunan Abu Dawud* Book 36, No. 4272; Retrieved from http://www.usc.edu/schools/college/crcc/engagement/resources/texts/muslim/hadith/abudawud/036.sat.html#036.4272.
25. David Robinson, *Muslim Societies in African History* (Cambridge: Cambridge University Press, 2004), 170.
26. Ibid., 170–171.
27. Quoted in A. Savyon and Y. Mansharof, "The Doctrine of Mahdism in the Ideological and Political Philosophy of Mahmoud Ahmadinejad and Ayatollah Mesbah-e Yazdi," *Inquiry & Analysis* No. 357 (MEMRI 2007): 5.
28. Retrieved from http://www.globalsecurity.org/wmd/library/news/iran/2007/iran-070926-irna01.htm.
29. See http://www.thememriblog.org/blog_personal/en/22035.htm.
30. "Shi'ite Supremacists Emerge from Iran's Shadows," *Asia Times* (September 9, 2005); Retrieved from http://www.atimes.com/atimes/Middle_East/GI09Ak01.html.

31. Noah Feldman, "Islam, Terror and the Second Nuclear Age," *New York Times* (October 29, 2006); Retrieved from http://www.nytimes.com/2006/10/29/magazine/29islam.html?pagewanted=all.
32. Ahiya Raved, "Messianic Leaders in Iran, Iraq," *Y-Net News* (November 6, 2006); Retrieved from http://www.ynetnews.com/articles/0,7340,L-3324216,00.html.
33. Jean-Pierre Filiu, "The Return of Political Mahdism," in *Current Trends in Islamist Ideology*, Vol. 8 (May 21, 2009); Retrieved from http://www.currenttrends.org/research/detail/the-return-of-political-mahdism.

Chapter 9

1. Bongars, *Gesta Dei per Francos*, 1, pp. 382 f., trans. in *A Source Book for Medieval History*, ed. Oliver J. Thatcher and Edgar Holmes McNeal (New York: Scribners, 1905), 513–517; Retrieved from http://www.ford ham.edu/halsall/source/urban2-5vers.html.
2. Jonathan Phillips, *The Crusades: 1095–1197* (London: Pearson Education, 2002), 5.
3. Jonathan Riley-Smith, ed. *The Oxford History of the Crusades* (New York: Oxford University Press, 2002), 217.
4. Phillips, *The Crusades*, 25.
5. Quoted in ibid.
6. Ibid., 19, 26.
7. Quoted in ibid., 169.
8. Ibid., 28.
9. Quoted in ibid., 41.
10. Ibid., 42.
11. Riley-Smith, *The Oxford History of the Crusades*, 122.
12. James E. Lindsay, *Daily Life in the Medieval Islamic World* (Indianapolis: Hackett Publishing, 2005), 79.
13. Hadia Dajani-Shakeel, "Some Medieval Accounts of Salah al-Din's Recovery of Jerusalem (Al-Quds)," in *Studia Palaestina: Studies in honour of Constantine K. Zurayk*, ed. Hisham Nashabe (Beirut Institute for Palestine Studies, 1988); Retrieved from http://www.fordham.edu/halsall/med/salahdin.html.
14. Charles M. Brand, "The Byzantines and Saladin, 1185–1192: Opponents of the Third Crusade," *Speculum*, Vol. 37, No. 2 (April 1962): 161–171.
15. Dajani-Shakeel, "Some Medieval Accounts."
16. Quoted in ibid.
17. Sayyid Qutb, *Social Justice in Islam*, trans. Hamid Algar (Oneonta, NY: Islamic Publications International, 2000), 271.

18. Ibid., 273.
19. Ibid., 267.
20. Ibid.
21. Ibid.
22. Ibid.
23. Ibid., 279.
24. Ibid., 281.
25. Ibid., 273.
26. Ibid., 271.
27. Ibid., 270.
28. Ibid.
29. Ibid., 273.
30. Ibid.
31. Ibid., 275.
32. Ibid.
33. Robert Irwin, "The Emergence of the Islamic World System 1000–1500," in *Islamic World,* ed. Francis Robinson (New York: Cambridge University Press, 1996), 48.
34. Quoted in Marvin E. Gettleman and Stuart Schaar, *The Middle East and Islamic World Reader* (New York: Grove Press, 2003), 49.
35. Gettleman and Schaar, *Middle East and Islamic World Reader,* 50.
36. Quoted in ibid.
37. Joseph De Somogyi, "A *Qasida* on the Destruction of Baghdad by the Mongols," *Bulletin of the School of Oriental Studies, University of London,* Vol. 7, No. 1 (1933), 41.
38. Gettleman and Schaar, *Middle East and Islamic World Reader*, 51.
39. De Somogyi, "A *Qasida* on the Destruction of Baghdad by the Mongols," 41.
40. Irwin, "The Emergence of the Islamic World System 1000–1500," 51.
41. Jonathan P. Berkey, *The Formation of Islam: Religion and Society in the Near East, 600–1800* (New York: Cambridge University Press, 2003), 182; see also, Irwin, "The Emergence of the Islamic World System 1000–1500," 49.
42. Reuven Amitai-Preiss, "Islam and Mongol Tradition: A View from the Mamluk Sultanate," *Bulletin of the School of Oriental and African Studies, University of London*, Vol. 59, No. 1 (1996), 1–3.
43. D. O. Morgan, "The Great Yasa of Chingiz Khan and Mongol Law in the Ilkhanate," *Bulletin of the School of Oriental and African Studies, University of London,* Vol. 49, No. 1, in honour of Ann K. S. Lambton (1986): 163.
44. Amitai-Preiss, "Islam and Mongol Tradition" (1996): 10.
45. Abu Mus'ab al-Suri and 'Umar 'Abd al-Hakim, *The Call for Global Islamic Resistance* (CTC/OTA Translation and Analysis, 2006), 104; Retrieved

from https://www.opensource.gov/portal/server.pt/gateway/PTARGS_0_0_200_203_121123_43/content/Display/6719634/pdffilenov2006.pdf.

46. Sayyid Qutb, *Milestones* (*Ma'alim fi'l-Tariq*), trans. anonymous (New Delhi: Islamic Book Service, 2002), 160.
47. Ibid.
48. Ibid., 51.
49. Transcribed from audio recordings retrieved from http://www.7cgen.com/index.php?showtopic=16411.
50. Abu Hamza, *Allah's Governance on Earth* (PDF version, 1999); Retrieved from http://www.scribd.com/doc/2411227/Allahs-Governance-on-Earth-Excellent-Book.
51. Muhammad Abdul Salaam al-Faraj, *The Absent Obligation: And Expel the Jews and Christians from the Arabian Peninsula*, ed. and trans. Abu Umamah (London: Maktabah al-Ansaar, 2000), 22; see also, Johanns J. G. Jansen, *The Neglected Duty: The Creed of Sadat's Assassins and Islamic Resurgence in the Middle East* (New York: Macmillan, 1986).
52. Francis J. West, *No True Glory: A Frontline Account of the Battle for Fallujah* (New York: Bantam Books, 2005), 14.

Chapter 10

1. Stephen L. Harris, *Understanding the Bible: Fifth Edition* (Mountain View, CA: Mayfield Publishing, 2000), 18–19.
2. Ibid., 20.
3. Ibid.
4. Matthew 4:8–11.
5. Translated and retrieved from http://www.fordham.edu/halsall/basis/VITA-ANTONY.html.
6. Ibid.
7. *Sahih al-Bukhari,* Vol. 8, Book 81, No. 772 translated and retrieved from http://www.usc.edu/schools/college/crcc/engagement/resources/texts/muslim/hadith/bukhari/081.sbt.html#008.081.771.
8. *Sahih Muslim*, Book 10, No. 3836; translated and retrieved from http://www.usc.edu/schools/college/crcc/engagement/resources/texts/muslim/hadith/muslim/010.smt.html#010.3836.
9. *Sahih Muslim*, Book 1, No. 109; translated and retrieved from http://www.usc.edu/schools/college/crcc/engagement/resources/texts/muslim/hadith/muslim/001.smt.html#001.0109.
10. Muhammad ibn Idris al-Shafi'i, *al-Risala fi Usul al-Fiqh: Treatise on the Foundations of Islamic Jurisprudence*, trans. Majid Khadduri (Cambridge, UK: The Islamic Texts Society, 1987), 288.

11. Ali Rabeea, "Bahraini hotels get around alcohol laws," *Al-Arabiya.Net* (September 12, 2007); Retrieved from http://www.alarabiya.net/articles/2007/09/12/39045.html.
12. Ibid.
13. "MPs Demand Total Ban on Alcohol in Bahrain," *Gulf Daily News* (April 30, 2008); Retrieved from http://www.gulf-daily-news.com/NewsDetails.aspx?storyid=216027.

Chapter 11

1. Quoted in Jake Sherman and Martin Kady, "Islam Group Ridicules Muslim 'Spies' Claim," *Politico.com* (October 14, 2009); Retrieved from http://www.politico.com/news/stories/1009/28283.html.
2. Retrieved from http://www.snopes.com/politics/obama/muslim.asp.
3. Marshall G. S. Hodgson, *The Venture of Islam: Conscience and History in a World Civilization, Volume One: The Classical Age of Islam* (Chicago: The University of Chicago Press, 1974), 207.
4. Jonathan P. Berkey, *The Formation of Islam: Religion and Society in the Near East, 600–1800* (New York: Cambridge University Press, 2003), 74.
5. Marshall G. S. Hodgson, *The Venture of Islam: Conscience and History in a World Civilization, Volume Three: The Gunpowder Empires and Modern Times* (Chicago: The University of Chicago Press, 1974), 259.
6. Ibid., 259–260.
7. Dankwart A. Rustow, "Atatürk as Founder of a State," *Daedalus*, Vol. 97, No. 3 (Summer 1963): 813.
8. Ibid.
9. Quoted in Joshua Teitelbaum, "'Taking Back' the Caliphate: Sharif Husayn Ibn Ali, Mustafa Kemal and the Ottoman Caliphate," *Die Welt des Islams*, New Series, Vol. 40, No. 3 (Nov. 2000): 423.
10. "Islam: Caliph's Beauteous Daughter," *Time Magazine* (November 9, 1931); Retrieved from http://www.time.com/time/magazine/article/0,9171,742555,00.html.
11. Mahmoud Haddad, "Arab Religious Nationalism in the Colonial Era: Rereading Rashid Rida's Ideas on the Caliphate," *Journal of the American Oriental Society*, Vol. 117, No. 2 (April/June, 1997): 264.
12. Ibid., 265.
13. Ibid., 268; as cited from Briton Cooper Busch, *Britain, India, and the Arabs, 1914–1921* (Berkeley: University of California Press, 1971), 62.
14. Haddad, "Arab Religious Nationalism in the Colonial Era," 273.
15. Ibid., 274.
16. Ibid.

17. Quoted in Haddad, "Arab Religious Nationalism in the Colonial Era," 275.
18. *Jihad Recollections*, Issue 2; Retrieved from http://www.scribd.com/doc/15508071/Jihad-Recollections-Issue-2?autodown=pdf [no longer available].
19. Retrieved from http://www.atajew.com.
20. Retrieved from http://www.ideofact.com/archives/000489.html.
21. Translated by Open Source.Gov; Retrieved from https://www.opensource.gov/portal/server.pt/gateway/PTARGS_0_0_200_975_51_43/content/Display/10520357?highlightQuer=eJwli0EKgDAMBL8SerL%2F8QNrSamQktBEehD%2FbtHbzMBs6d4b09ThQQUBj6G2SjQEHVxZZDHT1TsaTfhnRUVgzqT1d8hp6%2BAn5Rf1vR4g&fileSize=17049.
22. Translated by Open Source.Gov; Retrieved from https://www.opensource.gov/portal/server.pt/gateway/PTARGS_0_0_200_240_151207_43/content/Display/6355998?highlightQuery=eJzTqEosT8zILMpUcPRzUVCqdkwrSS1SKMlIVUhLzMlRyE9T8C8pyc9NzFNwTszJLMhILElVqFXSBAAQCRLU&fileSize=85576.

Chapter 12

1. Qur'an 2:144.
2. Qur'an 17:1.
3. Qur'an 53:13–18.
4. See "The Origins of the Islamic State," being a translation from the Arabic of the *Kitab Futuh al-Buldha* of Ahmad ibn-Jabir al-Baladhuri, trans. P. K. Hitti and F. C. Murgotten, *Studies in History, Economics and Public Law*, LXVIII (New York: Columbia University Press, 1916 and 1924): 207–211; Retrieved from http://www.fordham.edu/halsall/source/yarmuk.html.
5. Eric F. F. Bishop, "Hebron, City of Abraham, the Friend of God," in *Journal of Bible and Religion*, Vol. 16, No. 2 (April 1948): 94.
6. Jonathan P. Berkey, *The Formation of Islam: Religion and Society in the Near East, 600–1800* (Cambridge: Cambridge University Press, 2003), 81.
7. Bernard O'Kane, *Treasures of Islam: Artistic Glories of the Muslim World* (New York: Sterling Publishing, 2007), 37.
8. See Nasser Rabbat, "The Meaning of the Umayyad Dome of the Rock," *Muqarnas*, Vol. 6 (1989): 16–17.
9. Carol Herselle Krinsky, "Representations of the Temple of Jerusalem before 1500," *Journal of the Warburg and Courtauld Institutes*, Vol. 33 (1970): 4.
10. Donald P. Little, "Communal Strife in Late Mamluk Jerusalem," *Islamic Law and Society*, Vol. 6, No. 1 (1999): 72.
11. Berkey, *Formation of Islam*, 182.

12. Jonathan Riley-Smith, ed., *The Oxford History of the Crusades* (New York: Oxford University Press, 2002), 249–250.
13. Nabil Matar, "Two Journeys to Seventeenth-Century Palestine," *Journal of Palestine Studies*, Vol. 29, No. 4 (Autumn 2000): 39.
14. Ibid., 40.
15. Ibid., 40–42.
16. Ibid., 43.
17. Deborah J. Gerner, *One Land, Two Peoples: The Conflict over Palestine, Second Edition* (Boulder, CO: Westview, 1994), 13.
18. Ibid., 15.
19. Ibid., 16.
20. Ibid., 17.
21. Ibid.
22. Ibid., 18–19.
23. Ibid., 30–31.
24. Ibid., 43.
25. Sami Hadawi, *Bitter Harvest: A Modern History of Palestine, Fourth Edition* (New York: Olive Branch Press, 1991), 58.
26. Ilan Pappé, "The 1948 Ethnic Cleansing of Palestine," *Journal of Palestine Studies*, Vol. 36, No. 1 (Autumn 2006): 6.
27. Ibid.
28. Gerner, *One Land, Two Peoples*, 44.
29. Pappé "The 1948 Ethnic Cleansing of Palestine" (2006): 7.
30. Hadawi, *Bitter Harvest*, 85.
31. Ibid.
32. Peter Mansfield, "Nasserism," *The Oxford Encyclopedia of the Modern Islamic World*, Vol. 3, ed. John L. Esposito (New York: Oxford University Press, 1995), 232.
33. Ibid.
34. Ibid.
35. Gerner, *One Land, Two Peoples*, 111.
36. Ibid., 112.
37. Ibid.
38. Ibid., 113.
39. Hadawi, 226; see also James Scott, *The Attack on the Liberty: The Untold Story of Israel's Deadly 1967 Assault on a U.S. Spy Ship* (New York: Simon & Schuster, 2009).
40. Quoted in Montasser al-Zayyat, *The Road to al-Qaeda: The Story of Bin Laden's Right Hand Man*, trans. Ahmed Fekhry, ed. Sara Nimis (London: Pluto Press, 2004), 23.
41. Abdullah Azzam, *The Defense of Muslim Lands: The First Obligation of Iman*, trans. Brothers in Ribatt (e-book, no date), 23.

42. "Report: New Bin Laden Tape Emerges," *CNN.com* (January 24, 2010); Retrieved from http://www.cnn.com/2010/US/01/24/bin.laden.terror.tape/.
43. Ayman al-Zawahiri, *The Exoneration: A Treatise on the Exoneration of the Nation of the Pen and Sword of the Denigrating Charge of Being Irresolute and Weak*, trans. Open Source.Gov (2008), 38.
44. Yonah Alexander, *Palestinian Religious Terrorism* (Ardsley, NY: Transnational Publishers, 2002), 1.
45. Ibid.
46. Retrieved in English translation from http://www.thejerusalemfund.org/carryover/documents/charter.html.
47. Alexander, Palestinian Religious Terrorism, 1.

Chapter 13

1. See Bruce Lincoln, *Holy Terrors: Thinking about Religion after September 11* (Chicago: University of Chicago, 2003).
2. Sigmund Freud, *The Future of an Illusion*, trans. James Strachey (New York: W. W. Norton, 1961), 38.
3. Maya Müller, Robert E. Shillenn, Jane McGary, "Afterlife," *The Oxford Encyclopedia of Ancient Egypt*, ed. Donald B. Redford (New York: Oxford University Press, 2001, 2005); The Oxford Encyclopedia of Ancient Egypt: (e-reference edition), Oxford University Press, Arizona State University. 25 January 2010. http://www.oxford-ancientegypt.com/entry?entry=t176.e0013.
4. Stephen G. J. Quirke, "Judgment of the Dead," *The Oxford Encyclopedia of Ancient Egypt*, ed. Donald B. Redford (Oxford University Press, 2001, 2005); The Oxford Encyclopedia of Ancient Egypt: (e-reference edition), Oxford University Press, Arizona State University. 25 January 2010. http://www.oxford-ancientegypt.com/entry?entry=t176.e0367.
5. Jacobus Van Dijk, "Paradise," *The Oxford Encyclopedia of Ancient Egypt*, ed. Donald B. Redford (Oxford University Press, 2001, 2005); The Oxford Encyclopedia of Ancient Egypt: (e-reference edition), Oxford University Press, Arizona State University. 25 January 2010. http://www.oxford-ancientegypt.com/entry?entry=t176.e0550.
6. Stephen L. Harris, *Understanding the Bible: Fifth Edition* (Mountain View, CA: Mayfield Publishing, 2000), 22.
7. Psalm 88:6–13.
8. Daniel 12:2.
9. See, e.g., Lawrence H. Mills, *Zarathushtra, Philo, the Achaemenids and Israel* (New York: AMS Press, 1977).
10. Mary Boyce, *A History of Zoroastrianism: The Early Period* (Leiden: E. J. Brill, 1996), 237–239.

11. Ibid., 236.
12. Harris, *Understanding the Bible*, 24.
13. Ibid., 393.
14. Ibid., 392.
15. Matthew 18:9.
16. Matthew 13:40–43.
17. Revelation 20:4.
18. Qur'an 32:17.
19. Qur'an 88:10–16.
20. For references in the Qur'an, see, e.g., 52:20, 56:22, 55:72, and 44:54.
21. A. J. Wensinck, "Hur," *Encyclopedia of Islam, Second Edition*, ed. P. Bearman, Th. Bianquis, C. E. Bosworth, E. van Donzel, and W. P. Heinrichs (Leiden: E. J. Brill, 2009); Brill Online, Arizona State University, 22 December 2009. http://www.brillonline.nl.ezproxy1.lib.asu.edu/subscriber/entry?entry=islam_SIM-2960.
22. See, e.g., Qur'an 7:43, 15:45, 57:12, and 47:15.
23. See, e.g., for the eight gates al-Bukhari 4.54.479 and 4.55.644; for the special street: Muslim 40.6792; for the tree with infinite shade: Muslim 40:6784–6786; tents made of pearl: Muslim 40:6804–6806; for the *hur*: al-Bukhari 4.54.476.
24. Translated and retrieved from http://www.sunniforum.com/forum/showthread.php?29 728-Hadith-of-72-Virgins.
25. *Musnad Ahmed Ibn Hanbal*, No. 16553, translated from the Arabic by Jeffry R. Halverson; Retrieved from http://www.ekabakti.com/dosearch.php?txtSearch2=%C7%CB %E4%CA%ED%E4+%E6%D3%C8%DA%ED%E4+%D2%E6%CC%C9+&topic=ahmad&B1=Search.
26. Qur'an 3:157.
27. See, e.g., for Christianity: the writings on martyrdom by Origen, Tertullian, Eusebius's *Martyrdom of Justin and His Companions*, W. H. C. Frend, *Martyrdom and Persecution in the Early Church* (1965); for Judaism: *Memorbukh, the Midrash of the Ten Martyrs*, and Werblowsky and Wigoder, *The Oxford Dictionary of the Jewish Religion* (New York: Oxford University Press, 1997) 444; and for a general discussion of martyrdom: Samuel Z. Klausner, "Martyrdom," in *The Encyclopedia of Religion*, Vol. 9, ed. Mircea Eliade (New York: Macmillan, 1987), 230–237.
28. See (1) by plague: al-Muwatta 8.2.6 and 16.12.36, Bukhari 7.71.629, Abu Dawud 20.3105; (2) by disease of the stomach: al-Muwatta 8.2.6 and 16.12.36, Bukhari 7.71.629; (3) by drowning: al-Muwatta 8.2.6 and 16.12.36; (4) by collapsing building: al-Muwatta 8.2.6 and 16.12.36, Abu Dawud 20.3105; (5) by fire: al-Muwatta 16.12.36, Abu Dawud 20.3105; (6) by childbirth: al-Muwatta 16.12.36, Abu Dawud 20.3105; (7) by

protecting property: Bukhari 3.43.660, Muslim 1.0260; (8) by falling from horse or camel: Abu Dawud 14.2493; (9) by sting of poisonous creature: Abu Dawud 14.2493; (10) while defending family: Abu Dawud 40.4754.

29. This includes being killed for preaching the message of Islam, speaking the truth in defiance of a tyrant, refusing to compromise one's faith under compulsion or torture, et cetera. See E. Kohlberg, "Shahid," in *The Encyclopedia of Islam: New Edition*, Vol. IX, ed. C. E. Bosworth, E. Van Donzel, W. P. Heinrichs, and G. Lecomte (Leiden: E. J. Brill, 1997), 203–207.
30. See, e.g., Qur'an 2:154, 3:169, 3:157–158, 8:39, and 22:58–59; al-Muwatta 21.14.27 and 21.15.35, Bukhari 1.2.35, Muslim 20:4678 and 20:4634.
31. See Martin Lings, *Muhammad* (Cambridge: The Islamic Texts Society, 1991), 79–80.
32. B. Todd Lawson, "Martyrdom," in *The Oxford Encyclopedia of the Modern Islamic World*, Vol. 3, ed. John L. Esposito (New York: Oxford University Press, 1995), 58.
33. Abu Dawud, Book 14, No. 2535; translated and reproduced by http://www.usc.edu/schools/college/crcc/engagement/resources/texts/muslim/hadith/abudawud/014.sat.html#014.2535.
34. Bruce Lincoln, *Holy Terrors: Thinking about Religion after September 11* (Chicago: University of Chicago, 2003), 86.
35. Translated by Open Source.Gov; Retrieved from https://www.opensource.gov/portal/server.pt/gateway/PTARGS_0_0_200_746_51_43/content/Display/11511741?highlightQuery=eJzTKMssSs%2FMK1Zw9HNRyE0sKqks0gQASdoHBg%3D%3D&fileSize=60236.
36. Translated by Open Source.Gov; Retrieved from https://www.opensource.gov/portal/server.pt/gateway/PTARGS_0_0_200_746_1525_43/content/Display/11378178?highlightQuery=eJzTyMgvLcos1gQADRUC7A%3D%3D&fileSize=8931883.
37. Translated by Open Source.Gov; Retrieved from https://www.opensource.gov/portal/server.pt/gateway/PTARGS_0_0_200_746_1525_43/content/Display/11206694?highlightQuery=eJzTyMgvLcos1gQADRUC7A%3D%3D&fileSize=73584893.

Chapter 14

1. Angel Rabasa, Peter Chalk, Kim Cragin, Sara A. Daly, Heather S. Gregg, Theodore W. Karasik, Kevin A. O'Brien, and William Rosenau, *Beyond al-Qaeda: Part 1, The Global Jihadist Movement* (RAND, 2006): 12–14; http://www.rand.org/pubs/monographs/2006/RAND_MG429.pdf.

2. David Betz, "The Virtual Dimension of Contemporary Insurgency and Counterinsurgency," *Small Wars and Insurgencies*, 19: 4 (December 2008): 510–540.
3. Ann Swindler, "Culture in Action: Symbols and Strategies," *American Sociological Review*, Vol. 51, No. 2 (April 1986): 273–286.
4. Thomas H. Johnson, "The Taliban Insurgency and an Analysis of *Shabnamah* (Night Letters)," *Small Wars and Insurgencies,* Vol. 18, No. 3 (September 2007): 317–344.
5. Betz, "Virtual Dimension" (2008), 520.
6. Ibid.
7. Max Weber, *The Sociology of Religion*, trans. Ephraim Fischoff (Boston: Beacon Press, 1991), 139.
8. Donald E. Polkinghorne, *Narrative Knowing and the Human Sciences,* (Albany, NY: State University of New York Press, 1988), 107.
9. Ernest G. Bormann, "Fantasy and Rhetorical Vision: The Rhetorical Criticism of Social Reality," *Quarterly Journal of Speech*, Vol. 58, No. 4 (December 1972): 398.
10. H. Porter Abbott, *The Cambridge Introduction to Narrative* (Cambridge, UK: Cambridge University Press, 2002).
11. Specifically, the boxes are sized to indicate the betweenness centrality of a node in the network. A node has high betweenness centrality if it lies on a large number of shortest paths between pairs of other nodes in the network.
12. Gerald F. Smith, P. George Benson, and Shawn P. Curley, "Belief, Knowledge, and Uncertainty: A Cognitive Perspective on Subjective Probability," *Organizational Behavior and Human Performance*, Vol. 48, No. 2 (April 1991): 291–321.
13. William Paley, *Natural Theology: On the Existence and Attributes of the Deity, Collected from the Appearances of Nature* (Boston: Gould and Lincoln, 1860).
14. For example, William Greider, "Iraq as Vietnam," *The Nation* (April 15, 2004); http://www.thenation.com/doc/20040503/greider.
15. See A. Juthe, "Argument by Analogy," *Argumentation,* Vol. 19, No. 1 (March 2005): 1–27.
16. Smith, Benson, and Curley, "Belief, Knowledge, and Uncertainty" (1991): 302.
17. Rosalind Ward Gwynne, *Logic, Rhetoric, and Legal Reasoning in the Qur'an,* (London: Routledge Curzon, 2004), 110.
18. Sayyid Qutb, *Milestones*, trans. Anonymous (New Delhi: Islamic Book Service, 2002), 10.
19. See Angela Trethewey, Steven R. Corman, and Bud Goodall, *Out of Their Heads and into Their Conversation: Countering Extremist Ideology*

(Consortium for Strategic Communication Report #0901, September 2009); http://comops.org/article/123.pdf.

20. George W. Bush, "Remarks by the President upon Arrival," White House Office of the Press Secretary (September 16, 2001); http://georgewbushwhitehouse.archives.gov/news/releases/2001/09/20010916-2.html.
21. Alexander Cockburn, "The Tenth Crusade," *Counterpunch* (September 7, 2002); http://www.counterpunch.org/cockburn0907.html.
22. "Bible Gun Sights 'Inappropriate,'" *al-Jazeera English* (January 21, 2010); http://english.aljazeera.net/news/americas/2010/01/2010121868549281.html.
23. "Dexter Filkins: Arghanistan's 'Make or Break' Time," *Fresh Air* (National Public Radio, April 21, 2010); http://www.npr.org/templates/story/story.php?storyId=126108594.
24. Ned Parker, "Secret Prison Revealed in Baghdad," *The Los Angeles Times* (April 19, 2010); http://www.latimes.com/news/nationworld/world/middleeast/la-fg-iraq-prison19-2010apr19,0,7841354.story.
25. Cameron Shelley, "Analogy Counterarguments: A Taxonomy for Critical Thinking," *Argumentation,* Vol. 18 (2004): 223–238.
26. While al-Qaeda now argues that its actions are inextricably linked to the situation in the Holy Land (e.g., bin Laden's claim that the 2009 underwear bomber struck because of Palestine), this amounts to a post hoc rationalization because until recently, Palestine was not a predominant element of their ideology.
27. Gabriel A. Almond, R. Scott Appleby, and Emmanuel Sivan, *Strong Religion: The Rise of Fundamentalisms around the World* (Chicago, IL: University of Chicago Press, 2003).
28. Ibid., 57.
29. David Hackett Fischer, *Historians' Fallacies: Toward a Logic of Historical Thought* (New York: Harper & Row, 1970).
30. Ibid., 135.
31. For longer discussion of this rhetorical move, see Bud Goodall, "Obama's Nobel Speech Opens Narrative Possibilities," *COMOPS Journal* (December 14, 2009); http://comops.org/journal/2009/12/14/obamas-nobel-speech-opens-narrative-possibilities/.
32. Leslie A. Baxter, "A Dialectical Perspective of Communication Strategies in Relationship Development," in *Handbook of Personal Relationships*, ed. S. Duck (New York: Wiley, 1988), 257–273.
33. Jean Francois Lyotard, *The Postmodern Condition* (Minneapolis: University of Minnesota Press, 1980).
34. Jack Goody, *The Domestication of the Savage Mind* (Cambridge: Cambridge University Press, 1977).

Bibliography

Abbott, H. Porter. *The Cambridge Introduction to Narrative*. Cambridge, UK: Cambridge University Press, 2002.

Aghaie, Kamran Scot. *The Martyrs of Karbala: Shi'i Symbols and Rituals in Modern Iran*. Seattle: University of Washington, 2004.

Ahmed, Leila. *Women and Gender in Islam: Historical Roots of a Modern Debate*. Hartford, CT: Yale University Press, 1993.

Alexander, Yonah. *Palestinian Religious Terrorism*. Ardsley, NY: Transnational Publishers, 2002.

Almond, Gabriel A., R. Scott Appleby, and Emmanuel Sivan. *Strong Religion: The Rise of Fundamentalisms around the World*. Chicago, IL: University of Chicago Press, 2003.

Amini, Ibrahim. *Al-Imam al-Mahdi: Just Leader for Humanity*. Trans. Abdulaziz Sachedina. Ahlul Bayt Digital Islamic Library Project, n.d.

Ayoub, Mahmoud. *Redemptive Suffering in Islam*. New York: Mouton Publishers, 1978.

Azzam, Abdullah. *Signs of Ar-Rahman from the Jihad in Afghanistan*, ed. A. B. al-Mehri. Birmingham, UK: Maktabah, n.d.

Beck, Roger. *The Religion of the Mithras Cult in the Roman Empire: Mysteries of the Unconquered Sun*. New York: Oxford University Press, 2006.

Berkey, Jonathan P. *The Formation of Islam: Religion and Society in the Near East, 600–1800*. New York: Cambridge University Press, 2003.

Blichfeldt, Jan-Olaf. *Early Mahdism: Politics and Religion in the Formative Period of Islam*. Leiden: E. J. Brill, 1985.

Boyce, Mary. *A History of Zoroastrianism: The Early Period*. Leiden: E. J. Brill, 1996.

Burke, Kenneth. *On Symbols and Society*, ed. Joseph Gusfield. Chicago: University of Chicago Press, 1989.

Campbell, Joseph. *The Power of Myth*. New York: Anchor, 1991.

Cook, David. *Martyrdom in Islam*. Cambridge: Cambridge University Press, 2007.

Corman, Steven R., Angela Trethewey, and H. L. Goodall Jr., eds. *Weapons of Mass Persuasion: Strategic Communication to Combat Violent Extremism*. New York: Peter Lang Publishing, 2008.

Crone, Patricia. *Hagarism: The Making of the Islamic World*. Cambridge: Cambridge University Press, 1977.

Davis, Joyce M. *Martyrs: Innocence, Vengeance, and Despair in the Middle East*. New York: Palgrave Macmillan, 2003.

Donohue John J., and John L. Esposito, eds. *Islam in Transition: Muslim Perspectives*. New York: Oxford University Press, 1982.

Esposito, John L. *Voices of Resurgent Islam*. New York: Oxford University Press, 1983.

———., ed. *The Oxford Encyclopedia of the Modern Islamic World*. New York: Oxford University Press, 1995.

al-Faraj, Muhammad Abdul Salaam. *The Absent Obligation: And Expel the Jews and Christians from the Arabian Peninsula*. Ed. and trans. Abu Umamah. London: Maktabah al-Ansaar, 2000.

Fischer, David Hackett. *Historians' Fallacies: Toward a Logic of Historical Thought*. New York: Harper & Row, 1970.

Fisher, Walter R. *Human Communication as Narration: Toward a Philosophy of Reason, Value, and Action*. Columbia: University of South Carolina Press, 1989.

Freud, Sigmund. *The Future of an Illusion*. Trans. James Strachey. New York: W. W. Norton, 1961.

Gätje, Helmut. *The Qur'an and its Exegesis: Selected Texts with Classical and Modern Muslim Interpretations*. Trans. Alford T. Welch. Oxford: Oneworld, 1996.

Geertz, Clifford. *The Interpretation of Cultures*. New York: Basic Books, 1973.

Gerner, Deborah J. *One Land, Two Peoples*. Oxford: Westview, 1994.

Gettleman, Marvin E., and Stuart Schaar. *The Middle East and Islamic World Reader*. New York: Grove Press, 2003.

Giddens, Anthony. *The Constitution of Society*. Cambridge: Polity Press, 1984.

Goody, Jack. *The Domestication of the Savage Mind*. Cambridge: Cambridge University Press, 1977.

Guillaume, Alfred. *The Life of Muhammad: A Translation of Ishaq's Sirat Rasul Allah*. Karachi: Oxford University Press, 1955.

Gwynne, Rosalind Ward. *Logic, Rhetoric, and Legal Reasoning in the Qur'an*. London: Routledge Curzon, 2004.

Hadawi, Sami. *Bitter Harvest: A Modern History of Palestine, Fourth Edition*. New York: Olive Branch Press, 1991.

Halverson, Jeffry R. *Theology and Creed in Sunni Islam: The Muslim Brotherhood, Ash'arism, and Political Sunnism*. New York: Palgrave Macmillan, 2010.

Harris, Stephen L. *Understanding the Bible: Fifth Edition.* Mountain View, CA: Mayfield Publishing, 2000.

Hodgson, Marshall G. S. *The Venture of Islam: Conscience and History in a World Civilization, Volume One: The Classical Age of Islam.* Chicago: The University of Chicago Press, 1974.

———. *The Venture of Islam: Conscience and History in a World Civilization, Volume Three: The Gunpowder Empires and Modern Times.* Chicago: The University of Chicago Press, 1974.

Horgan, John. *The Psychology of Terrorism.* New York: Routledge, 2005.

Ibn Kathir. *Stories of the Prophets.* Trans. Sayed Gad. El-Mansoura, Egypt: Dar al-Manarah, 2000.

Jaber, Hala. *Hezbollah: Born with a Vengeance.* New York: Columbia University Press, 1997.

Jansen, Johanns J. G. *The Neglected Duty: The Creed of Sadat's Assassins and Islamic Resurgence in the Middle East.* New York: Macmillan, 1986.

Kepel, Gilles. *Jihad: The Trail of Political Islam.* Trans. Anthony F. Roberts. New York: I. B. Tauris, 2002.

———. *Muslim Extremism in Egypt: The Prophet and Pharaoh.* Trans. Jon Rothschild. Berkeley: University of California Press, 2003.

Lewis, Bernard, Charles Pellat, and Joseph Schacht, eds. *Encyclopedia of Islam.* Leiden: Brill, 1991.

Lincoln, Bruce. *Holy Terrors: Thinking about Religion after September 11.* Chicago: University of Chicago, 2003.

Lindsay, James E. *Daily Life in the Medieval Islamic World.* Indianapolis: Hackett Publishing, 2005.

Lings, Martin. *Muhammad: His Life Based on the Earliest Sources.* Cambridge, UK: The Islamic Texts Society, 1991.

Lyotard, Jean Francois. *The Postmodern Condition.* Minneapolis: University of Minnesota Press, 1980.

MacIntyre, Alasdair. *After Virtue: A Study in Moral Theory.* South Bend, IN: University of Notre Dame Press, 1984.

Michael, Robert. *History of Catholic Anti-Semitism: The Dark Side of the Church.* New York: Palgrave Macmillan, 2008.

Mills, Lawrence H. *Zarathushtra, Philo, the Achaemenids and Israel.* New York: AMS Press, 1977.

Moussalli, Ahmad S. *Radical Islamic Fundamentalism: The Ideological and Political Discourse of Sayyid Qutb.* Beirut: American University of Beirut Press, 1992.

al-Mubarakpuri, Safi ur-Rahman. *Ar-Raheeq al-Makhtum (The Sealed Nectar): Biography of the Noble Prophet.* Riyadh, SA: Maktaba Dar-us-Salam, 1995.

Nashabe, Hisham, ed. *Studia Palaestina: Studies in Honour of Constantine K. Zurayk*. Beirut: Institute for Palestine Studies, 1988.

Nasrallah, Sayyed Hassan. *Voice of Hezbollah: The Statements of Sayyed Hassan Nasrallah*, ed. Nicholas Noe, trans. Ellen Khouri. New York: Verso, 2007.

O'Kane, Bernard. *Treasures of Islam: Artistic Glories of the Muslim World*. New York: Sterling Publishing, 2007.

Oxtoby, Willard G., ed. *World Religions: Western Religions*. New York: Oxford University Press, 2002.

Paley, William. *Natural Theology: On the Existence and Attributes of the Deity, Collected from the Appearances of Nature*. Boston: Gould and Lincoln, 1860.

Paz, Octavio. *In Search of the Present: 1990 Nobel Lecture*. San Diego: Harcourt Brace Jovanovich, 1990.

Peterson, Daniel C. *Muhammad: Prophet of God*. Cambridge, UK: William B. Eerdmans, 2007.

Phillips, Jonathan. *The Crusades: 1095–1197*. London: Pearson Education, 2002.

Polkinghorne, Donald E. *Narrative Knowing and the Human Sciences*. Albany, NY: State University of New York Press, 1988.

Qutb, Sayyid. *Milestones*. Trans. Anonymous. New Delhi: Islamic Book Service, 2002.

———. *Social Justice in Islam*. Trans. Hamid Algar. Oneonta, NY: Islamic Publications International, 2000.

Redford, Donald B., ed. *The Oxford Encyclopedia of Ancient Egypt*. New York: Oxford University Press, 2005.

Reza, Sayed Ali, trans. *Nahjul Balagha: Peak of Eloquence*. Elmhurst, NY: Tahrike Tarsile Qur'an, 1985.

Richard, Yann. *Shi'ite Islam: Polity, Ideology, and Creed*. Trans. Antonia Nevill. Oxford: Blackwell, 1995.

Riley-Smith, Jonathan, ed., *The Oxford History of the Crusades*. New York: Oxford University Press, 2002.

Robinson, David. *Muslim Societies in African History*. Cambridge: Cambridge University Press, 2004.

Robinson, Francis, ed. *Islamic World*. New York: Cambridge University Press, 1996.

Roy, Olivier. *Globalized Islam: The Search for a New Ummah*. New York: Cambridge University Press, 2004.

Saad-Ghorayeb, Amal. *Hizbu'llah: Politics and Religion*. London: Pluto Press, 2002.

Scott, James. *The Attack on the Liberty: The Untold Story of Israel's Deadly 1967 Assault on a U.S. Spy Ship*. New York: Simon & Schuster, 2009.

al-Shafi'i, Muhammad ibn Idris. *al-Risala fi Usul al-Fiqh: Treatise on the Foundations of Islamic Jurisprudence.* Trans. Majid Khadduri. Cambridge, UK: The Islamic Texts Society, 1987.

Weber, Max. *The Methodology of the Social Sciences.* Trans. and ed. Edward A. Shils and Henry A. Finch. New York: Free Press, 1904/1949.

———. *The Sociology of Religion.* Trans. Ephraim Fischoff. Boston: Beacon Press, 1991.

West, Francis J. *No True Glory: A Frontline Account of the Battle for Fallujah.* New York: Bantam Books, 2005.

al-Zayyat, Montasser. *The Road to al-Qaeda: The Story of Bin Laden's Right Hand Man.* Trans. Ahmed Fekhry, ed. Sara Nimis. London: Pluto Press, 2004.

Index

Abbas ibn 'Ali (647–680), 85–87
Abbasids, 103, 112, 118, 120, 139, 154
'Abdul-Hamid II (1858–1918), 140, 146
Abraham (Ibrahim), 2, 6, 38, 47, 151, 154, 157
Abu Bakr (573–634), 54, 76, 83, 139, 140, 199, 203
Abu Jahl, 52, 173
Abu Sufyan (560–650), 51, 71, 84, 104
Adam and Eve, 37, 42, 83, 87, 129–130, 151
Afghanistan, 41, 53–55, 64, 123, 180, 196, 204–205
Ahmadinejad, Mahmoud, 64, 89, 106
Ahmed ibn Hanbal (780–855), 5, 172, 175
al-Ahzab (confederates), 71–74
'Aisha (613–678), 60–61, 83
Akhenaten, 27
alcohol, 125, 131–135
'Ali ibn Abu Talib (599–661), 51, 54, 75, 77, 83, 84, 85, 86, 154, 203–204
analogy, 79, 132–133, 135, 148, 191–193, 198–200
  counterarguments, 198–199
angels, 49, 51–52, 54–55, 79, 81, 86, 97, 127, 128, 129–130, 169, 174, 186, 192
animist. *See* pagan
Ansar of Medina, 51, 52, 58, 70, 105
anti-Semitism, 67–69, 144, 145, 146, 157
al-Aqsa, 33, 113, 114, 150, 151, 152, 153, 154, 155, 156. *See also* Noble Sanctuary (*al-Haram al-Sharif*)
archetype, 9, 12, 15, 16, 20, 21–22, 107, 108, 117, 120, 121, 124, 131, 135, 176, 179, 183–184, 187–190, 195, 197, 203–205
  definition of, 21, 187
argument(s)
  from analogy, 191
  observational, 191, 198
  from parallel case, 191
  from sign, 191
Arnold, Benedict (1741–1801), 68
Ashura, 85, 87, 88, 89, 104
Asiya (wife of Pharaoh), 29–30
Atatürk, Mustafa Kemal (1881–1938), 137, 138, 140, 141–142, 144–147, 194
Awlaki, Anwar, 62, 122, 124
Azzam, 'Abdullah Yusuf (1941–1989), 53, 54–55, 162, 192

Baghdad, 12, 112, 118, 120, 123, 139, 198
Bahrain, 90, 133–134, 194

Bani Nadir, 60, 69, 70–71, 73, 75, 76, 77, 78, 79
Bani Qaynuqa, 59, 69, 70, 76, 78
Bani Qurayza, 69, 71–74, 77, 78, 79
al-Banna, Hasan (1906–1949), 121
barbarian, 120, 184, 187, 188, 189, 190
Basiji, 91–92. *See also* martyrdom
Battle of 'Ayn Jalut, 119, 120, 122, 156, 201
Battle of Badr, 7, 49–56, 70, 79, 184, 186, 192, 193, 201
Battle of Jaji, 55–56
Battle of Khaybar, 63, 68, 71–80, 184, 185
Battle of Uhud, 40, 60, 70
betrayal, 57, 67, 72, 79, 80, 102, 184, 185
Betz, David, 9, 180, 181, 190, 195
Bilal (580–640), 41
Bin Laden, Usama, 13, 19, 34, 46, 48, 53, 55, 56, 78, 162, 201, 203, 204
binaries, 201–202
Book of Revelation (Apocalypse), 2, 68, 100, 102, 128, 129, 130, 169, 170
Bormann, Ernest (1925–2008), 182–183
British Empire, 68, 105, 114, 116, 124, 141–143, 144, 145, 157–158, 185, 187, 205
Burke, Kenneth (1897–1993), 18, 22, 23, 24, 26
  and *The Rhetoric of Hitler's Battle*, 18–20
  and symbolic action, 19
Bush, George W., 34, 78, 90, 123, 196
Byzantine Empire, 41, 44, 69, 98, 110, 113, 153, 199, 201
Cairo, 31, 54, 86, 90, 98, 139, 154, 156, 161
Caliphate, 19, 21, 79, 84, 85, 118, 123, 137, 138–143, 144, 146–147, 180, 194, 199
Campbell, Joseph (1904–1987), 16, 17, 22
  and *The Power of Myth*, 16
Canaan, 96, 126, 152–153
champion, 50, 107, 110, 112, 113, 117, 120, 183, 184, 185, 189, 190, 192, 194, 195, 201, 203, 204, 205
Chinvat bridge (*al-Sirat*), 168, 174
Christianity, 6, 28, 38, 78, 80, 82, 98–100, 101, 115, 116, 119, 126, 127, 128
colonizer, 32, 114, 116, 117, 120, 121, 122, 143, 161, 163, 176, 184, 187, 188, 190
conflict with God (deity), 35–36, 184
Constantine the Great (272–337), 100
Constitution of Medina, 69–70, 76
Crusades, 13, 21–22, 78, 109, 110–117, 120, 121, 124, 155, 156, 164, 176, 193, 196, 199, 201
  pork eating crusader, 196–197. *See also* colonizer
Cyrus the Great (576–530), 97, 110, 127, 168

Dajjal (Anti-Christ), 69, 102, 128
David (*Daud*), 150
David and Goliath, 4, 16, 50, 56. *See also* King David
Day of Judgment, 39, 40, 42, 102, 130, 168, 169, 170, 173–174
deity, 16, 21, 24, 35, 38, 39, 47, 50, 82, 98, 99, 100, 125, 126, 169, 184, 187, 188, 189

deliverance, 21, 47, 48, 56, 96, 106, 107, 108, 163, 164, 184, 186, 192, 193, 194
Dhu'l-Fiqar, 86, 104, 107
Dhul-Janah, 86
Dome of the Rock. See *al-Aqsa*
Dönme, 137, 144–145

Egypt, 28, 30–33, 35, 41, 43, 45, 53, 62, 63, 64, 86, 89, 90, 105, 110, 112, 114, 117, 119, 126, 128, 129, 135, 139, 141, 143, 152, 153, 155, 156, 159, 160–161, 164, 166, 199. *See also* Cairo
Eucharist, 170

fallacy of presentism, 200
Fahmideh, Mohammed Hossein (1967–1980), 91
al-Faraj, Muhammad 'Abdel-Salam (1954–1982), 47, 90, 120, 123
Fatimah az-Zahra (605–632), 30, 40, 83
Fatimids, 110, 112, 122, 139, 154–155
Fisher, Walter, 16, 17, 22
  and narrative fidelity, 24–25
  and narrative probability, 24
freemasonry, 145, 147
Freud, Sigmund (1856–1939), 166

Gabriel (Jibreel), 2, 31, 51, 70, 72–73, 101, 151
Gaza, 34, 156, 159, 160, 161, 163, 175
Geertz, Clifford (1926–2006), 17
Germany, 18–20, 141, 145, 157, 158
al-Ghazali, Abu Hamid (1058–1111), 87, 155
Giddens, Anthony, 25
Gog and Magog, 102
Goodall, H. L., 22
Gnosticism, 82, 99, 102

Hadith, 2, 4, 5, 7, 41, 47, 51, 62, 66, 76, 101, 102, 104, 131, 132, 143, 150, 151, 165, 171, 172–173, 189, 195
Halverson, Jeffry R., 6, 12
Hamas, 162, 163, 195
Hamza ibn 'Abdel-Muttalib (568–625), 40, 51, 52, 54, 86
Harun al-Rashid (766–809), 144. *See also* Abbasids
Hassan ibn 'Ali (625–670), 84, 85
Heaven (*jannah*), 17, 30, 38, 51, 86, 100, 101, 102, 128, 129, 130, 150, 151–152, 165–176
Hebron (*al-Khalil*), 150, 154, 155, 157
Hell (*gehennom*), 41, 59, 82, 84, 130, 167–169, 170, 171, 176
Herodotus (484–420 BCE), 28
Hezbollah, 76–77, 78, 90–91, 92, 107, 163, 193
hijra (migration), 46, 49–50, 58, 69, 83, 131, 150
Hitler, Adolf (1889–1945), 15, 18–19
  and *Mein Kampf*, 19–21
Horus, 27, 126
Houris (*hur al-'ayn*), 171–173, 175, 176
Hubal, 38, 45
Hulagu Khan (1217–1265), 117–119, 120, 123
Husayn ibn 'Ali (626–680), 30, 77, 85–87, 88, 89, 90, 91, 92, 103, 104, 142, 193, 201
Hussein, Saddam (1937–2006), 78, 193

Ibn Kathir (1301–1373), 4, 6, 28, 29, 30, 101, 172
Ibn Taymiyyah, Ahmed (1263–1328), 43, 119–121, 172

Ibn Ubayy, 'Abdallah (unknown–631), 59–62
ideology, 6, 22, 34, 44, 47, 77, 90–92, 148, 157, 161, 180–181
imposter, 57, 58, 65, 66, 120, 144, 147, 184, 187, 188, 189, 190, 197, 203, 205
invasion, 109, 120, 124, 183, 184, 185–186, 187, 188, 194–195
Iran, 41, 64, 77, 78, 81, 87–89, 90–91, 95, 106–107, 133, 134, 156, 193. *See also* Safavids
Iraq, 22, 32, 33, 41, 63, 64, 78, 85, 88, 89, 90, 91, 102, 103, 107, 117, 119, 122–124, 139, 159, 176, 191, 193, 196, 197, 198, 199, 204. *See also* Baghdad
Israel (state), 32, 33–34, 76, 77, 78, 79, 89, 91, 92, 107, 116, 149, 157, 158–160, 161–165, 175, 187, 193, 194–195

jahiliyyah, 13, 37–48, 54, 131, 143, 170, 173, 184, 185, 186, 187, 192
Jesus of Nazareth (5 BCE–30 CE), 2, 3, 17, 27, 29, 37, 67–68, 82, 92, 95, 98–99, 100–103, 106, 127–128, 150, 151, 154, 156–157, 169, 170
Jerusalem (*al-Quds*), 32, 79, 97, 98, 109, 110–111, 112–114, 116, 117, 118, 122, 142, 149, 152, 153–155, 156–157, 158, 159, 160, 161–162, 167, 169, 199, 201. *See also* Night Journey
Jews, 18, 19, 21, 33–34, 37, 44, 50, 59, 60, 62, 63, 67–80, 84, 95, 97, 99, 110, 111–112, 113, 116, 117, 129, 144–146, 150, 153, 154, 156, 157–160, 164, 167–168, 169, 170, 173. *See also* Zionism
jinn (spirits), 37, 52, 130
Job, 126–127, 129, 130
Jordan, 33, 141, 142, 159, 160, 161
Judas Iscariot, 67, 68, 101

Karbala, 22, 88, 89, 90, 91, 92, 93, 103, 184, 186, 199
  battle of, 81, 83–87, 108, 188, 193, 201
Khamenei, 'Ali, 64, 106
Khan, Abdul-Ghaffar (1890–1988), 205–206
Khan, Genghis (1162–1227), 117, 119, 120, 121
Khan, Ghazan (1271–1304), 119–121, 184
Kharijites, (*Khawarij*), 43, 84, 119, 203–204. See also *takfir*
Khomeini, Ruhullah (1902–1989), 64, 77, 88–92, 106, 133, 193, 194. See also *Velayat-e Faqih*
King David (1040–970 BCE), 96–97, 99, 101, 153

Lebanon, 32, 33, 76–77, 90–91, 107, 159
Lenin, Vladimir (1870–1924), 45
Lincoln, Bruce, 4, 174

al-Mahdi, 81, 88, 95–96, 102–107, 181, 184, 186–187, 193
al-Mahdi, Muhammad Ahmad (1844–1885), 105, 187
Mamluks, 114, 117, 119, 121, 155–156, 201
al-Manar, 77
al-Maqdisi, Abu Muhammad, 63
martyrdom, 9, 13, 29, 30, 48, 54–55, 56, 77, 85–87, 89, 92–93, 99,

102, 103, 104, 110, 122, 123, 145, 165–166, 167–168, 170, 171, 172–174, 175, 176–177, 184, 186, 189, 190, 193, 195. *See also* suicide-bombings
Marx, Karl (1818–1883), 45, 161, 166, 202
Mary (mother of Jesus), 27, 29, 82, 100, 101, 102, 155, 157
master narrative, 1, 6, 7, 9, 11–15, 17–18, 20, 22–25, 179–180, 181–188, 190–198, 201, 202, 203, 204, 205
  countering Islamist extremist usage, 195–205
  definition of, 13–14
  method for understanding, 26
Mecca, 2, 5, 21, 22, 38, 40, 41–42, 49–52, 56, 58, 59, 60, 69, 71, 72, 74, 83, 88, 104, 112, 142, 144, 150, 151, 152, 154, 156, 170, 171, 173
Messiah (*Masih*), 2, 86, 95, 96–110, 128, 145, 168, 169, 170
Mongols. *See* Tatars
Morocco, 6, 15, 63
Moses (Musa), 2, 27–31, 34–35, 58, 74, 78, 98, 151, 152, 154, 182, 192, 201
Muawiyyah (602–680), 84–85, 154, 203
Muhammad (the Prophet, 570–632), 1, 2, 3, 4, 5, 12, 16, 21, 28, 37–39, 40, 41–42, 48, 49–52, 58–61, 65, 69–76, 77, 83–84, 86, 90, 95, 102, 104, 113, 120, 124, 129, 137, 138–140, 150–152, 153, 154, 156, 170, 172, 186, 189, 192, 203
Mullah Omar, 201, 203
Munkar and Nakir, 174
Musaylimah, 199, 203
Muslim Brotherhood (Egypt), 32, 62, 90, 138, 163, 193

Nakba, 111, 117, 149, 158–164, 184, 185, 186, 187, 194–195. *See also* Palestine
narrative, 1, 2–3, 4, 5, 6–7, 11, 12, 13, 14–15, 16–25, 179–185, 190, 195, 200, 202, 203, 205
  definition of, 1, 14, 23–24
  and desire, 19–21
  different from story, 13–14
  eschatological, 180–181
  master. See *master narrative*
  strategic, 179–183
  trajectory, 20–21
Nasser, Gamal Abdel (1918–1970), 33, 34, 43, 45, 160–162, 164
Night Journey (*Isra* and *Mi'raj*), 113, 150–152
noble sacrifice, 92, 93, 176, 184, 186, 188, 190
Noble Sanctuary (*al-Haram al-Sharif*), 33, 151, 153, 154, 155, 156, 160
Nur al-Din Zangi (1118–1174), 112

Obama, Barack, 3, 137–138, 144, 194, 199, 201, 202
observational arguments, 191
occultation (*ghaybat*), 88, 103, 104, 106
Odin, 50
online forums. *See* web sites
Ottoman Turks (Empire), 105, 114, 138, 139, 140–141, 143, 144, 145, 146, 147, 156, 157, 194, 199–200

pagan (*mushrik*), 21, 22, 37, 38, 40, 42, 49, 50, 51, 53, 56, 59, 62, 120, 121, 168, 169, 170, 171, 173, 184, 186, 201

Pakistan, 32, 44, 53, 55, 64, 175, 205
Palestine, 41, 53, 69, 71, 76, 77, 91, 97, 110, 114, 116, 117, 118, 119, 124, 127, 141, 142, 143, 149–164, 167, 168, 185. See also *Nakba*
Pharaoh (*fir'aun*), 27–36, 52, 65, 89, 98, 166, 182, 184, 185, 192, 198, 201
presidential elections, 89, 146, 194
prophet(s), 2, 3, 4, 21, 28, 29–30, 35, 37, 38, 42, 47, 48, 57, 68, 74, 82, 84, 87, 96, 101, 150, 151, 154, 157, 184, 187, 188–189, 192, 199, 203. *See also* Muhammad

al-Qaeda, 13, 18, 34, 46, 47, 55, 62, 63, 78, 121, 147, 175, 185
al-Qaeda in the Arabian Peninsula (AQAP), 62, 122
al-Qaeda in the Land of the Islamic Maghreb (AQLIM), 146–147
qibla, 150
Quraysh tribe, 38, 41, 42, 50–51, 52, 71, 74, 105, 129, 142. *See also* Abu Sufyan
Qutb, Sayyid (1906–1966), 6, 42–48, 54, 78, 114–117, 121–122, 124, 145–146, 187, 190, 192, 193

rhetorical vision, 9, 179, 182–183, 188, 190, 195, 198, 203, 205
Richard the Lionheart (1157–1199), 113–114
Rida, Rashid (1865–1935), 143
ruse, 57, 65–66, 120, 133, 135, 137, 144, 147, 184–185, 187–188
Russia, 54, 55, 68, 116, 141, 144, 157

Sadat, Anwar (1918–1981), 32–33, 36, 89, 90, 120, 192
al-Sadr, Muqtada, 107
Safavid Empire, 87–88, 108, 120, 156
Sagan, Carl (1934–1996), 11
St. Anthony (251–356), 128–129
Saladin al-Ayyubi (1138–1193), 98, 112–114, 115, 117, 118, 121, 155, 201, 204
Sasanian Empire, 41, 44, 82, 87
Satan (*Shaytan*), 52, 58, 125–135, 184, 188, 194
Saudi Arabia, 32, 46, 53, 90, 122, 133, 134, 142, 150, 159, 161, 166, 172, 199
savior, 82, 96, 99, 100, 106, 107–108, 109–110, 184, 188, 193
September 11 attacks, 1, 11, 25, 56, 147
Set (Seth), 27, 125, 126, 127
Shah Ismail (1487–1524), 87, 88
Shah Mohammad Reza Pahlavi (1919–1980), 89, 90
al-Shafi'i, Muhammad Idris (767–820), 132–133
shari'ah, 21, 33, 43, 46, 63, 77, 120, 121, 135, 138, 142, 146
Sharon, Ariel, 33–34
sheol, 167. *See also* Hell
Six-Day War (*naksa*), 56, 160, 161, 164. See also *Nakba*
Somalia, 63, 78, 134
Star Wars, 15, 16
story, 1, 5, 11, 12, 13–15, 16, 17, 18, 20, 21, 22, 24, 181–182, 187, 192
  definition of, 13
story form(s), 19, 20, 21–22, 25, 26, 35, 47, 48, 50, 55, 56, 57, 65, 66, 79, 80, 92, 104, 107–108, 109, 117, 120, 121, 124, 133, 135, 144, 147, 163, 164, 176, 180, 183, 184, 185, 186, 187, 188, 189, 190, 192, 194, 205

Sudan, 105, 143, 187
suicide-bombings ("self-martyrdom"), 77, 91–92, 162, 163, 165, 175, 176, 189
Sumayyah (unknown–615), 41, 173
Syria, 41, 50, 70, 71, 77, 88, 91, 112, 118, 119, 143, 153, 156, 159, 161

takfir (excommunication), 43, 119, 204
Taliban, 34, 175, 180, 182, 183, 197
Tanzim al-Jihad (Egyptian al-Jihad), 33, 90, 91. *See also* al-Faraj, Muhammad Abdel-Salam
Tatars (Mongols), 43, 110, 117–124, 139, 156, 183, 184, 188, 193, 194, 201
three R's of Islamist extremism, 180, 191,194, 205
Torah, 2, 28, 29, 30–31, 41, 57, 74, 151, 168
Tower of Babel, 30
traitor, 67, 79, 80, 184
trickster, 79, 131, 135, 184, 187, 188
Turkey, 6, 138, 141, 142, 144, 145, 146, 147, 200. *See also* Ottoman Turks (Empire)
Twelver Shi'ites, 5, 64, 76, 87–88, 90–91, 95, 103–104, 106–107, 139, 187, 193
Tylor, E. B. (1832–1917), 38

Umar ibn 'Abdul-Aziz (682–720), 84
Umar ibn al-Khattab (590–644), 54, 76, 83, 84, 98, 113, 132, 139, 140, 153, 154
Umayyads, 84–86, 87, 89, 102, 104, 139, 154, 188. *See also* Muawiyyah
United Nations, 63, 106, 158, 159, 161, 163
United States of America, 1, 13, 14, 25, 32, 34, 62, 63, 67, 78, 89, 90, 107, 121, 122, 123, 124, 133, 134, 138, 142, 144, 149, 158, 161, 162, 175, 180, 187, 191, 194, 196–197, 199, 201, 204
usury (*ribba*), 41
Uthman ibn Affan (579–656), 83, 84, 102, 139

velayat-e faqih, 88–90, 106, 187, 193
vertical integration, 179–182, 190, 195

Wahhabism, 42, 119, 142, 172, 199, 201
Weber, Max (1864–1920), 17, 18, 22, 181
web sites (extremist), 34, 62, 63, 64, 65, 78, 145, 147, 175, 176
women, 29, 30, 40, 41, 61, 73, 85, 86, 89, 110, 115, 117, 123, 159, 165, 175

Yahweh (Elohim), 28, 34, 38, 41, 58, 74, 82, 96, 97, 99, 110, 126–128, 130, 153, 160, 167, 170
Yazid (645–683), 85–87, 89–90, 104, 193, 201
Yemen, 5, 62, 63, 122, 129, 161, 172
Young Turks, 140–141, 144

al-Zawahiri, Ayman, 45, 54, 55, 62, 147, 162, 204
Zeus, 100, 126, 167
Zionism, 32, 33, 76, 78, 117, 121, 124, 137, 138, 141, 145, 157–160, 163–164, 187. *See also* Israel
Zoroastrianism, 37, 41, 81–82, 97, 100, 127, 168, 174